AMERICA IN THE MODERN WORLD

THE TRANSCENDENCE OF UNITED STATES HEGEMONY

STEPHEN BURMAN

University of Sussex

HARVESTER WHEATSHEAF

NEW YORK   LONDON   TORONTO   SYDNEY   TOKYO   SINGAPORE

First published 1991 by
Harvester Wheatsheaf,
66 Wood Lane End, Hemel Hempstead,
Hertfordshire, HP2 4RG
A division of
Simon & Schuster International Group

© 1991 Stephen Burman

Typeset in 10/12 pt Bembo by Photo-graphics,
Honiton, Devon

Printed and bound in Great Britain by BPCC Wheatons Ltd, Exeter

British Library Cataloguing in Publication Data

Burman, Stephen
America in the modern world: The transcendence of
United States hegemony.
I. Title
973.92

ISBN 0-7450-0363-X (cloth)
ISBN 0-7450-1098-9

1 2 3 4 5 94 93 92 91

For Candida and Eve

WITHDRAWN

AMERICA IN THE
MODERN WORLD

CONTENTS

Preface   ix

CHAPTER ONE   Theories of imperialism   1
CHAPTER TWO   Imperialism and the United States   24
CHAPTER THREE   The superpowers: politics, economics
                   and survival   46
CHAPTER FOUR   The capitalist powers: discord and
                   harmony   67
CHAPTER FIVE   America and the Third World   89
CHAPTER SIX   The 1960s: the acme of American
                   power   111
CHAPTER SEVEN   Nixon and Carter: responses to decline   131
CHAPTER EIGHT   Reagan and the resurgence of America
                   in the 1980s   153
CHAPTER NINE   America in the 1990s: dangers and
                   opportunities   175

Select Bibliography   197
Index   211

PREFACE

In the past few years we have witnessed changes which will prove to be of lasting significance in international affairs. The revolutions in Eastern Europe and the Soviet Union, for example, are fundamental not only for those societies but also in their implications for the rest of the world. They signal nothing less than the end of the international order that has governed the post-war era. Since the United States was the principal architect of that order, its passing will have fundamental implications for America's role in the modern world.

It has been widely suggested that this transformation will reduce the USA to the status of an ordinary country, indeed that the signs of decline are already everywhere apparent. And yet the euphoria surrounding American-inspired and led victory in the Gulf war has, paradoxically, given rise to visions, or nightmares, of a resurgent, militaristic America dominating the new world order to an extent that will make its hegemonic role in the post-1945 era look pale by comparison.

In this book I reject both extremes, but argue that the 1990s do offer great opportunities for the USA to retain its status as the leading power in the world. There are many dangers to the American position in a transition of this magnitude, notably the weaknesses of its domestic economy, but the fundamental trends of the collapse of communism and the globalization of the market economy favour continuing American influence. World politics will become more complex as it moves away from a system dominated by the bipolarity of superpower confrontation and towards a global market system. Collaboration rather than domination will have to become the mode of operation in inter-national affairs, and no single country will enjoy the unquestioned pre-eminence that the USA achieved after the Second World War. But the increasing interdependence attendant on the globalization of capitalism will not obviate the need for political leadership if it is to produce a stable and prosperous order rather than descend into destructive competition and anarchy. Although the thrust of change is economic and international, leadership will have to be political and national, and the United States is the only country equipped with the combination of attributes to fulfil such a role.

The construction and maintenance of a widespread and successful coalition under UN auspices to meet the challenge of the Gulf crisis augur well for American understanding of the needs of leadership in a multipolar world and its willingness to assume that mantle. The era of American hegemony may be passing, but it is being transcended rather than overturned, and the opportunities for continued leadership presented by the 1990s mean that the American century has not yet run its course.

This book derives from a seminar I have taught at the University of Sussex for the last ten years. I am indebted to my past and present students for their valuable input as we together tried to comprehend the implications of this turbulent decade for America's role in the world. I owe special thanks to Michael Dunne, who initially devised the course, and who has been a sympathetic, generous and supportive colleague throughout. In this, as in everything, my greatest debt is to Candida Lacey. Her love, support, patience and care have been indispensable and inexhaustible – and at a time when she had much else to be exhausted about. And finally, my thanks to Eve for arriving just in time to keep everything in perspective. She especially should not be held accountable for any errors in this book; the responsibility is mine alone.

CHAPTER ONE

———————— · ————————

THEORIES OF IMPERIALISM

It would take us far beyond the scope of this book to present a comprehensive survey of the theories of imperialism,[1] and it is not the purpose of this chapter to investigate these theories for their own sake. However, much discussion of foreign policy is too narrow in scope because it focuses unduly on the policy-making process itself.[2] While this provides information of value, it also identifies the study of foreign policy too much with the practice of it. The benefits of detail then become outweighed by the costs of lacking a broad analytical framework which can increase our understanding of the forces impinging on policy-makers, forces of which they are often unaware. The theory of imperialism offers such a framework, and its application to a particular period and country can, equally, enhance its validity and help rescue it from the arid abstraction to which it is prone. Our primary focus is on the role of America in the modern world and not just its foreign policy in a conventional sense, and we will achieve a deeper understanding of that role if we begin by drawing out those aspects of the theory of imperialism that are relevant to it.

The first problem is that of definition. The term 'imperialism' is employed with a disconcertingly wide range of meanings: while at its core there is invariably some connotation of one state being dominated by another, this can be viewed normatively in either a positive or a negative light. Further, at its narrowest the term can be confined to those situations characterized by possession of formal colonies, while at its widest it can encompass many forms of exploitation including those which, far from entailing formal domination, appear to be characterized by the freest of market relations. But if this suggests that exploration of differing definitions is fruitless, it remains the case that we need some framework within which to structure any discussion. The test of such a framework is whether it generates interesting problems and insights, not whether the definitions it employs are true or false in an abstract sense. It is in this context that the most interesting

1

dichotomy emerges: that between Marxist and non-Marxist theories of imperialism. Although there are differences within each camp, the basic question dividing them remains the most important for our purposes: whether or not imperialism is a consequence of capitalism; whether capitalism causes imperialism. It is in the light of their answers to this question that we will look first at a variety of non-Marxist theories and subsequently at the range of Marxist responses.

The first non-Marxist approach does not in fact deny a connection between imperialism and capitalism, but, contrary to the Marxist view, argues that far from capitalism causing imperialism it actually serves to eliminate it from the world stage. This view derives from classical economics, from the works of Adam Smith which provided the rationale for free trade,[3] and more particularly from those of David Ricardo who developed the idea of comparative advantage,[4] but it has been given renewed emphasis by contemporary advocates of the free market.[5] The principle of comparative advantage states that, if all countries concentrate on producing and exporting those goods in which they are relatively most efficient and importing those in which they are relatively less efficient, they will be better off than if each country tried to meet all its needs from its own production.[6] In other words, specialization and exchange is preferable to self-sufficiency, and this remains valid even if one country is more efficient at producing all goods than the other, as long as it concentrates on producing the good where its relative advantage is greater.[7]

The question is, what is the relationship of capitalism to this principle of comparative advantage? The answer lies in the nature of markets. Clearly, comparative advantage can only operate in a system of free trade, and while this is not synonymous with markets that cross national boundaries, it is difficult to envisage truly free trade without a market system. The association between capitalism and free trade is also an historical one. Although there have been periods of competitive protection, the underlying trend of the capitalist era has clearly been to reduce trade barriers. The argument then is that the free movement of goods, services and factors of production upon which capitalism depends makes that system in its nature antithetical to the possession of colonies, whose defining characteristics in this context are monopolistic and restrictive. So, as an example, while few would deny that Britain was a capitalist society even at the height of its imperial power, the logic of its economic system was actually working to undermine its colonial structures.

There is tension here inasmuch as although powerful 'capitalist' states may often develop a tendency to exert monopolistic control over foreign markets, this tendency is not compatible with the capitalism on which their prosperity ultimately depends. Monopolistic privilege associated with imperialism thus provides only an illusion of advantage; the greater prosperity actually derives from free movement of goods and services. Moreover, this prosperity is of a Pareto-optimal type in which all are made better off and none worse.[8] As the principle of comparative advantage demonstrates, not only will weaker economies benefit from free trade, but the strong will actually gain more from the working of free trade than from the restrictiveness of colonialism. This is the lesson that the USA absorbed in its period of dominance of the world economy after 1945. By forswearing to use its power to develop formal possessions overseas and by relying instead on its capacity to win in an open world economic system, it produced a period of unprecedented growth and prosperity not only for itself but also for the other participants in this system. The contrast with the effects of the more restrictive approach taken by the Soviet Union in its sphere of influence is striking.

The critical distinction then is between monopolies and markets, and in this context capitalism is a progressive economic system which breaks down barriers and leads to the triumph of the market. It was on this basis that Schumpeter argued that imperialism was an atavism, a relic from an earlier age when social structures were dominated by aristocratic and military classes whose *raison d'être* was to make war and extend their sway over as much territory as possible.[9] The historical victory of the bourgeoisie presaged the elimination of these older structures and the emergence of a free, competitive and non-exploitative world economy. In the modern world we are witnessing the rapid internationalization of capitalism and the emergence of a single world economy, and the forces driving these processes are revealed by the principle of comparative advantage. This then is a class analysis but one which draws conclusions diametrically opposed to Marxist ones.

This is an argument that can bear a good deal of historical weight, especially in the era of American hegemony. It also has the advantage of undermining the vulgar argument that inequality itself is a sign of exploitation. Much of the criticism of America's role in the world derives from the notion that its absolute wealth relative to most other countries must put it in an exploitative relationship to them because it permits a regime of unequal exchange.[10] However, there can be no such thing as unequal exchange in a free market system. If we exclude monopolistic power by definition, the value of goods and services traded has no intrinsic value beyond the price for which they can be exchanged in the marketplace. Rather the issue is whether the process of free exchange makes all parties better off than they would be without it; and they must be, since otherwise they would not participate. In so far as the USA has been responsible for the modern regime of free trade, it has on this argument promoted not only its own wealth but also that of other countries. There is thus a happy marriage between the self-interest of the USA as the hegemonic power and the collective interest of countries participating in the world market economy, a harmony that continuing inequality does nothing to diminish.[11]

Before we conclude that capitalism is the solution rather than the problem, however, we should bear in mind that this argument is based on an ideal type of capitalism, one characterized by the perfect competition necessary to the working of the market system and to the welfare benefits it entails.[12] Perfect competition requires a variety of unrealizable assumptions, such as the absence of information costs, an infinite number of producers and so on. In practice, capitalism is imperfectly competitive, and this opens the door to an abuse of power that may undermine the harmony of interests implicit in the model of perfect competition. It also raises the spectre of conflicting economic interests of a zero-sum kind between nation-states; in short, of a variety of imperialism. If capitalism is compatible with varying degrees of imperfect competition and if the problem is monopoly power, then the critical issue becomes whether capitalism has any inbuilt tendency to produce monopoly or whether its dynamic is in fact to enhance competition and move towards perfect competition, even if that is ultimately unrealizable. If the former then we revive the suggestion that capitalism does indeed cause imperialism and discover the mechanism by which this is so. If the latter, then Schumpeter's argument as to the progressive nature of capitalism is enhanced.

Whichever tendency we claim to detect – and, not surprisingly, both have their advocates – politics has to be brought into the debate in order to correct the fallacy often associated with a *laissez-faire*, pro-capitalist perspective: namely, that the beneficial effects of the market can only arise if it is allowed to operate independently of political constraints. In fact neither capitalism nor any other economic system can operate in a vacuum. Political pressures can be mobilized to reinforce or counteract whichever tendency is thought to be in operation. Thus if perfect competition is thought to be the ideal, international agreements can be concluded by nation-states to promote as near an approximation of it as possible, even if economic agents like multinational companies would themselves prefer to promote monopolistic arrangements.[13] On the other hand, if a government feels that free trade will operate against its national interest, it can introduce restrictions irrespective of the theoretical plausibility of the principle of comparative advantage.

The point is that, regardless of the direction in which politics affects the economic sphere, economic activity must always operate in a political framework, a framework which it affects but which is also subject to other pressures, particularly in the international sphere. The introduction of the nation-state into this equation obviously complicates matters greatly. At the very least it suggests that the purely economic analysis we have encountered so far can provide only an incomplete understanding of the phenomenon. The principle of comparative advantage and the economic emphasis it represents, while an important factor, can therefore be only the starting point of any non-Marxist theory of the relationship between capitalism and imperialism. It is the interaction between economics and politics which is the hub of the matter.

A second group of theories of imperialism go not only beyond Marxist and classical arguments which suggest the primacy of economics but even beyond the interactionist position, to suggest that it is in politics that the explanation of imperialism lies. In its historical form the political perspective is wary of generalization since it derives from analyses of concrete developments such as the scramble for Africa between the European powers in the late nineteenth century.[14] The conclusion drawn from the study of this era was that trade followed the flag rather than the other way around, and economic competition arose only in situations created initially by an impulse that was political or strategic in nature. The nature of that impulse is in fact susceptible to generalization beyond the study of specific events, and its systematic elaboration is encapsulated by the theory of political realism.[15] Realism assumes a pessimistic theory of human nature which doubts perfectibility in human relations generally and those between nation-states in particular.[16] It assumes that the fundamental human motivation is the search for security and the quest for power.[17] Egoism is tempered by loyalty to groups, initially to the family or tribe, but in this context to the nation-state. It follows that the relations between states are characterized by conflict in a world of scarce resources. Indeed, the international environment in which these motivations become manifest is fundamentally anarchic with the potential for a Hobbesian 'war of all against all'[18] in which order is achieved, if at all, by the realities of power rather than by the higher virtues of morality and justice.[19]

In this perspective imperialism is a function not of capitalism, but of the existence of nation-states. The nature of such states is taken to be expansionary and competitive, since they need to have this character to survive in a world of scarcity. This is true of all states irrespective of their internal social structures, and because it derives from basic truths located in an unchanging human nature it is also true across all historical epochs.[20] On this view, the imperialism of the USA and the Soviet Union would be essentially of the same character.

The constraining factor is not the impulse to expansion, since this is universal; it is rather the degree of power a state possesses to manifest this impulse. Imperialism then becomes a function of the differential in power between states. All states have the same motivation, but only some have the resources to realize their ambitions, and it is only when the differential is sufficiently great as to give one state pre-eminence that imperialism follows.

This expansionary impulse can be given an aggressive or defensive gloss. It is not necessary for all states to seek unlimited expansion for its own sake for the argument to stand. All that is necessary is for one state to assume expansionary intentions on the part of others. For once this assumption is made, it follows that the best form of defence is attack designed to prevent the other states realizing their expansionary intentions. Indeed, it is not even necessary to be certain that the assumption of aggression is valid. It only has to be feasible. Even if the intentions of other states are uncertain, as long as the possibility of expansionism exists it becomes rational for a state to expand in order to prevent others from doing so. This is why military planners are enjoined to judge other states by their capability and not their intentions. Uncertainty as to intentions is an inevitable element of the international system, and as long as this is true states will seek to minimize the life-threatening risks involved in international relations by securing their survival through pre-emptive expansion. Hence the curious phenom-enon, characteristic of US foreign policy as well as that of other countries, in which aggressive intent is denied on their own part but is assumed to be true of other states, and expansionism is justified by the need to defend against the *possible* aggressive intent of others. This provides a rationale for expansionism if the assumptions on which it is based are accepted. Since those assumptions resolve only to the existence of uncertainty, it becomes apparent how unassailable that rationale can appear.

It is equally clear that if all states adopt this logic, a cycle of aggression is instituted that has no inherent restraint. In fact restraint can come only from recognition of the power of opposing states to impose sanctions against aggressive action. Hence we arrive at a classical notion of the balance of power as the only protection against unlimited conflict.[21] But clearly international action would be difficult, if not impossible, if this were the only constraint on unlimited aggression. Normal behaviour depends on a series of expectations built up from experience. The analogy with individual action is helpful here. In principle all individuals are capable of aggression, but this does not lead each of us to act protectively, whether in an aggressive or a defensive fashion, all day and every day. We base our behaviour on the expectations of others that we develop from close contact, expectations constantly reinforced by experience. These expectations are also based on a calculation of the interests of those we deal with. There are inevitably interests to be served by co-operation as well as by aggression; but beyond this there must also be an element of trust, and it is important to realize how fragile this component of daily life can be. We may feel perfectly safe in our day-to-day environment, but placed in an unfamiliar environment, a dark alley at night, our survival instinct quickly becomes paramount. And for nations the environment must inevitably resemble more the dark alley than the safe everyday world.

We are left then with a combination of trust, expectation, rational calculation of common interests and a balance of power as determinants of the behaviour of nation-states. And the last factor is predominant because the point at issue is the very survival of the state, a point on which the potential for compromise is limited and which is even more basic than economic interest. Since these characteristics are so deeply rooted, it would be unwise, because doomed to failure, to try to construct an international system by attempting to alter the nature of nation-states. The object, and the best safeguard for peace, is to construct an appropriate balance of power, since instability will only arise out of imbalance. The only alternative method of keeping order is a system of benign dictatorship.[22] Given the assumption we have made about the nature of nation-states, it would seem that a benign dictatorship is a contradiction in terms, but it is a relevant proposition since many would argue that this was exactly the role played by the USA in the post-war reconstruction of the capitalist world system. If this view is accepted, the problem for US policy, and indeed the underlying theme in international relations in recent years, has been to accommodate the relative growth in power of other nation-states under this benign regime, and to manage the transition from hegemony to a multipolar world based on a balance of power without a period of severe destabilization.[23]

If balance of power is the key motif in the political perspective on imperialism, then it has to be admitted that even such an apparently abstract construct contains psychological assumptions about behaviour. And, as we have seen, political realism does indeed rest on a concept of imperialism as an expression of basic human drives. Again there are two sets of possibilities: these drives can be of the aggressive type favoured in realist theory and variously deriving from a will to power, basic animal survival instincts, the need for security or fear of domination; alternatively, they may be more benign, ranging from altruism to a concept of a burden which stems from a religious impulse to bring enlightenment, salvation or civilization to 'inferior' peoples.

Neither group is strictly economic or political in origin, although they do of course manifest themselves in these spheres. What they do have in common, however, is a claim to universality. The problem with this is that, to the extent that each cluster of impulses is the opposite of the other, they cannot both be universally true; or, rather more precisely, if it is claimed that both sets are invariably present in human nature, how are we to distinguish which should be invoked to explain any given phenomenon? Any such 'explanation' must be tautological, a *post hoc* rationalization of events, employing the most suitable item from a wide selection of universals, rather than a falsifiable proposition.

This psychological basis of political theories shares a weakness with all propositions which claim universality: if the explanatory factors are universally present, how can they explain change? It is evident that, whatever our precise conception of imperialism, it is a phenomenon characterized as much by a process of historical change as by any constant qualities across time and space. In so far as it is this process of change which is the object of interest, universals, where they are not simply rationalizations, are underlying factors whose nature is truistic rather than profound. The limited value of concentrating on them is reinforced by the determinism that also follows from their claimed universality. By definition, if these traits are universal and the basic expressions of human nature, then they are unchangeable. If imperialism follows from these characteristics, it too must be unchangeable. Following this line of reasoning leads to a fatalism that can easily become a justification of the very phenomenon it attempts to explain. For these reasons the psychological premises of political theories of imperialism which couch explanation in terms of the imperatives of human nature should always be treated with great scepticism.

In summary, there are two groups of non-Marxist theories of imperialism: economic and political. The political perspective carries the weight of conventional wisdom and has plausible roots in the very nature of nation-states. It is the economic view which is more iconoclastic, however: not only does it suggest that capitalism, far from causing imperialism as Marxists would have it, in fact undermines it by promoting free markets that are antithetical to imperialism, but it also suggests, by implication, that the development of the free market is a global phenomenon which will eventually undermine the integrity of sovereign nation-states themselves and thus the very basis of imperialism as seen from the political perspective. Clearly, the relationship between the economic and the political dimension is not a simple one, and it is the nature of the interaction between the two which is the basic theme we shall explore in subsequent chapters. This theme applies equally to the Marxist perspective where the interaction is construed quite differently. Before we consider this, however, we should look at the ideas of J. A. Hobson on imperialism.[24] Hobson was a liberal writer of the early twentieth century whose work may be viewed as providing a bridge between Marxist and non-Marxist approaches and containing elements of both, as well as being a precursor of the Keynesian perspective on political economy which became so influential later in this century.

The premise of Hobson's approach, as of Keynes', was to contradict Say's law which states simply that supply creates its own demand.[25] This axiom underpins a great deal of classical economic theory and implies that, if the market is allowed to operate without hindrance, the economy will be self-regulating in that it will achieve equilibrium at a level which fully employs the factors of production. Hobson suggests that a capitalist economy in fact has a tendency towards imbalance, and that imperialism arises out of this. The imbalances are caused by the inequality that is endemic to capitalism. Inequality means that the rich have capital, but they have nowhere to invest it because the poor do not have the income to create sufficient demand for the goods that the capital would produce if invested. This lack of effective demand creates a pool of surplus capital looking around for a source of investment which will realize an adequate rate of profit. Since this is impossible to find at home because of the inequality which created it in the first place, the owners of capital look abroad in search of a return.

The consequent development of new markets overseas has the beneficial effect of ensuring growth and thus preventing stagnation in the domestic economy. But this is bought at the price of exacerbating inequality, since the benefits of investment abroad accrue primarily to the wealthy: the rich get richer and the poor get what is left. Rather than solving the problem, therefore, overseas investment only defers it and makes the economy increasingly dependent on finding new markets to continue to absorb the ever-increasing quantities of 'surplus' capital which cannot be employed at home. As the need to secure overseas markets becomes imperative, so it brings with it the other adverse consequence of this 'solution': the state is drawn in to guarantee opportunities for investment overseas. These guarantees are effected by the deployment of military force to secure territory within which investment may safely take place: in other words, investment opportunities are guaranteed by imperialism.

The solution which Hobson proposes is a redistribution of domestic income in order to increase effective demand. This involves giving more money to those poorer elements of society which will spend their marginal income rather than investing it. If done to the proper extent, the effect will be to create domestic equilibrium and thus obviate the need for overseas expansion with all its attendant imperialist panoply. But it is in this liberal solution to the problem rather than in the diagnosis of its source that Hobson differs from Marxist analysis. His reformist answer removes the underlying imperative to imperialism without abolishing capitalism. The rejoinder of Lenin was that, if capitalism could reform itself to this extent, it would not be capitalism. This degree of reform implies a massive and voluntary forgoing of profit by the capitalist class to the benefit of workers. Marxists argue that there is no possibility of the capitalist class acquiescing to this voluntarily. The changes required will only be made when the crisis becomes so bad that no alternative solution will work. And at this point the solution will have to be imposed by the proletariat in a fashion that sweeps away the logic of capitalist development along with the class which benefits from it.

The history of liberal democracies in the twentieth century suggests that this may be unduly apocalyptic. The Keynesian post-war solution to the capitalist crisis of the 1930s was based on an expansion of the role of the state which involved precisely the type of redistribution of income which Hobson had advocated. The effect of this was not simply to benefit the poorer sections of the community, although in a democratic polity they were able to make their interests felt; it was also to address the problem of underconsumption,[26] which threatened the stability of the capitalist system after the war, as it had done in the 1930s. The Marxist error was to underestimate the capacity of the state to intervene in the economy in order to protect its stability. Often such action appeared to work against the interests of capital: for example, by increasing taxes to pay for the welfare state. And for this reason many capitalists opposed the growth of the welfare state and its attendant redistribution of income. However, such redistribution did have the consequence, intended or otherwise, of increasing effective demand and thereby securing the collective interest of the capitalist class.[27] The capacity for reform which this shift evidenced demonstrated the flexibility of the capitalist system, a trait which Marxist analysis has consistently underestimated. It also provided a major alternative to overseas expansion as a means of stabilization, and thus cast doubt on the *necessity* of overseas expansion for the survival of capitalism. This issue of necessity is the crucial one in the Marxist perspective, and it is to this that we now turn.

The variety of perspectives that have been taken on imperialism within the Marxist frame of reference is considerable.[28] Once again, it is not our purpose to survey all of them, but to draw out the distinctions which have the greatest relevance for America's position in the modern world. The fundamental question, to which Marxists have given different answers, is whether imperialism is necessary to the survival of capitalism. Among classical theorists who laid the foundations of the Marxist approach, the argument in favour of necessity is most closely associated with Rosa Luxemburg,[29] while Lenin and Bukharin are representative of the alternative line which suggests that, although imperialism grows organically out of capitalism and is indeed synonymous with it at a certain stage of its development, to speak in terms of necessity is to misconceive the problem.[30] In order to draw out the significance of these distinctions we will consider each line of argument in turn.

Luxemburg's argument is perhaps closest to classical Marxism in its attempt to understand the imperative which pushes capitalism to produce imperialism. The object is to establish that there is a logically necessary connection between the two rather than merely a contingent association. The approach is therefore analytical rather than historical. Its basis is the so-called realization problem: namely, how can capital continue to realize profit on the investment of the surplus generated by the capitalist system of production?[31] The problem arises from the tendency, identified by Marx, for the rate of profit to fall as capitalism develops. To see why this tendency occurs, consider the following:

$$P = \frac{s}{c+v}$$

$$= \frac{s/v}{c/v+1}$$

where: $P =$ rate of profit
  $s =$ surplus value
  $c =$ constant capital (that part which does not vary with output)
  $v =$ variable capital (that part which does vary with output)

The organic composition of capital is constituted by the relative proportions of constant and variable capital in the whole. As surplus is accrued, the organic composition rises as the proportion of constant capital rises. The latter must rise since the surplus value must be invested in new and more productive forms of constant capital in order to ensure survival in a competitive market. This inbuilt tendency for growth in constant capital means that absolute profit must also grow in proportion if the rate of profit is not to fall.[32] There is, however, no guarantee that it will do so. Indeed, given the operation of the law of diminishing marginal returns, it is most unlikely that profit will expand indefinitely in proportion to capital. Hence the profit rate is likely to fall. If this happens, at some point it ceases to be worthwhile to invest; and if investment collapses for lack of an adequate return, economic stagnation follows. The social system then runs into crisis and eventually collapses. Thus the basic condition for the revolutionary transformation of capitalism is met. For Marx this tendency was the hidden flaw which would undermine capitalism and bring about its transcendence by a system of production which was not prone to collapse in this way. But this tendency is an abstraction, of course, and applies only to a static model. Historically, a variety of counter-tendencies have operated to prevent the collapse which many Marxists saw as inevitable, a view derived from an infatuation with this tendency which quite incorrectly elevated it to the status of a law.

The analytic virtue of identifying this tendency is much more modest. It shows that, if there were no counter-tendencies, the system would collapse under the logic of its own development. In other words, it shows that counter-tendencies are necessary to the survival of capitalism. If this identifies the problem, then the question is, what changes in the parameters of the model will provide the solution? The first is to increase the intensity of exploitation of labour: that is, to increase the proportion of surplus value extracted from a given output. This means in effect cutting the wages of workers. This is, however, a limited option. The natural working of a competitive market will, according to Marx, tend to reduce wages to subsistence level. It is by definition impossible to go beyond this point, and indeed it is a constant struggle for capital even to approach it when workers are organized in trade unions. Reliance on this option would inevitably cause great discontent among the labour force if pursued over a prolonged period, to the point where the ensuing class conflict would, far from restoring the health of the economic system, threaten its very existence.

The second option is to increase productivity, and thus the surplus available, by means of technical progress. It can be assumed that the opportunity for technical progress is built in to the system through the mechanism of reinvestment of the surplus. The only question is whether it is sufficiently rapid to produce the gains in productivity needed to offset the change in the organic composition of capital. The answer to this is partly a function of the organization or management of the production process, the incorporation of technical innovation and so on, and to this extent it is susceptible to the influence of capital. It is also partly a function of the rate of technical progress itself, a factor which, though strictly exogenous to the production process, can be influenced indirectly through the control of research and education, and by the financial incentive which an open market offers for the exploitation of technical innovation.

The likelihood of this course offsetting the tendency of the profit rate to fall is also much influenced by the degree to which it is associated with the complementary option of the development of new products. This refers less to the diversification by corporations into products which, though new to them, are already existing, since this will only accentuate the declining marginal rate of return in the market for that product; more significant is the employment of new technology to create entirely new products and thus new markets which it may be assumed will in their immature stage produce a high marginal rate of return. The extraordinary procession of new consumer durables through this century from automobiles to videos, from personal computers to compact discs, may be taken as evidence of the vital role which this form of change has played in offsetting the potential decline in the profit rate. One need only pause to imagine a capitalist economy deprived of all these products and reliant on those of a century ago to become aware of the impact of these phenomenal changes on the rate of profit.

A third form of diversification, and one which is more directly relevant to imperialism as a solution to the problem of the declining rate of profit, is diversification into new, overseas markets. This need not involve any technical progress and may thus act as a substitute for as well as a complement to it. Export of finished goods is again a limited response to the problem because it is difficult to imagine that other countries could permit trade deficits on the scale required to resolve the problem for an economy of the relative size of the United States. It would also be impossible for them to generate sufficient demand unless their own economies were developed, and dependence on imported goods from the USA would not be conducive to the required level of development. The import of capital to engender internal growth might provide a solution, however, and by the same token the export of capital rather than goods is much more likely to resolve the realization problem for a large economy such as the USA.

If some combination of these developments is required in order to counteract the tendency of the profit rate to fall, then the particular mix adopted has great significance for a country's role in the world. Reliance on technical innovation, for example, may well have wholly benign consequences, whereas if the emphasis is placed on increasing the exploitation of labour, social stability is at the very least put in jeopardy. However, it is with the last option, the export of capital, that imperialism is associated. If the origin of this tendency is economic, the consequence is not. This is because capital is not exported into a vacuum. It will only be invested if there is an environment conducive to its growth. Such a stable, secure environment, specifically one in which the rights of private property will be recognized, cannot be assumed in overseas territory subject to different sovereignty. And this is the core of the issue – economic investment must always take place in an environment the nature of which is essentially a political question.

Even if we accept the Marxist premiss that it is economic motivation which provides the basic dynamic, this does not mean that politics becomes somehow secondary. On the contrary, provision of a secure political environment becomes of paramount importance if the economic dynamic is to work itself out. And this is particularly the case where capital extends its intervention into territory with different sovereign control. The issue therefore becomes less one of sovereignty than one of effective control. In the heyday of European imperialism this problem tended to be solved by an extension of formal sovereignty over the territory to which capital was exported. In the American era such extension of formal authority has been eschewed and reliance has been placed on informal and indirect forms of manipulation to produce the secure environment. For our purposes the point to recognize is that the form of control is less important than the logic of intervention which creates it. The form will vary considerably with a variety of historical circumstances and can range from mild financial inducement to full-blown military intervention. The varying consequences of these forms of control are clearly not trivial and will be considered later; at this stage the essential point is that some form of control is necessary to provide the environment in which capital can thrive.

In considering these solutions to the realization problem we must note that they are not really solutions at all. Rather they are palliatives which provide only temporary respite. They do not alter the logic of the declining rate of profit; by staving off economic collapse they simply postpone the day when its consequences become apparent. They have to be continually renewed, and the mix employed may therefore vary over time. At one stage technical innovation may produce a respite, at others imperialism may provide the easier way out. There is nothing in the Marxist analysis to determine which combination will be employed; this is an historical question. What this line of analysis does claim to reveal, however, is the essentially unstable nature of capitalism because of its dependence on these palliatives for its stability, indeed for its continuing survival. This underlying instability should not, however, blind us to just how long term the effectiveness of these palliatives might be. On the contrary, technical progress and product innovation show no signs of being eliminated. And the limit to the imperialist solution of capital export will only be reached when the market itself reaches its limits: that is, when capitalism has become truly global and there is no outlet for the surplus capital to be exported to.[33] Internationalization is proceeding rapidly and is of great significance for America's role in the modern world. At this stage however, far from presaging the revolutionary overthrow of capitalism, globalism is reinvigorating it. The merit of Luxemburg's approach is to remind us that, even in its present triumphal stage, the dynamism of capitalism contains inherent instabilities. But this is a truth whose practical consequences appear likely to be so deferred as to be irrelevant.

The contradiction between the pessimistic logic of the analysis and the revolutionary intentions of the Marxist approach has been resolved by reference to a concept of competitive expansion that again demonstrates the importance of the political dimension of this problem. Capital is not exported in the abstract but under the aegis of nation-states; capital itself carries a national character, as do the benefits that export of capital brings. These benefits therefore become a competitive phenomenon by which nation-states seek a maximum share for themselves. The conflicts to which such competition gives rise can and have spilled over into violence and war. It is in this aspect of the expansionary process – its historical manifestation, rather than its abstract logic – that its limits as a remedy for the realization problem will be reached. The argument is then that the disruption and misery arising out of this national competition will produce instability and revolution well before the theoretical limit of the market is reached.

In the early years of the twentieth century this explanation of the tendency to war shown by European powers carried great plausibility. It was clearly essential that such competitive conflict be eschewed if the solution of capital export was to be effective. Alternative and less destructive methods of securing access for capital had to be found. It may be argued that the post-1945 order, by replacing the destructive balance of power system of the pre- and inter-war years with a benign American hegemony in which such inter-state rivalry could be kept in check by US power, has given this solution an extended lease of life. The question remains, of course, as to what will happen when this hegemony wanes: will the capitalist system revert to the forms of competition which prevailed in the first half of this century, or will collective interests be asserted even in the absence of a single hegemonic nation-state? These are the critical issues to which the Marxist analysis directs us, and the answer to them which will emerge in subsequent chapters will govern the future of America's role in the modern world.

This strand of Marxist analysis is therefore an alternative underconsumption theory to Hobson's, but one stripped of his liberal illusions as to the prospect of reform.[34] If true, it does indeed reveal the nature of many developments in twentieth-century capitalism, including imperialism, as counter-tendencies to the falling rate of profit, and thus demonstrates their essential contribution to the survival of capitalism.

It also provides a clear justification for viewing the spectrum of forms of inter-state domination as an essentially unitary phenomenon because each makes the same contribution to the world capitalist system, albeit with practical consequences which vary greatly. The problem with this type of analysis, however, is that having identified the realization problem as the core of the issue it must, logically, also leave open such a wide range of solutions to it. The danger inherent in this is functionalism. With so many solutions to choose from, it is easy to reason from the effects of whichever happens to be operative, and to claim that it exists *because* of its effect on the survival of capitalism. Such circular argumentation when applied to imperialism elevates it from an undeniable historical phenomenon to an historical necessity, but does so in a fashion that is simply not logically coherent.[35]

It follows from this that imperialism is neither a necessary nor a sufficient condition for the survival of capitalism. Since it is precisely the indispensability of imperialism that this line of argument began by trying to demonstrate, it becomes clear that the argument has undermined itself. The role of imperialism in this context becomes all the more problematic when we consider the nature of the alternatives, such as technical progress, which appear to be more easily renewable and productive. Even if we concede the general analysis of capitalism to be correct at the level of necessity, it does not follow that the implications for imperialism can be sustained at the same level. Imperialism then becomes an impulse, a possibility, an option but nothing more. The realization problem may be real, but the corollary that it must give rise to imperialism is not sustainable. Whether this option will be taken up is an historical matter, a more contingent one than this approach allows. Any approach which is to do justice to the importance of imperialism must start from its historical character and abandon the search for logical solutions. The history of capitalism in the twentieth century has displayed a degree of flexibility that defies any attempt to fit its character into the logical straitjacket of this type of Marxist analysis. The alternative strand of Marxism, associated with Lenin, is indeed historical in approach, and we must therefore consider whether it avoids these pitfalls.

The historical nature of the Leninist analysis is revealed in its approach to the basic question of the relationship between capitalism and imperialism. The two are defined as synonymous, with the division between them being purely historical.[36] Imperialism is not an independent phenomenon, but nor is it a necessary outcome of the imperatives of capital accumulation. Rather it is the form that capitalism takes at a certain stage of its development. This stage is associated crucially with the growth of monopoly as the typical form of capitalist organization.

The answer to the Schumpeterian question of the monopolistic tendencies of capitalism is unequivocal: the natural progression of capitalism is from a market to a monopoly system, an argument supported as much by reference to historical fact as to analysis of the nature of markets. Indeed, the whole emphasis of the Leninist approach is on historical description of the features of the monopoly stage. These refer not just to the development of a critical mass of monopolistic firms, but also to the merging of banking and industrial capital to form finance capital, the consequence of which is enhanced mobility and not just increased power. The other features which follow from the monopoly stage are the export of capital with its attendant politico-military infrastructure, the development of multinational corporations and the territorial division of the world between the leading capitalist powers. This division operates on a highly competitive basis, competition which grew out of hand and resulted in the Great War of 1914.

If the approach is descriptive rather than analytical, there remains an implicit theoretical basis for it. This follows the conventional Marxist perspective which argues that the basic dynamic of the capitalist system is the drive for capital accumulation as the guarantee of its survival: capital either expands or dies. This drive is manifested in a search for maximum profit, which can be secured through cheaper materials or labour or through higher productivity. The ceaseless search for profit leads capital to seek markets, materials and investment opportunities wherever it may find them, with little heed paid to national boundaries. But the extension beyond these boundaries requires in its turn support from the state to secure the appropriate environment. This view may seem virtually indistinguishable from the alternative, more analytical strand of Marxism. But the distinction lies in the fact that, while this approach shares the view of the drive for accumulation as a necessity for the survival of the system, it sees imperialism as only one tendency by which this drive may become manifest. It is the historical circumstances which will determine whether there is more or less overseas expansion, more or less inter-state rivalry and so on. The appropriate metaphor is of a river which will always flow to the sea, but whose exact course will be determined by a variety of external factors such as the shape of the land. Similarly with the drive for maximum profit: nothing is explicable without it as the underlying dynamic, but the form that it takes depends on contingent factors such as the prevailing system of nation–states, the development of transport, weapons technology and many others. So Lenin's 'theory' combines this basic drive with a description of how it works itself out at a given stage of history.

This perspective then, because it avoids the attractions of excessive determinacy inherent in the analytical approach, carries a greater degree of plausibility. The problem with it, however, is that it goes too far in the other direction. Because it leaves so many possible avenues open and leaves the nature of imperialism subject to so many other, non-economic forces, we are bound to ask whether the Marxist theory provides anything other than the most general guidance on this topic. We can ask, for example, whether the theory permits combinations of circumstances such as would eliminate imperialism from capitalism altogether. Lenin wrote at the time of the Great War, in part as an attempt to understand why it had arisen. At that time the inevitability of some form of imperialism did not seem to be in question. Developments since then must pose the problem anew. Despite the continuing growth of finance capital, multinational corporations, capital export and the other features of the monopoly stage which Lenin outlines, it is no longer clear that these need give rise to the intense inter-state rivalry which he saw as the precursor of social collapse and revolution, and which indeed acted in just such a way in Russia itself. Accurate as it was for Russia in its own time, the relevance of Lenin's approach came from acute analysis of a specific time and place. The more general applicability of the approach depends on its general principles rather than the quality of its contemporary analysis, and it is in this area that we are left with such little guidance.

This point can be illustrated by reference to Lenin's debate with Kautsky over the issue of ultra-imperialism.[37] Kautsky used the term to argue that, rather than fight each other interminably in pursuit of rival imperialist goals, capitalist powers would learn to co-operate with each other in order to dominate the rest of the world. It would be rational for them to seek to share the spoils rather than risk losing all in the search for absolute victory. At the time of the Great War, with the powers fighting each other to a standstill, the argument seemed to be with Lenin, as it did in the 1930s when, as seen through this prism, absolute domination even at the cost of war is precisely what the Nazi philosophy sought, as indeed did Japan in its own sphere. Today, however, the ground has shifted. Even before the momentous events in the Soviet Union and Eastern Europe began to break down the old rivalries, arguments for co-operation rather than conflict as the dominant mode of operation between the capitalist powers since 1945 had been strong. The rapid globalization of the capitalist world economy is being achieved, admittedly not without inter-state competition, but clearly within a shared framework as to the limits of conflict, and with a recognition that collective interests are paramount because no one state can emerge victorious from unrestrained competition. This is a truth which results not only from the increased interdependence of the world economy, but also from the hegemony of one power, the USA, which has been able to exert sufficient influence to prevent rivalry getting out of hand. But it is also a lesson which has been painfully learned from the history of conflict in this century.

The point to be made at this stage is not so much whether Lenin or Kautsky is correct, whether conflict or co-operation is paramount in the relations between capitalist powers at any given point; it is rather that both perspectives are equally consistent with basic Marxist principles. If such principles are compatible with diametrically opposed outcomes, in what sense can they be said to provide any explanation of these outcomes? They do not lack plausibility, but that is really the problem: they can provide a plausible account, in terms of the needs of capitalism, of whatever happens. But this is the plausibility of functionalism, the plausibility of *post facto* rationalization, not of explanation. In explaining everything by reference to the imperatives of capital accumulation, the Marxist perspective explains nothing and relies for its appeal on the calibre of its historical description rather than the analytical principles which are claimed to underlie it. In sum, the problem with the Marxist theory of imperialism is that, in so far as it seeks a determinate theory based on the logic of capital accumulation, it demonstrates by its own analysis that such a general principle is inadequate to provide an explanation at the level of necessity. But in so far as it abandons any pretence at explanation at this level and accepts the historical character of the phenomenon, its account becomes so eclectic as to be empiricist, a form of description rather than of explanation. A position in the middle ground is clearly what is required, but it is precisely this which is so difficult to sustain in the face of the competing pressures of the Marxist framework. Its principles must therefore be viewed at best as hypotheses, rather than as a store of catch-all rationalizations which can always be plundered to provide a functionalist 'explanation' of the inevitable triumph of the needs of capital.

What, in conclusion, can we derive from these theories of imperialism which will assist us in understanding the role of America in the modern world? The first lesson is that it is a mistake to attempt, as most theories do, to give analytical primacy to a single factor, whether economics or politics. The subject defies such simple analysis because the essence of any explanation will be the interaction of economics and politics, a process as complex as its forms are varied. It is, however, the dynamism of the capitalist economic system which provides the best starting point for analysis. One aspect of this dynamism is revealed by the principle of comparative advantage, which demonstrates the gains in wealth that free trade can bring. Whether these are sufficient in themselves to undermine imperialism is, as we have seen, a good deal more problematic. Comparative advantage is important because it helps to explain the dynamic in trade which exists for the globalization of the capitalist system; its weakness as a form of explanation is that it is too narrow in scope to provide a convincing answer as to whether the advantages it demonstrates will in fact be brought about. That is a political question which we need a broader theory to address.

Marxism, of course, claims to provide just such an explanation. Its focus is the imperative for capital accumulation to which the capitalist mode of production gives rise, an imperative which must transcend national boundaries if the system is to survive. The claim that this drive for accumulation must manifest itself in imperialism cannot be sustained in a logical sense even if the premiss is accepted, since there are too many alternative solutions available to the problem of realization that it creates. But there can be little doubt that in recent history it has played a significant part in determining the policies of nation-states. This might be taken to suggest that it is indeed economics which governs politics in international affairs, and this is an interpretation to which the Marxist framework leaves itself open. Properly construed, however, this approach demonstrates how a political framework is indispensable if the imperative to accumulation is to be satisfied. Again it does not follow that such a framework must take an imperialist shape, since there are alternatives which meet the criterion of creating an environment in which capital accumulation is free to proceed. But it does suggest that the economic dynamic of capitalism and the political framework which permits it should be seen as form and content, each inconceivable without the other.

The mistake, or perhaps the shortcoming, of the Marxist approach is to assume that provision of such a framework for accumulation is all there is to the political dimension of this problem. To cite only the most obvious limitation, the Marxist theory is a theory of capitalist development and therefore has little direct applicability to non-capitalist nation-states. It is here that political theories, most notably those falling under the rubric of realism, although often one-sided themselves, can provide a useful corrective. The importance of the drive for security can hardly be doubted as a factor determining the policies of nation-states, capitalist and otherwise, in the contemporary world. It is this defensive aspect of realism, rather than the more aggressive notions of an unfocused, transhistorical 'will to power', which carries conviction as an explanation. This is all the more true in the nuclear age when security can literally mean survival, an imperative which is logically prior to all others and which can produce an identity between the need to preserve a particular political system, or even a particular regime, which is not an absolute imperative, with the requirement to preserve the very existence of the state itself, which is.

If we accept that the imperatives both for economic expansion and for security have a part to play in determining the behaviour of capitalist nation-states, then we must also accept that each implies the other: economic expansion is inconceivable without a conducive political framework, and equally political security is unachievable without an adequate economic base. We must also recognize that in particular instances it will often be impossible to unravel which factor is vital. Although analytically distinguishable, a given policy will in more cases than not achieve both ends simultaneously, since they will rarely contradict each other. This, finally, is the reason we should abandon as misconceived any attempt to attribute to a single factor the explanation of America's behaviour in the modern world. Rather we should adopt an approach which investigates the variety of ways in which these elements combine to explain American behaviour in different spheres. Prior to such an investigation, however, we must consider how these theories of imperialism can be applied directly to the case of the United States, and assess their value in deepening our understanding of the role it has played and will play in the modern world.

Notes

1. There are a number of such surveys available, including, T. Kemp, *Theories of Imperialism*, London: Dobson, 1967; D.K. Fieldhouse, *The Theory of Capitalist Imperialism*, London: Longman, 1967; A. Hodgart, *The Economics of European Imperialism*, London: Edward Arnold, 1977; W.J. Mommsen, *Theories of Imperialism*, London: Weidenfeld & Nicolson, 1981; M. Wolfe (ed.), *The Economic Causes of Imperialism*, London: Wiley, 1972; M. Barratt-Brown, *The Economics of Imperialism*, London: Penguin, 1974; A. Thornton, *Doctrines of Imperialism*, London: Wiley, 1965; N. Etherington, *Theories of Imperialism: War, conquest and capital*, London: Croom Helm, 1984.
2. C.F. Hermann, C.W. Kegley, Jr and J.N. Rosenau (eds.), *New Directions in the Study of Foreign Policy*, Boston, Mass.: Unwin Hyman, 1987.
3. A. Smith, *The Wealth of Nations*, Oxford: Clarendon Press, 1976, book IV.
4. D. Ricardo, *On the Principles of Political Economy*, London: Dent, 1965.
5. M. Friedman, *Capitalism and Freedom*, Chicago, Ill.: University of Chicago Press, 1982; F. Hayek, *The Road to Serfdom*, London: Routledge, 1944.
6. P.A. Samuelson and W.D. Nordhaus, *Economics*, New York: McGraw-Hill, 1989, 13th edn, pp. 901–5.
7. *ibid.*
8. R.G. Lipsey, *An Introduction to Positive Economics*, London: Weidenfeld & Nicolson, 1989, 7th edn, p. 380.
9. J.A. Schumpeter and P. Sweezy (eds.), *Imperialism and Social Classes*,

Oxford: Blackwell, 1951; J.A. Schumpeter, *Capitalism, Socialism and Democracy*, London: Unwin, 1987, 6th edn.

10. A. Emmanuel, *Unequal Exchange: A study of the imperialism of trade*, London: New Left Books, 1972; R. Sau, *Unequal Exchange, Imperialism and Development: An essay on the political economy of capitalism*, London: Oxford University Press, 1978.

11. It may even be argued that a degree of inequality is necessary for growth in the world economy just as it is in national economies, for without it no country or agency would have the investment resources necessary to economic development.

12. D. Begg, S. Fischer and R. Dornbusch, *Economics*, London: McGraw-Hill, 1987, 2nd edn, pp. 161–78.

13. The General Agreement on Tariffs and Trade (GATT) is a case in point.

14. R.E. Robinson, J.A. Gallagher and A. Denny, *Africa and the Victorians: The official mind of imperialism*, London: Macmillan, 1961; W.R. Louis (ed.), *Imperialism: The Robinson and Gallagher controversy*, London: New Viewpoints, 1976.

15. The modern classic statement of the realist position is H.J. Morgenthau, *Politics Among Nations: The struggle for power and peace*, New York: Knopf, 1985, although the tradition is generally traced back to Thucydides, *The History of the Peloponnesian War*, New York: Galaxy Books, 1960.

16. R. Gilpin, 'The richness of the tradition of political realism', *International Organization*, 38, 2, spring 1984, p. 290.

17. S. Gill and D. Law, *The Global Political Economy*, Hemel Hempstead: Harvester Wheatsheaf, 1988, p. 25.

18. *ibid.*

19. Gilpin, *op. cit.*

20. R. Gilpin, *War and Change in World Politics*, New York: Cambridge University Press, 1981.

21. H.J. Morgenthau, *op. cit.*, part four. See also the special issue of the *Review of International Studies*, 15, 2, April 1989.

22. An alternative formulation that is particularly relevant to the United States is 'hegemonic stability'. See M.C. Webb and S.D. Krasner, 'Hegemonic stability theory: an empirical assessment', *Review of International Studies*, 15, 2, April 1989, pp. 183–98.

23. T. Geiger, *The Future of the International System: The United States and the world political economy*, Boston, Mass.: Unwin Hyman, 1988.

24. J.A. Hobson, *Imperialism: A study*, London: Nisbet, 1902; G. Arrighi, *The Geometry of Imperialism: The limits of Hobson's paradigm*, London: New Left Books, 1978.

25. Samuelson, *op. cit.*, pp. 410–11.

26. M. Bleaney, *Underconsumption Theories: A history and critical analysis*, London: Lawrence & Wishart, 1976.

27. T. Skocpol, 'Political responses to capitalist crisis: neo-Marxist theories of the state and the case of the New Deal', *Politics and Society*, 10, 1980, pp. 155–210.

28. V.G. Kiernan, *Marxism and Imperialism: Studies*, London: Edward Arnold, 1974; C.A. Barone, *Marxist Thought on Imperialism: Survey and critique*, London: Macmillan, 1985; A. Brewer, *Marxist Theories of Imperialism: A critical survey*, London: Routledge, 1980; R. Owen and R.B. Sutcliffe, *Studies in the Theory of Imperialism*, London: Longman, 1972.

29. R. Luxemburg, *The Accumulation of Capital*, London: Routledge, 1951: R. Luxemburg, 'The accumulation of capital: an anti-critique', in N. Bukharin, *Imperialism and the Accumulation of Capital* (ed. K. Tarbuck), London: Allen Lane, 1972.
30. V.I. Lenin, 'Imperialism: the highest stage of capitalism', in *Selected Works*, vol. 1, Moscow: Foreign Languages Publishing House, 1950; N. Bukharin, *Imperialism and the World Economy*, London: Merlin, 1972; N. Bukharin, *Imperialism and the Accumulation of Capital* (ed. K. Tarbuck), London: Allen Lane, 1972.
31. The surplus arises because under capitalism labour is paid in wages a sum that is less than the value of what it produces. The difference or surplus is appropriated by the capitalist class as profit, which then becomes available for reinvestment.
32. Somewhat more precisely, the condition is that it should not rise faster than the ratio of s/v (increased productivity). If it does, then the denominator in the second line of the equation is rising faster than the numerator and the profit rate falls.
33. Although not a consideration generally incorporated into the Marxian perspective, the drive for unlimited growth which it reveals has clear implications for the environment. It may well be that the ecological limits of the expansion of capital are reached before the class contradictions associated with it arrive at crisis point. In short, the revolution it predicts may have to be green before it is red.
34. Bleaney, *op. cit.*
35. On Marxism and functionalism, see G.A. Cohen, *Karl Marx's Theory of History: A defence*, London: Oxford University Press, 1979; G.A. Cohen, 'Marxism and functional explanation', in J. Roemer (ed.), *Analytical Marxism*, London: Cambridge University Press, 1986, pp. 221–34; J. Elster, 'Cohen on Marx's theory of history', *Political Studies*, 28, 1, March 1980, pp. 121–8; J. Elster, 'Marxism, functionalism and game theory', *Theory and Society*, 2, July 1982, pp. 453–82; J. Elster, *Making Sense of Marx*, London: Cambridge University Press, 1985.
36. Lenin, *op. cit.*
37. K. Kautsky, 'Ultra-imperialism', *New Left Review*, 59, Jan.–Feb. 1970, originally published in German, 1914.

CHAPTER TWO

———— · ————

IMPERIALISM AND THE UNITED STATES

In this chapter we shift the emphasis away from the relatively abstract discussion of competing theories of imperialism towards consideration of their value in explaining the position of the United States in world affairs in the present era. We begin with the paradox that, although the categories and insights developed by the theory of imperialism are the most appropriate for explaining America's role in the modern world, it is not the case that America should necessarily be described as an imperialist power. Perhaps it would be more accurate to suggest that it does not matter a great deal whether the USA is called imperialist or not; the term is open to such a wide range of interpretations that the decison as to whether the US role in the world is best described as imperialist becomes redundant. It is a loaded question which can be resolved by manipulating the meaning of the term to produce the desired answer, a form of labelling invariably employed for polemical rather than analytical reasons. To avoid such labelling is not to beg the question; it is rather to avoid asking the wrong question.

This issue could be addressed primarily from a historical perspective.[1] In a literal sense, that of possessing colonies, American history does not contain sufficient examples for it to qualify as a significant imperial power. The height of such activity may be placed at the turn of the century and the war with Spain;[2] but even here perhaps it was the debate as to the significance for American identity of whether it was becoming an imperial power that was more important than the actual outcome of the conflict.[3] This debate has persisted throughout the existence of the republic and derived its initial impetus from the fact that the United States itself was born out of an anti-colonial revolution and came to symbolize, to itself at least, the idea of freedom as emancipation from old-world colonialism. It is hardly surprising, therefore, that the adoption of a leading world role after 1945, with all its potential for inter-state domination that would amount to imperialism

24

in all but name, should have posed particularly acute dilemmas for the United States.

If the circumstances and ideology of its founding did much to generate dilemmas for the USA as a world power, the relative 'emptiness' of the North American continent, though of course an ideological construct rather than a physical fact, gave sustenance to a strand of isolationism which stressed that the USA should concentrate on developing its own land and avoid entanglements with the corruption of the old world. Equally, this very concept of an empty continent crying out to be filled by American civilization lends itself to a quite different interpretation of American history, and one which overturns any supposed imperial dilemmas for the United States. Such an interpretation is most notably associated with William Appleman Williams, who argued that the United States has always been an expansionist power and, by implication, an imperialist one.[4] In the first part of its history, expansionism took the form of extending the frontier within North America, often through violence. Thereafter the same impulse was manifest in expansion of the 'frontier' overseas, generally through informal extension of US power over other countries rather than through acquisition of colonies. Both periods are therefore aspects of the same impulse to empire that Williams sees as the defining characteristic of the American experience.[5] The basis of this imperial dynamic and the source of the continuity of American policy is its capitalist economic system, which subjected policy-makers to its imperative for growth if stability was to be preserved.[6]

Although it did enjoy a certain vogue among revisionist historians, this sweeping interpretation of American history is now generally viewed with a great deal of scepticism. Its principal defect is a functionalism of the type discussed in Chapter 1 with reference to Marxist theories of imperialism. In attemping to explain everything by means of a single category it actually explains nothing, since its explanatory principle is necessarily pitched at a level of such generality that it can invariably be manipulated to accommodate any objection and leave the central thesis unscathed. It amounts in fact to a philosophy of history rather than a falsifiable hypothesis, its character more theological than analytical.[7]

While the inadequacies of Williams' approach should not, of course, lead us to doubt the value of historical perspectives in general, our problem is to attempt to grasp the nature of the current role of the USA in world affairs. Any historical approach which claims to assist in this task by drawing lessons from the past must, like Williams, presume a degree of historical continuity if not a unity in American behaviour.[8] Our premiss will be that the position of the USA in the post-war world has been sufficiently different from what went before as to justify the idea that the problems facing it became qualitatively different from that point onwards. Indeed, for our concerns it is primarily the period since 1960 that provides the most appropriate frame of reference because it is since reaching the apogee of its power then that the USA has had to grapple with the major problem facing it in the contemporary world: how to cope with its relative decline as a world power.

The question then becomes whether the post-war international system in which the USA has played such a dominant role justifies characterization as an imperialist order. Again the issue is not whether this is the case in any literal meaning of the term, since clearly it is not. More useful is to invoke Raymond Aron's distinction between an imperial power and an imperialist one.[9] The difference lies in the degree of coercion involved in the maintenance of a sphere of influence, and the extent of control over the domestic politics and society of other countries within that sphere. Aron's argument is that the USA is an imperial power because in its sphere of influence its sway has been maintained via consensus and a sense of its legitimacy that obviates the need for domestic interference in other countries; whereas the USSR is imperialist because in its sphere it has controlled the domestic lives of client-states through the threat, and occasionally the use, of force. There is room for considerable debate on this characterization of the USA: American involvement in armed conflict in defence of its interests is hardly unheard of in the post-war era, and what is known of the extent of American covert interference in the domestic politics of other countries by the CIA and other agencies does not promote easy acceptance of such a benign view of US power.[10] None the less, in what might be seen as the core of its sphere of influence, in Western Europe and Japan, the argument that US domination has been consensually based and legitimate appears valid, particularly in comparison with Soviet rule in the eastern part of Europe.

The point is less to accept Aron's definition than to use it to open up the concept of imperialism. His distinction suggests the possibility of a continuum in the degree of control exercised within a system of nation-states.[11] At one extreme would be the case of complete independence involving equality of states but little co-operation between them, a situation difficult to sustain since it would imply a degree of disorder amounting to anarchy. The next stage would be interdependence characterized by relative equality between states but also by co-operation between them. The third stage of the continuum would be hegemony whereby one state achieved dominance but maintained stability through consensus. The other extreme would be the situation of empire where domination was maintained by force, a situation that would again be at least potentially unstable since always subject to the possibility of revolt. Within this framework the status of the USA in the post-war world comes closest to being that of a hegemonic power, and it is the meaning of this which therefore warrants further exploration.

'Hegemony' is a term that can easily be used simply as a euphemism for imperialism, and it is therefore subject to the same diversity of meaning. The underlying issue to which it relates, however, is that of order, of how stability is maintained in international affairs. If complete independence between states is likely to produce anarchy on the one hand, and empire will eventually result in revolt on the other, then the alternatives which are likely to produce stability are twofold and both of relevance to the United States. The first alternative is a balance of power between states. The balance, of terror perhaps, between the US and Soviet blocs has been a major characteristic of the post-war international system. But this in turn has depended on control by the two superpowers of their respective blocks and it is in relation to its own sphere of influence that hegemony becomes the defining feature of US power.

Hegemony is characterized, as we have seen, by leadership based on active consent rather than rule by force or the threat of force, and consent itself rests upon a perception of common interests by nations within the US sphere. The first such interest has been defence from an external enemy, namely the Soviet Union, against which only the USA has had the resources to provide nuclear protection. Secondly, there has been a common perception of the advantages of a capitalist economic system, a perception not necessarily shared by all sectors of the population, but by a sufficiently broad and powerful constellation of forces to facilitate an era of international economic co-operation under US tutelage. The cement holding these strategic or political and economic interests together in a unified structure has been a common ideological outlook on the contemporary world, a factor of particular importance when the mode of co-operation is consensual and one in the creation and maintenance of which the USA has taken the leading role. It was upon its strength in all three dimensions that the USA was able to construct the hegemonic role that produced stability in the Western world.

What has now become the pressing issue is whether this stability can be maintained in the face of the momentous shifts of power and resources that have taken place in recent years both within the West and in what was the communist bloc. Important to an understanding of the possibilities here is an awareness of the fact that American success in international affairs grew out of its domestic stability.[12] The post-war welfare compromise which neutralized the fundamental conflicts of a class-based society in the USA was in itself a hegemonic victory for a capitalist class, one which permitted America to reach out to its counterparts in other capitalist countries and create an international environment which would facilitate the replication of the class compromise achieved in the USA. The vital element which this introduces into the concept of international hegemony is that it should be seen as a process of organic growth, of an extension of modern capitalism rather than simply the interplay of sovereign states.[13] It is this systemic orientation rather than the more familiar but narrowly conceived state orientation which gives the concept of hegemony its force in application to the American case, since it reveals the substance on which the spread of American power has been based.

The consensual implications of the concept of hegemony must be treated with caution because without qualification they neglect both the fact of continuing conflict within American society and the contributions to class compromise made by social democracy in other Western countries, contributions which have produced social systems arguably superior in this respect to the American one. It also neglects the possibility that, even if the compromise reached in the USA is perceived as relatively benign, its extension may not be: it has demonstrated a potential for authoritarianism in transposition, particularly in less developed countries, that has been sufficiently widespread to suggest that such tendencies are inherent in the system, even if less manifest at the core of the US sphere of influence than at its periphery.[14] Despite these caveats an historically unprecedented period of economic growth has been the hallmark of the era of American hegemony, and it is the collective interest in the extension of capitalism which has produced stability, notwithstanding the fact that the political arrangements of this period were indispensable to the creation of prosperity.[15]

The question has become whether this stability can be maintained. Some advocates of hegemonic stability theory would argue that decline is inevitable as hegemony is subject to a cyclical logic throughout history.[16] Others, somewhat more concretely, suggest that the mechanism of decline is the burden of expenditure which falls on the hegemon in maintaining collective security, a burden which has through history undermined economic competitiveness. This is a proposition of clear relevance to the position of the United States today.[17] An alternative basis for decline would be to question the assumption of the benign nature of the hegemonic role and suggest that ultimately hegemons decline for the same reason that empires do: that they are perceived as acting exploitatively.[18] To apply this to the United States would not require us to deny that for a period it did provide the classic collective good of order and stability. But it would lead us to recognize that it did so because these goods and the system of free trade they involved were of benefit to the USA itself rather than because of any benign intention to help the world community. Any collective element to the benefits provided was therefore purely contingent on US self-interest.[19] Were this to be the case, it would follow that other nations would dispense with US leadership once they were in a position to do so, even if the American-led system was of the Pareto-optimal type; it would also follow that the USA would resist any such attempts.

The importance of this is to illustrate the dialectical nature of American post-war hegemony. While there have been collective benefits, there has also been exploitation; consequently, while there has been consensus, there is also the potential for conflict. The key to which dimension will prevail lies less in the inherent properties of hegemony in general than in the substance of the system that American hegemony has created. And here the problem is acute, since the threat to American leadership comes primarily from the very economic success which that leadership helped to bring about. The basis of American hegemony has been the extension of the capitalist system, the inherent universality of which provided the USA with the legitimacy it required to maintain its position.[20] But globalization has necessarily entailed the growth of other economic powers capable of challenging US dominance, and there is a sense therefore in which the USA, as the sponsor of global capitalism, may prove to have been its own gravedigger by setting in motion the very forces that will undermine its position.

The question of whether American hegemony can be maintained clearly depends to a significant extent on the relation between capitalism and American behaviour in the world, and it is to this question that the Marxist theory of imperialism is applicable. The specific debate centres, as we saw in Chapter 1, on the extent to which imperialism is necessary to the survival of capitalism. In terms of the American case, the question becomes whether it is an imperative or no more than contingent to the American domestic social system. The significance of the debate is that it indicates the parameters which govern the USA's responses to its changing position in world capitalism.

The strongest case that could be made is that the accumulation process and the whole social structure which rests upon it would collapse without the fruits of imperialism to nourish them. The alternative, weak argument is that, while the USA may be viewed as an imperialist power, its character as such does not derive from its internal social system, which would not be affected in other than cosmetic fashion if the exploitative aspect of its foreign policy were to be removed. The argument between these two extremes would be to suggest that, although not necessary to its survival, imperialism is a natural outgrowth of the dynamics of a capitalist society. Its implementation remains a matter of policy since it could be dispensed with, but it is an option behind which powerful pressures arise from the social structure and which would therefore require equally powerful counter-pressures from outside to prevent its development.

As we have seen, the strong argument is associated with Rosa Luxemburg and her analysis of the realization problem under capitalism, the principal point of which is to suggest that capital must be exported if the profit rate is to be maintained. It is the case that the USA has been a major exporter of capital for much of the post-war period, and the argument may therefore possess a certain plausibility at first sight. However, even in the period of capital export, the magnitude of the outward flow was never great enough relative to the size of the domestic economy to sustain the necessity thesis.[21] Nevertheless, if the reproduction of the economic system could not be said to rest on so disproportionately small a phenomenon, this is not to say that the export of capital could not and did not have significant consequences. For example, the capital flow was frequently substantial relative to the size of the receiving economies, since they were invariably so much smaller than the US economy. The result was to lead the states in the receiving countries to take a close interest in the process of investment. Their policies therefore became the concern of the US government because they would affect the pursuit of its object of protecting the integrity of that investment. Because the importance of the issue was often considerable to the host country, the scope for conflict and thus for substantial US involvement in the internal political structure of other states became considerable.

On the question of magnitude, one may similarly argue that the implications for foreign policy arise not at the macro level but more at the level of individual corporations.[22] It is generally the case that American-based multinational corporations attain a higher profit rate on overseas than on domestic operations, and up to a third of the profits of large corporations have been made overseas.[23] The move to transfer production and therefore capital overseas to take advantage of lower costs was a major trend in economic development in the post-war period, and it has only recently been counterbalanced by the inward flow of Japanese and European investment arising out of the US balance of payments deficit in the 1980s. The consequence of internationalization is that many large corporations have become thoroughly dependent on their overseas operations to maintain profit levels, and this remains the case even if the sums involved are not large in relation to the US domestic economy as a whole. These corporations therefore have a significant interest in the stability and receptivity of the overseas environment.[24]

While recognizing the dangers of too instrumental a view of the US state,[25] it does seem reasonable, both intuitively and historically, to accept that the state will prove responsive to the needs of these corporations, and not just in banana republics dominated by single companies. These needs will influence high policy and US government action in promoting a congenial environment for capital export in the major economies of the world.[26] The question therefore becomes one not of necessity but of probability. The state does not *have* to protect and promote the profits of multinational corporations, but in the absence either of some massive counterpressure, or of the incapacity of the state to influence events, neither of which conditions has been met, there is every likelihood that it will do so. Consequently, if the criterion for imperialism is relaxed from one of necessity to probability, and the focus is shifted from general macroeconomic relationships to that of the interaction between groups of corporations and policy-makers in government, the classic Marxist theory regains at least some of its value as an explanation of the behaviour of the US state.

For much of the post-war period, however, the major problem with applying the Marxist theory of imperialism to the USA has been one of direction rather than magnitude.[27] While there undoubtedly was a massive outflow of capital in the early part of the period, and this could well be seen as easing the realization problem, this capital soon began, as was intended, to produce further capital as the initial investment generated profit. Much of this, again as intended, was repatriated to the USA. Eventually the quantity repatriated came to exceed new outward investment and there was a net inflow of capital into the country. The consequence was that the movement of capital associated with imperialism increased the domestic surplus rather than decreasing it. In other words, it exacerbated the realization problem rather than resolving it. The only way it could have been otherwise was if the profit made overseas had been invested elsewhere overseas in a continually expanding network. This did indeed happen but, unsurprisingly, many corporations chose to return much of the profit to domestic shareholders. Although it confounds the Marxist argument, this suggests a more commonsense notion of hegemony, that of tribute, with the dominant state receiving wealth from the periphery as a consequence of its power. The process may have been manifested in economic investment and return rather than the military conquest and plunder traditionally associated with imperialism, but in this respect the essentials are the same. If we accept this notion, however, we are again confronted with the problem of magnitude since, though significant to some corporations, this inflow never in itself reached a size which would make it essential to the workings of the domestic economy. It was a welcome bonus rather than a life-sustaining force.

If the argument is unsustainable in terms of necessity when applied to the USA, then we are brought back to the alternative, organic perspective. On this, American imperialist activity is seen as evolving naturally from the process of domestic economic competition.[28] It is competition which forces firms to maximize profit in order to survive, and one possible path of meeting this goal is extension of economic activity overseas. It will be followed if it is the easiest path available, and eschewed if the costs are higher than the alternatives. But there will always be alternatives, and which is followed is a question of the relative costs and benefits applicable to each. The distinctive feature of the path of overseas investment is the requirement it entails for security in a potentially hostile environment, and it is to provide this that the state becomes directly involved in the political and economic affairs of other countries. The failure of the necessity argument need not then imply that hegemony will be voluntarily or easily ceded. To the extent that it is based on exploitation its elimination will require struggle on the part of oppositional forces in the receiving territories. The point is, however, that such struggles do have a prospect of success since, although the USA will resist, it can compromise if pushed sufficiently hard because the interests it has at stake, while important, are not vital. If one avenue of profit generation is closed off, alternatives can always be found.

Arguments concerning the importance of the export of capital take on an air of unreality, however, when applied to the recent history of the United States because of the massive turnround in America's economic position in the world which took place under the Reagan administration. From being the biggest exporter of capital at the start of the 1980s, by their end the USA had become the world's biggest debtor. The policies which produced this state of affairs were not the result of acquiescence in economic decline on the part of the US government. On the contrary, they were the product of a concerted effort to reassert American economic power in the world. The paradox is that these policies, which arose from a resurgence of the imperialist mentality in the 1980s after the retrenchment of the 1970s, have in fact accelerated American relative economic decline by turning the USA into a debtor nation. This turn of events certainly undermines the Marxist argument by which the status of the USA as the leading imperial power rests on the effect on the rest of the world of its drive to export capital. The realignment of economic and political power currently affecting the USA threatens to bring it to a position which is the inverse of Japan, which enjoys growing economic power but not as yet a commensurate political or strategic role. The USA may now be involved in a reversal of the usual position, as seen from the Marxist perspective, in which economic power underpins political, and instead is having to use its continuing political and strategic power to help attain those goals that economic power alone can no longer achieve.

This suggests that in the American case there has been a trajectory in which economic pre-eminence provided the initial impetus towards the assumption of a leading world role after the devastation of war. In the early stage politics was drawn in to provide security for the economic expansion. But as the situation has evolved politics has become increasingly important and has gradually taken over the leading role. As other powers have recovered their economic position under the protection of the US strategic umbrella, America has become the victim of its own success and faced inevitable relative economic decline. It has therefore become more and more reliant on political power to redress or at least slow down this decline. A variety of strategies have been adopted by different US administrations, but they share this common goal of arresting or reversing economic decline by essentially political means. How long US hegemony can be sustained on this basis, or whether, as the Marxist argument would suggest, relative economic weakness will ultimately prove decisive, remains to be seen. At the very least such a trajectory would demonstrate that, even if they have to be compatible in the very long run, as the Marxist argument has it, the balance between economic and political power is not static. The relationship evolves and an infinite variety of combinations is possible.

The export of capital is not the only aspect of economic activity relevant to this question. But if we consider trade of goods and services we are again confronted with the problem of magnitude.[29] The USA has traditionally been much less dependent on trade than other capitalist countries. At the height of its power, trade constituted in the region of 5 per cent of GNP, and although this has risen to 10 per cent in recent years it remains much less than that of Japan or the leading European countries. Whichever direction the trade balance tipped, therefore, into deficit or into surplus, it could not be argued that protection of the freedom to trade, which is what imperialism means in this context, was as indispensable to US interests. This is not to say, however, that the rapid growth of a deficit in the trading of goods and services which the USA has experienced in the 1980s is not of significance. Apart from symbolizing the newfound weakness of American capacity in the production of consumer goods compared particularly to Japan, and a structural imbalance between consumption and investment that is a sure sign of economic decline, it has also prompted the countervailing inflow of capital which has transferred an increasing proportion of American-based industry and commerce to foreign ownership, a trend whose long-term effects could be profound.

Since the bulk of US trade is with other advanced capitalist economies of Europe and Japan, we must also ask if the question of surplus or deficit on trade is not secondary to the question of whether such trade can be viewed as exploitative at all.[30] If we presume that one connotation of imperialism must be an element of exploitation, it is difficult to reconcile this with the free trade between equals which characterizes most of the US overseas account. The principle of comparative advantage, with its benign implications, would appear to have more applicability. Far from trade being the basis of imperialist political involvement, we appear to be witnessing the development of a series of trading relationships based on mutual advantage that is threatening to outstrip the control of any political agency. This may cause a reduction in US political domination of the capitalist world economy, but if this is the result of the transcendence of all national political power by the development of a global market, as opposed to the replacement of the USA by an alternative hegemonic power, then trade may indeed prove to be the ultimate anti-imperialist phenomenon, as Schumpeter argued. Against a development of this magnitude the theoretical significance of the US trade balance, favourable or otherwise, is minimal and suggests that, while the pattern of America's trading may be a significant indicator of relative economic decline, it does not provide grounds for an imperialist impulse on the part of the US state.

The need to secure a supply of raw materials to feed its massive output has often been cited as the basis for an imperialist American foreign policy.[31] In fact the USA is unusually self-sufficient in raw materials, although that has been less true since the early 1970s when it first became dependent on imported oil. Again, magnitude is not necessarily the most appropriate measure of dependence. Some materials may be vital to the economy, or perhaps to security needs, even if the amount required is very small. An example would be some rare substance necessary to the production of sophisticated military equipment. The issue here is one of quality rather than quantity. The possibility of alternatives is also relevant, however. Even if a given material is necessary for existing production, it does not follow that alternatives could not be developed were access to it stopped. Dependence on any material, whether domestically located or otherwise, is rarely absolute. The market system is actually very conducive to the process of substitution: elimination of access to a given raw material would alter relative prices and in most cases mobilize the production of substitutes. It is also important to question in whose interest denial of access would be. Less developed countries, which may be the source of these materials, certainly have an interest in altering the terms of trade to their benefit. But this argues for controlling supply to raise price; it does not suggest an interest in eliminating trade by cutting off supply altogether. It might be argued, therefore, that the idea that the USA would need to become involved in overseas countries to secure the supply of raw materials is superfluous, since in the vast majority of cases the operation of self-interest in an international market system will resolve any supply problems.

This is perhaps too dismissive, and for a reason which has more general significance. The more plausible rationale for intervention in respect of raw materials is that of access rather than specific need. In an uncertain world the 'need' of the USA is not for a particular raw material, but to insure its position against the consequences of unforeseen events which might abruptly deny access to a whole range of materials and preclude substitution. Reliance on the market mechanism to produce the required goods at a price is not acceptable if the integrity of the market itself is not secure. Intervention then is not undertaken to protect current supplies of raw materials, or indeed to protect current profit flows. Rather it is an attempt to guarantee the existence of an international market system which will in turn permit the free movement of goods and profits. It is, in other words, an attempt to maximize the options available to the USA, to provide maximum flexibility to pursue its chosen course under the widest possible variety of circumstances.

The costs of providing this flexibility rise in proportion to the degree achieved, and always have to be balanced against the potential rewards. The cost of absolute security and total access under all circumstances would be absolutely prohibitive. Policy on intervention may therefore be seen as the outcome of the balance struck between the costs of external involvement and the potential rewards. This is in itself a rationale for unlimited intervention, or rather it places no inherent limits upon it, since the more the USA controls the external environment, the more secure it will be. The constraints are imposed by actors in that environment resisting US attempts at control. The conclusion to be drawn from this is that intervention is a matter of desirability rather than necessity, and is determined as much by the balance of power between states as by a unilateral American drive for expansion. Greater security is always more desirable than less, and this in itself provides the impulse for intervention, but the degree of security required for the economic system to continue functioning is not absolute; policy therefore remains primarily a matter of choice based on a calculus of costs and benefits rather than the outcome of any absolute imperative to domination.

It is also clear that, even if the motivation for intervention is the economic one of securing supplies of raw materials or ensuring the freedom of capital to penetrate overseas territories, economic actors cannot themselves provide this security. The market mechanism may be benign in its effects once established, but its establishment and survival is irreducibly a political phenomenon since only the state can provide the guarantee of access that capital seeks. Since there is no inherent limit on the accumulation process, the logic of this position is that the state will intervene up to the limits of its power to secure the widest possible parameters within which profits can be sought. The underlying purpose of policy is to create an environment in which the pursuit of profit is possible, and this gives the USA the incentive to influence the political system of all territories where this pursuit is threatened. In a world environment characterized by uncertainty, this provides a very extensive rationale for intervention and one which courts the danger of over-extension that has indeed been a characteristic of US involvement in the modern world, most notably in Vietnam. It is even possible that it is only by over-extension that the limits set by the balance of power can be determined. In sum, we can recognize that the question of raw materials, while not compelling in itself, does reveal the way in which a massive edifice of intervention can be built upon a relatively narrow foundation. The relationship between economics and politics which this suggests resembles that of the chicken and the egg. If economic factors provide the content of the relationship, politics has to provide the form. Which comes first is therefore not only unravellable, but also less important than the fact that each element is inconceivable without the other.

Military expenditure is a necessary component of the American state's role as conceived in this approach. While the process of extending the boundaries within which US capital is free to operate is multi-faceted, force, or the capacity to employ it, is an essential element. But military expenditure on the scale this implies has domestic economic consequences which may outweigh any role it has in securing economic access overseas. The question this poses is whether substantial military expenditure helps or hinders the development of the domestic economy. The Marxist argument is counter-intuitive.[32] It again derives from the proposition that a capitalist economy is prone to recession because of the tendency of the profit rate to fall below the point at which investment is sufficient to maintain full employment. The problem is to some extent cyclical but in common with a Keynesian perspective it is argued that the real solution can only be achieved through counter-cyclical intervention by the state to iron out the fluctuations and maintain economic activity at or close to the full-employment level. In particular this involves state spending at low points in the cycle to boost effective demand and restore producers' profitability.

The role of military mobilization at the onset of US involvement in the Second World War in ending the depression of the 1930s is invariably cited as evidence of the effectiveness of this strategy. But even in the post-war era a strong correlation can be demonstrated between the level of military expenditure and the growth of GNP,[33] with perhaps the most spectacular example being the boom of the early and middle Reagan years which was largely fuelled by massive increases in defence spending. Such evidence suggests that military expenditure has been the principal method by which the US government has staved off the depressive tendency built into the capitalist mode of production. It has in this way played a critical role in the survival of that mode of production irrespective of any role it has played in facilitating the overseas expansion of capital, although of course without the rationale of possible overseas intervention it could not have had this domestic impact.

Before we accept this conclusion, however, alternative arguments must be considered. In the first place, even if the recent role of military expenditure has been as described above, it does not follow that it was necessary to the survival of the system if other non-military options were available as alternatives capable of performing the same function. The most obvious alternative is social expenditure, both on welfare and on other public services such as infrastructure. Since the government has in fact spent considerable sums in these areas as well as the military, it is clear that they are all available in service of the same macroeconomic function. The question then becomes what determines the balance between the different forms of expenditure. The case could be made in terms of objective need: the country only needs so many roads, and there are only so many people who need welfare, while the threat to national security must always be the primary goal, since if it is not guaranteed other needs cannot even be addressed. While there is no doubt some irreducible minimum set by objective need in all these areas, it is equally the case that needs are constructed by society, that their character is in fact more a matter of preference than objective constraint. They are the subject of government policy which, ideally, should consist of that set of options which best reflects the preferences of society at large.

The preferences of all sections of society are not given equal weight in these calculations, however. The beneficiaries of welfare expenditure are by definition poor and, almost equally inevitably, not well organized to affect political outcomes. The beneficiaries of military expenditure are, first, the services, which are a cohesive and well-organized political constituency; and, second, the industrial corporations which receive defence contracts, again a group with the resources to be able to prosecute their interests very effectively. The two together, the military–industrial complex, represent an alliance formidable enough to exert a shaping influence over the whole pattern of government expenditure. And their influence is all the greater because they can attach their interests to the universally shared goals of peace and security in the face of an external threat, whereas the ideological connotations of welfare expenditure do not reverberate in a society characterized by an ethic of individual responsibility and reward through work. In sum, although alternative forms of government expenditure necessary to maintain effective demand do exist, they are unlikely to be taken up as long as the balance of domestic political power remains as it has been in recent years. This argument is made all the more compelling by the fact that the success of the military–industrial complex breeds further success as vested interests of many members of Congress become attached to it because the economic health of their districts have come to depend on military expenditure.[34]

The availability of other forms of government expenditure which could maintain effective demand at the full-employment level does not then translate into a practical alternative, given the realities of political power in the USA. It does not therefore of itself undermine the historical role that military spending has played in maintaining the stability of the economic system. But the very strength of the political constituency supporting military expenditure gives rise to the possibility that spending will rise even beyond the level required for macro-economic stability. The consequence would be to make such spending inflationary. Its function as a counter-cyclical device implies flexibility, whereby its level rises at the low point of the macroeconomic cycle, but also falls as the economy reaches full employment. The strength of the vested interests supporting military spending are inimical to such flexibility. There is also no guarantee that the external threats which are the ostensible rationale for this expenditure will conform neatly to the pattern dictated by its macroeconomic function. Military expenditure therefore has a double-edged quality as a tool of economic management, since it has characteristics which can foster inflation as easily as they can forestall depression.

Military spending can also distort the distribution of resources within the economy in such a way as to reduce overall efficiency and output.[35] One perennial problem has been that of waste and inefficiency in the production of military goods. This has resulted in part from the prevalence of cost-plus contracts in defence industries, which are justified on security grounds but which signally fail to provide protection against cost overruns. More generally, the absence of market constraints in an area which has rarely been exposed to the full rigours of competition have bred notorious examples of waste, extravagance and inefficiency among defence contractors. Even more important in its effect on economic development is the high level of military spending on research and development. A very large proportion of the research activity of the United States is directed towards military problems, far higher than the proportion of military output in GNP. By its nature, research is a limited activity which none the less has substantial consequences for the productivity of the production process. The diversion of resources, both human and material, away from research into development of market-oriented products has led to a relative decline in the productivity of the US economy, only partially offset by the ability to sell military hardware overseas. Most striking in this context is the fact that of the leading industrial nations the two which have enjoyed the most rapid economic growth since the war, West Germany and Japan, have devoted the lowest proportion of their GNP to military activity and the highest to civilian research and development.[36] While not conclusive, this does support the intuitively plausible idea that military expenditure has become more of a burden on, than a stimulus to, the US economy.

The burden of military expenditure goes beyond its distorting effect on research, investment and thus productivity. The costs of maintaining the level of forces overseas that are required by superpower status have become a burden on the US economy in a more direct sense. While other capitalist economies have developed under the security umbrella provided by the USA since the war, they have contributed a less than proportionate share to the maintenance of the military alliance. Even though its economic pre-eminence has waned, the USA has continued to bear the bulk of the costs of providing military protection for the Western alliance. The continuing political domination this facilitates may well be the only remaining means by which the USA can maintain its hegemonic position. If so, the burden will have beneficial effects. But in the short run the USA appears to be caught in a vicious circle. The military costs of empire undermine its economic effectiveness; it therefore becomes more dependent on the political authority that its military pre-eminence gives. But maintaining this requires an ever-increasing economic cost which only accentuates the relative economic decline, thus increasing the dependence on military power, and so on. As we have seen, it has been argued that this dilemma is one in which all great powers become entrapped as military expenditure necessary to maintain an empire inevitably becomes a drag on the productive economy for which no amount of imperial tribute can compensate.[37] It is not necessary to embellish the argument with a dialectic of historical inevitability to recognize that the USA is experiencing difficulties in this respect which derive at least as much from its structural position in the post-war world as from the specific policies it has followed.

The role of military expenditure is therefore a complex phenomenon which defies reduction. It has both domestic and international effects, strategic as well as economic ones. In some aspects it has been indispensable to domestic economic prosperity and to US hegemony abroad; in others it has caused inflation, reduced economic productivity and proved so burdensome as actually to undermine US influence overseas. The argument that it is a necessary element of an imperial structure without which American capitalism could not survive is therefore clearly far too simple. Its historical importance in shaping America's role in the modern world is undeniable and to that extent it has been intrinsic to that role, but its effects have been so mixed that the concept of necessity cannot be sustained. Once again the usefulness of the Marxist perspective has been to suggest an approach which reveals this multi-faceted nature rather than to provide a convincing argument in itself.

The final aspect of imperialism which is of relevance to America's role is its ideological effect. This is again a domestic one and refers to the ideas of patriotism which are both a precondition for, and a consequence of, imperial status. Besides providing the cohesiveness necessary for effective international action, patriotism provides a type of social cement which helps hold domestic society together around a set of shared values. If capitalism in itself engenders individualistic, competitive values, there has to be some ideological counterweight if society is to cohere. Capitalism is a vulnerable, unstable social system because it is characterized by the juxtaposition of an ideology of democracy and equality with the inequality that is a necessary outcome of market competition. The tension between these two elements is partially reconciled by a consensus on values which provides a diversion from the contradictions involved in class-based inequality. The strength of American nationalism or, more precisely, the strength of an ideology of Americanism has, it is argued, accounted for the weakness of socialism in American life and the poverty of the working-class challenge to its social structure.[38] The concept of the US as an exceptional country with a unique mission in the world heightens this consensual element and diminishes the impact of a divisive economic system. The rallying effect which military engagements have generated in the post-war years has been plain to see, often, as in the Grenada invasion, with an intensity which seemed quite out of proportion to the engagement itself.

The principal ideological effect of imperialism revolves less around specific events, however, than around the pervasiveness of the ideology of anti-communism. America has defined itself and its role in the modern world in terms of its opposition to communism; the external threat has been seen as so extreme as to endanger its very existence, and American identity has been bound up with defence against this threat. In the nature of so basic a struggle, the enemy and the social system it represents have come to be defined as evil incarnate, while America itself has become the repository of all virtue. A Manichaean perspective which divides the world into black and white, good and evil, has thus come to typify the American view of world events. This leaves little room for subtlety or questioning of the common national purpose. Debate becomes a luxury and a danger when society is engaged in a life and death struggle. McCarthyism is the most extreme manifestation of this mentality, but it is an ever-present undercurrent in American life throughout the post-war era.

But ideology too is not a factor whose effects are immutable. Perspectives on particular countries can change dramatically, as was memorably illustrated at the time of the Nixon–Kissinger opening with China in the early 1970s. More importantly, the power of ideology to prompt and justify intervention abroad and to create cohesion at home cannot always be assumed. The Vietnam war is a case in point. In its early stages American involvement was not only prompted by the ideological mission of anti-communism, it also provided the classic rallying point of a patriotic war. But as it progressed, the consensus broke down in the face of rising casualties and an apparent lack of progress towards victory. At this point the ideology that had been a tool to help prosecute the war was inverted in character and became a resource deployed effectively by critics of the war. The same ideology which provided the image of America sacrificing itself to fight a just war against communist aggression undermined US involvement when it became apparent to many that it did not correspond to the reality of the nationalist struggle of the Vietnamese. Idealism was transformed into cynicism and hypocrisy as the hallmark of US involvement in the eyes of critics, a view which spread domestic turmoil as it came to be shared by more sections of the population. American ideology set a standard for its behaviour in the world which goes well beyond the canon of national self-interest. It has tied the mundane motives of national interest to the higher purpose of promoting good against evil. This has provided an effective rallying point and one which has maximized the freedom of action of policy-makers, allowing them to justify often unsalubrious activity in the name of the higher purpose. But when the gap between the ideal and the actual was too starkly exposed, disillusion and dissension were all the greater for resulting from the actions of a God that had failed.

Although the example of Vietnam demonstrates clearly the double-edged nature of American ideology, its effects could be contained once the particular problem was resolved by US withdrawal. Immediately this had been achieved the process of ideological rehabilitation began[39] and attention turned to binding wounds with a balm of ideological consensus. This process became notably successful under the renewed Reagan onslaught on the 'Evil Empire' of Soviet communism in the early 1980s. Success was possible because the real enemy, communism, remained abroad even after the argument that it was the driving force in Vietnam was discredited. Recent transformations in the social and political structures of the communist states of Europe therefore pose a much greater threat to American ideology than anything that has gone before. To put it starkly, if the American mission was to resist the designs for world domination of a godless communism, then what role is left for the USA if this threat ceases to be credible as formerly communist states are transformed into democracies? The problems of tying American identity in the world to anti-communism are becoming acute when the basis of that identity is eroding so rapidly.

The reconstruction of national identity this calls for is a momentous task. No doubt enemies will continue to be found and will provide an alternative basis for national cohesion, but none is likely to have the pervasive effect of international communism. Perhaps reversion to an isolationist mentality will be the alternative as America, its mission accomplished, forgoes its dominant presence on the world stage and retreats to more parochial concerns, though the internationalization of capitalism makes this an unlikely option for any country, let alone one with the leadership potential of the United States. Whatever the outcome, there is no doubt that some form of national consensus will have to be forged, and to this extent the Marxist argument as to the necessity of ideology carries weight. What cannot be sustained, however, is the view that this must be a rigid and unchanging imperial ideology. Any ideology which lacks flexibility is as likely to sow dissension as to reap harmony, and its grasp on reality can become so outdated by events as to make it worse than useless as an interpretative mechanism by which the society understands its role in the world. Once again the phenomenon proves more complex than the initial insight generated by the Marxist analysis will allow.

To sum up, the Marxist argument that imperialism is so integral to the logic of the development of American capitalism that without it that system would collapse is not sustainable. The problem of capital flows which is at the heart of the necessity argument is particularly problematic: on the issues of trade and raw materials the basic criterion of size is not met; and while both military spending and the ideological dimension of imperialism are of undoubted importance, their effects are in consequence multi-faceted, serving under some circumstances as much to destabilize American capitalism as to preserve it. The central point, and one which the Marxist argument consistently underestimates, is the flexibility of capitalism as a social system. The historical variety of societies we call capitalist, from puritan New England to the latter-day hedonism of Southern California, to name examples drawn only from the USA, should alert us to the fact that the determining features of capitalism, private property, wage labour, competitive markets and so on, exercise their influence in only the most general of ways. When seeking explanations of the factors governing American policy responses to the fundamental problem facing it as a world power, that of relative decline, the available choices exist in a space only the broadest parameters of which are set by the need to reproduce the capitalist system in America.

None the less, by directing our attention to the dynamic of capital accumulation the Marxist approach does perhaps provide the best starting point for analysing American behaviour, so long as it is understood as a basis for comprehending a complex reality on which other levels have as great a determining effect, and is not taken as an attempt to reduce that reality to a single, economic dimension. This remains true despite the danger of an untheorized eclecticism raised by the abandonment of a single governing principle, and it is for this reason that this discussion has focused on an assessment of this framework. If its strength is to inform an understanding of the expansionist and exploitative dimension of American behaviour in its sphere of influence, it is correspondingly weaker in explaining the consensual aspect that lies at the heart of American hegemony. Its limitations are even more evident, however, in explaining US behaviour towards powers outside its sphere of influence where the balance of power and strategic and military factors are paramount. The most important such area is in American relations with the other superpower of the post-war era, the Soviet Union. To obtain a fuller understanding of the factors governing America's role in the modern world, therefore, this relationship must be considered directly. This is the purpose of the next chapter.

Notes

1. C. Coker, *Reflections on American Foreign Policy*, London: Pinter, 1989.
2. H. Wayne Morgan, *America's Road to Empire: The war with Spain and overseas expansion*, New York: Wiley, 1965; D. Healy, *US Expansionism: The imperialist urge in the 1890s*, Madison, Wis.: University of Wisconsin Press, 1970; P.S. Foner, *The Spanish–Cuban–American War and the Birth of US Imperialism*, New York: Monthly Review Press, 1972.
3. G.F. Linderman, *The Mirror of War: American Society and the Spanish–American War*, Ann Arbor, Mich.: University of Michigan Press, 1974; M.B. Young (ed.), *American Expansionism: The critical issues*, Boston, Mass.: Little Brown, 1973; R.E. Welch, Jr (ed.), *Imperialists vs Anti-Imperialists: The debate over expansionism in the 1890s*, Itasca, Ill.: Peacock, 1972; N.A. Graebner (ed.), *Manifest Destiny*, New York: Bobbs Merrill, 1968.
4. W.A. Williams, *The Tragedy of American Diplomacy*, New York: Dell, 1972, 2nd edn.
5. W.A. Williams (ed.), *From Colony to Empire: Essays in the history of American foreign relations*, New York: Wiley, 1972.
6. W.A. Williams, *The Roots of the Modern American Empire: A study of the growth and shaping of social consciousness in a marketplace society*, New York: Random House, 1969.
7. J.A. Thompson, 'William Appleman Williams and the "American Empire"', *Journal of American Studies*, 7, 1, 1973, pp. 91–104.
8. Many historians would, of course, deny that it is possible to draw such lessons or that it is the purpose of the study of history even to attempt to provide them.
9. R. Aron, *The Imperial Republic*, Englewood Cliffs, NJ: Prentice Hall, 1974, part II, chapter IV.
10. P. Agee, *Inside the Company: CIA diary*, London: Penguin, 1975; P. Agee and L. Wolf (eds.), *Dirty Work: The CIA in Western Europe*, London: Lyle Stuart, 1978.
11. A. Watson, 'Systems of states', *Review of International Studies*, 16, 2, Apr. 1990, pp. 99–110.
12. S. Gill, *American Hegemony and the Trilateral Commission*, London: Cambridge University Press, 1989, chapter 3.
13. R.W. Cox, 'Gramsci, hegemony and international relations: an essay in method', *Millennium*, 12, 2, 1983, pp. 162–75.
14. D. Snidal, 'The limits of hegemonic stability theory', *International Organisation*, 39, 1985, pp. 579–614.
15. There are two schools among those who subscribe to hegemonic stability theory. The difference between them lies in whether they place emphasis on economic or political factors as the principal source of stability. See M.C. Webb and S.D. Krasner, 'Hegemonic stability theory: an empirical assessment', *Review of International Studies*, 15, 2, Apr. 1989, pp. 183–198.
16. R. Gilpin, *War and Change in World Politics*, Cambridge: Cambridge University Press, 1981; R. Gilpin, *The Political Economy of International Relations*, Princeton, NJ: Princeton University Press, 1987.
17. P. Kennedy, *The Rise and Fall of the Great Powers: Economic change and military conflict from 1500–2000*, London: Unwin Hyman, 1988.
18. I. Grunberg, 'Exploring the "myth" of hegemonic stability', *International Organisation*, 44, 4, autumn 1990, pp. 431–77.

19. C. Kindleberger, 'Dominance and leadership in the international economy: exploitation, public goods and free rides', *International Studies Quarterly*, 25, 2, 1981, pp. 242–54.
20. Cox, *op. cit.*
21. A. Szymanski, 'Capital accumulation on a world scale and the necessity of imperialism', *Insurgent Sociologist*, 7, 2, spring 1977, pp. 35–53.
22. R. Gilpin, *US Power and the Multinational Corporation*, New York: Basic Books, 1975; R. Gilpin, 'The multinational corporation and American foreign policy', in R. Rosencrance (ed.), *America as an Ordinary Country: US foreign policy and the future*, Ithaca, NY: Cornell University Press, 1976.
23. A. Szymanski, *The Logic of Imperialism*, New York: Praeger, 1981, chapter 5.
24. N. Poulantzas, *Classes in Contemporary Capitalism*, London: New Left Books, 1973.
25. N. Poulantzas, *Political Power and Social Classes*, London: New Left Books, 1978.
26. Gilpin, *US Power and the Multinational Corporation, op. cit.*
27. A. Szymanski, 'Capital accumulation', *op. cit.*
28. H. Magdoff, 'How to make a molehill out of a mountain', *Insurgent Sociologist*, 7, 2, spring 1977, pp. 106–12.
29. S.M. Miller *et al.*, 'Does the US economy require imperialism?', *Social Policy*, 1, 2, 1970, pp. 13–19.
30. *ibid.*
31. H. Magdoff, 'The logic of imperialism', *Social Policy*, 1, 2, 1970, p. 27; Miller *et al.*, *op. cit.*, p. 27; Szymanski, *Logic of Imperialism.*, *op. cit.*, pp. 152–68.
32. P. Baran and P. Sweezy, *Monopoly Capital*, Harmondsworth: Penguin, 1968.
33. T. Weisskopf, 'Theories of American imperialism: a critical evaluation', *Review of Radical Political Economics*, 6, 3, 1974, pp. 41–60.
34. S. Melman, *The Permanent War Economy: American capitalism in decline*, New York: Simon & Schuster, 1974.
35. Szymanski, *Logic of Imperialism.*, *op. cit.*, chapter 15.
36. *ibid.*, p. 519.
37. Kennedy, *op. cit.*
38. D. Bell, *Marxian Socialism in the United States*, Princeton, NJ: Princeton University Press, 1967.
39. N. Chomsky and E. Herman, *Manufacturing Consent*, New York: Pantheon, 1988.

CHAPTER THREE

THE SUPERPOWERS: POLITICS, ECONOMICS AND SURVIVAL

In this chapter we will consider the distinctive character of the relationship between the USA and its most powerful rival in the modern world, the USSR. In doing so we will elaborate on the theme of the relationship between economic and political explanations of America's role in the world. More specifically, the superpower relationship will illuminate that dimension of America's behaviour which derives from its participation in an international system in which competition between nation-states is endemic to their nature and derives from properties of that system, as opposed to being a consequence of its nature as a capitalist society.

Many enduring features of the relationship between America and the Soviet Union were formed at the birth of the communist revolution, on which the USA took an actively hostile stance. However, the character of the relationship was fundamentally changed by the emergence of the two countries as the leading powers in the world after the devastation of the Second World War. While both had played a role in world affairs before the war, their involvement took a qualitative leap after it, and for a substantial part of the post-war era their dominance grew and was unchallenged. The relationship that was formed in the immediate post-war years has been the subject of massive debate among historians, a debate marred by the fact that argument has been marshalled on all sides as much with a view to supporting the political stance of the participants as to revealing the nature of its ostensible subject. It is not necessary or desirable to summarize the course of the historiographical debate in this context, only to extract some aspects relevant to our theme.[1]

The debate on the cold war has been characterized primarily by the question of blame: who was responsible for the hostility and tension in the relations between the USA and the Soviet Union? In keeping with the Manichaean perspective on world affairs widespread even among American historians, the critical issue became which country was defending freedom and which represented evil. In the early historiography the answer was unequivocally that the USSR was the aggressor. It has to be admitted that this was not a difficult thesis to substantiate. The suppression of democracy in Eastern Europe, notably events in Czechoslovakia and Poland, provided ample evidence that the Soviet Union was not a bystander to events, but had a clear and determined strategy in the area which would not be unduly distracted by Western notions of elective democracy. The interpretation placed on Soviet behaviour was more open to question. It was seen as the actions of a power bent on world domination, the first stage in a grand design to submit the world to communist rule centred on Moscow, the product of an imperial ambition outreaching even that of Germany under Hitler. The role of the USA was therefore seen as passive, or rather reactive. As the only country with the power to resist this grand design, it was dragged into world events to contain the threat to freedom posed by Soviet ambitions. The Marshall Plan and all the other elements of the strategy of containment that was adopted were therefore sacrifices made by the USA in the struggle against tyranny.

In the 1950s the idea of such selflessness being the guiding light of America's role in the world was widely accepted, and played its part in creating the political will required to underwrite a huge increase in US involvement in world affairs. This view was a product of, and a contribution to, a period of strong ideological consensus within the USA.[2] When that consensus broke down across a wide span of US culture, as it did in the 1960s, it is not surprising that as part of this cultural transformation there arose a reassessment by historians of America's role in the cold war.[3] This revisionist perspective was in some respects merely the obverse of what had gone before. Where the USSR had been the aggressor whose designs caused the tension of the cold war, now the roles were reversed. In the first place, the actions of the USSR in Eastern Europe were seen as those of a security-conscious rather than an expansionist nation, one seeking merely to protect its legitimate security interests, not to plot world revolution. The intense and uncompromising desire of the Soviet Union to establish a *cordon sanitaire* on its western flank seemed hardly unreasonable in view of the devastation that had been wreaked upon it from that direction, and not just in the Second World War. Security in this area had been shown to be literally vital to Soviet survival, and if the sensibilities of some of those living in the area were given scant regard in the attempt to ensure it, this was an unfortunate consequence of a savage history and not evidence of an expansionist mentality. What the USSR was seeking was a sphere of influence in which it could provide for its own defensive security. This was a goal accepted and shared by the Western powers at the time, and it was only after the cold war had broken out that it came to be interpreted as a strategy of unlimited aggrandizement.

Other episodes in Soviet intervention in world affairs failed to support the expansionist thesis. Its behaviour in the Spanish Civil War and the uprisings in China showed, it was argued, a strongly pragmatic and nationalist approach rather than one governed by abstract ideological considerations. In part this reflected its lack of material capacity to influence world events. And this was particularly relevant at the origins of the cold war. The Soviet Union, though a victor, had during the Second World War experienced a level of suffering and devastation incomprehensible to an American mentality that had never been subject to either on anything like the same scale. With its economy decimated and its military exhausted, the idea of the Soviet Union embarking immediately on a path of world domination became ludicrous to many writing in the 1960s, and the wonder was that so many Americans, and indeed Western Europeans, could have been manipulated into taking it seriously.

If the Soviet Union was not responsible for the cold war, it follows that it was the USA that was to blame, and the revisionist historians did not flinch from this conclusion. They displayed some relish in overturning the view of America as merely reactive, and stressed instead its own expansionist aims. The cold war and the mentality it embodied were seen as myths expressly designed to divert attention from, and provide a covering rationale for, America's own aggressive agenda in the post-war world. Evidence that the USA began planning for its own post-war hegemony while the war was still on supported the calculated nature of US actions.[4] The fact that these plans revolved around undermining the restrictions placed on US influence by the British empire, the reconstruction of Western Europe in America's liberal capitalist image, and the reconstitution of Japan as an active member of the capitalist world, testifed to the comprehensiveness of the world-view which underlay them. The role of the Soviet Union in these plans was not as a serious short-term threat: calculations of Soviet capacity were too realistic for that. Instead the ideological differences with the Soviets were seen as an ideal basis for making the Soviet Union the enemy-without that would provide the USA with the leverage needed to marshal the forces of world capitalism to its advantage. This leverage was needed to influence US domestic opinion, which at the time was both friendly towards the Soviet ally and tending to isolationism, as much as to exert control over other sovereign nations in the capitalist camp. Hence the carefully planned speeches of Truman and others setting out the strategy of containment, powerfully constructing a world-view that justified unlimited US intervention overseas in the name of preventing the spread of communism.

If the rhetoric of this strategy was moralistic, excessive and Manichaean, the actions behind it were more calculated but no less compromising. The use of the atomic bomb, for example, was seen as a ruthless attempt to pre-empt Soviet involvement in the Far Eastern theatre[5] because it carried the threat of substantial territorial gains by the Soviets which would compromise US ambitions to dominate the region through the agency of a revitalized, capitalist Japan. Similarly, though much less dramatically, relations with another ally, Britain, though couched in terms of friendship and solidarity, were conducted with some ruthlessness.[6] Loans to assist in British reconstruction were made, to be sure, but the price extracted was substantial. The proposed American sphere of influence included much territory still part of the British empire. Britain's imperial prerogatives were clearly not conducive to the free access of American capital to these territories and so had to be eliminated, a goal which US resources as banker to another country impoverished by the war effort allowed America to achieve. Again Marshall Aid, previously seen as one of the great acts of humanitarianism in international affairs, was reinterpreted as a necessary mechanism to ensure the redevelopment of Western Europe along capitalist lines, thus making it available for profitable US investment.

It was the needs of capitalist expansionism, whether of a Marxist variety or not, which were the theoretical basis on which this argument for US responsibility for the cold war lay. The particular fear driving US policy-makers was not an abstract concern with the declining rate of profit; it was a quite concrete anxiety at the prospect of a return to the depression of the 1930s once the stimulus of war spending, which had transformed the US economy, was eliminated. The creation of a threat from the Soviet Union justified the maintenance of a high level of military expenditure with all the benefits this brought in maintaining full employment domestically. A highly developed military machine also provided the back-up that was vital to obtaining outlets for US capital in new territories across the world. Given that the stability, if not the survival, of American society would have been threatened, as it had been in the 1930s, without the stimulus provided by these factors, it becomes apparent just how essential the creation of the cold war myth was to America's plans for its own hegemony.

The debate has moved on since the 1960s when its animus was the re-evaluation of America's world role caused by the Vietnam war.[7] The excesses of the conservative and revisionist positions have given way to more measured assessments, improved in terms of scholarship by employment of a wider range of sources.[8] If the early perspective amounted to little more than an apologia for an aggressive ideology, it was challenged by a revisionism that was economistic and Amerocentric, motivated as it was by the equally ideological desire to provide an intellectual basis for a challenge to US involvement in Vietnam that was seen as a direct outgrowth of the cold war mentality. Preoccupation with the question of blame produced unduly simplistic and one-sided analyses, and it now seems a framework best avoided.

On balance, the implications of this early period are that the USA acted in a relatively restrained fashion given the unprecedented pre-eminence it enjoyed after a war that had severely debilitated every other power. While it would be naive to suppose that it did not have a design which involved considerable expansion of its own interests, it remains the case that it did not push expansion to the limits of its material and military capacity. Policy was governed by a tension between acceptance of spheres of influence between the USA and the USSR on the one hand, and a desire to roll back communism to the point of its elimination on the other. The result was a compromise in which rhetorical extremism was tempered to some extent by practicality.[9] Hegemony in the capitalist world was certainly the goal, and it was indeed achieved. But the degree of restraint in its achievement at least leaves open the possibility that it was a benign hegemony which favoured those subject to it by bringing prosperity to them as well as to the USA, in whose interest it was constructed.

One factor which became increasingly important in making for distinctiveness in the relations between the USA and the Soviet Union was the role of strategic considerations. What set the relations between the superpowers apart was not just their size and conventional military strength, it was this combined with the virtual nuclear monopoly they came to enjoy once the USSR developed effective delivery systems for nuclear weapons. This monopoly was the greatest source of influence for each power over the partners in its own camp because it meant that they alone could provide the nuclear umbrella that was the only source of real security in the modern world. But it also gave rise to the intransigent character of the superpower relationship. In their military planning each side inevitably had to allow for the worst case, and the existence of nuclear weapons meant that this was total annihilation, a quite unprecedented threat and one which governed the superpowers' responses to each other over the whole range of their relationship. It gave rise, for example, to the zero-sum outlook in which any advance for one side was seen as an equal loss for the other, a perspective which left little room for compromise. It blurred too the distinction between defence and aggression: when dealing with an enemy capable of annihilation any advance made by the enemy threatened to alter the balance of power in an irretrievable manner. It followed that the best form of defence against this possibility was to attack first in order to prevent any enemy advance. The US strategy of global containment was not therefore susceptible to restraint, and carried within it the seeds of unlimited aggression. This tendency was accentuated by domestic political considerations in which the paranoia of the right[10] created pressures for pre-emptive action on politicians who would otherwise have sought moderation. The danger of all this was the development of an irrational, overreaching policy that would accentuate world instability in circumstances where the consequences could dwarf anything that had gone before.

These dangers require more detailed examination, but they were particularly apparent on the American side, and to see why we must consider the intellectual underpinnings of the US perspective on the Soviet Union. These contributed as much to the high level of tension surrounding superpower relations as did the objective possibilities of nuclear conflict. The most cogent exposition of the USA perspective in the early post-war years was given initially by George Kennan,[11] and then elaborated more systematically, and more aggressively, in a review of national security policy that resulted in the document known as NSC–68.[12] The premiss was that the Soviet Union was a different kind of society, not because of the scope of its power but because of its ideological make-up and its internal social structure. The Marxist ideology of Soviet society made it necessarily committed to the goal of world revolution, a goal interpreted as meaning world domination by the Soviet Union as the fountainhead of world socialism. This was not an aim that had to be deduced from Soviet behaviour; it was an admitted, avowed and explicit aim that was intrinsic to the revolution which created Soviet society. For it to be dropped would undermine the whole justification for that society.

In a neat reversal of the Marxist argument concerning the necessity of imperialism to capitalism, it was to the contrary the social structure of a Marxist society which required unlimited expansionism for its legitimacy and survival. The totalitarian nature of that social structure, besides being a necessary concomitant of that ideology, also enhanced Soviet capacity to realize the goal of world revolution.[13] The absolute control of legitimate force, the economy, propaganda and politics by the central authority implied a much greater capacity for mobilization in pursuit of any goal than was possible in a pluralist society like the USA. The checks and balances on power in America, although necessary to the preservation of democracy, also had the unwanted consequence of weakening the USA in the struggle with its implacable antagonist. The Soviet Union therefore presented itself as a formidable opponent with both a deep-seated ideological purpose and the resolution needed to pursue it effectively.

The implication of this conception of Soviet society for superpower relations was that the USSR posed a qualitatively different threat from any other power. Conflict between it and the USA was seen as a conflict of whole social systems, not a matter of differences on specific issues. This meant that the concept of a balance of power, which was the usual key to security in international relations, did not operate in this context. Balance implied compromise, a form of international checks and balances, based on the idea that conflict between nation-states, although often intense, had limits to its scope. In the struggle between capitalism and communism, Soviet ideology would not and could not countenance compromise. A process of endless and unlimited struggle was therefore inevitable because in a nuclear era the USA was the only country with the power to stop the domination of the world by communism. Resistance was therefore a task it had no choice but to undertake, both in order to ensure its own survival and on behalf of freedom everywhere, since in effect the two were synonymous. The US policy of containment was therefore seen as the only possible response that was commensurate with the type of threat the Soviet Union posed. It was, in principle, an unlimited response because the threat was unlimited, extending beyond the international balance of power and into the domestic structure of American society. The commitment to resist Soviet expansionism wherever and whenever it occurred was not then solely the rhetorical product of an America relishing its newfound status as the leading world power; it was also the natural consequence of this analysis of the unique character of Soviet society.

If the analysis of Soviet society was the source of the containment strategy, it had properties which went well beyond these origins. It was, first, a political rather than an economic explanation, and as such it provided a refutation of those economic theories which purport to explain American expansionism. However, it also challenged conventional political theories inasmuch as they derive, as we saw in Chapter 1, from properties of all nation-states. This analysis, because it focuses on the ideological drive to expansion inherent in Marxism, suggests that it is only states governed by this ideology that are possessed of this drive. The implications for the US role in the world are therefore twofold: first, economic theories of expansion are ruled out on principle, and thus most of the criticism of USA expansionism is undermined; second, by dividing nations into two categories according to ideology, it leaves space for non-aggressive nation-states if they have the appropriate ideology. This, of course, permits the view of the USA as the reactive partner in the superpower relation. It thus creates the paradoxical image of a peace-loving nation without any dynamic to expand abroad, which would prefer to cultivate its own garden, but which in fact is drawn into unlimited involvement in world affairs in order to protect its legitimate interests by the nature of the threat it faces. This perspective on the Soviet Union therefore amounts to an impressive ideological *tour de force* in itself.

The double effect of this analysis, as both an explanation and a legitimation of America's role in the modern world, is not achieved without cost, however. It contrasts strongly with a traditional view of international relations as based on a mixture of co-operation and conflict. By eliminating all shades of grey from the analysis it enhances its ideological resonance, but it also imposes an onus on America to intervene wherever communism could be seen as a possible beneficiary of conflict, which in practice meant a responsibility to intervene everywhere. This was bound not only to prove burdensome in a material sense, even allowing for America's vast military capacity, but seemed likely only to perpetuate the tension it sought to eliminate. Its very one-sidedness carried within it the seeds of hubris, especially when allied to that same overweening military power. By reacting in kind to the perceived threat, it ran the risk of turning the USA into the mirror-image of the society it claimed to abhor.

Herein lay fertile ground for the development of a mentality which could tolerate no dissent, a trait which reached paranoid heights in the imagined and concocted dangers associated with McCarthyism.[14] The ways in which those who claimed to defend America against the communist threat actually subverted its democratic process have been well documented. But it will not do to blame the phenomenon on the delusions of particular individuals. The McCarthyite persecution grew naturally, if not logically, out of a cold war mentality developed by more sober souls. The architects of containment, particularly those responsible for NSC–68, cannot escape responsibility for the excesses to which their construction gave rise. After all, part of the reason for its employment was to overcome internal opposition to American involvement in world affairs. And there is no doubt that the anti-communism of the 1950s did indeed have a strong unifying effect on the American class structure and succeeded in generating the unquestioning consensus that foreign policy-makers sought, even if its more hysterical manifestations made many of them uneasy. Kennan himself rejected the extreme interpretations which were put upon his doctrine of containment by the authors of NSC–68.[15] He preferred to try to reconcile it with a balanced foreign policy which employed various and subtle tactics in the endless struggle against communism that he had identified as necessary. The elegance of Kennan's prose in defending moderation should not, however, blind us to the fact that the more extreme interpretation in NSC–68 of what the USA needed to do to counter the communist threat was arguably more consistent with the premisses upon which his analysis was based.

Of course, events contributed to the acceptance of the NSC–68 conception of the post-war world, most notably the Korean invasion of 1950. Indeed, without this it may well have been that NSC–68 and its recommendations for greatly increased defence expenditure by the USA would not have been implemented.[16] Certainly American involvement in Asia may have taken a different path, with fateful consequences for countries beyond Korea itself, notably Vietnam.[17] Even so it is equally the case that the self-confirming nature of the analysis of the Soviet Union contributed much to American involvement in Korea and fed the conspiratorial fantasies of right-wing anti-communism in America.[18] The fact that the perspective was based on the supposed fundamental traits of the USSR rather than on its behaviour meant that Soviet behaviour was interpreted in terms of what it *must* be doing rather than what it *seemed* to be doing. If the Soviet Union was compelled by its ideology and internal structure to pursue expansionism, any apparent deviation from this strategy could easily be seen as a devious means of weakening American resolve in the struggle against communism.

It followed from the analysis that any attempts at co-operation rather than confrontation were ruses designed to buy time for the long-term strategy of world revolution, as was the use of proxies such as the Koreans or the Chinese, because the commitment to world revolution was considered by definition to be the indispensable basis of Soviet society. Once the premisses articulated by the foreign policy establishment were accepted they exerted such a compelling influence as to blind the USA to the actuality of Soviet behaviour. They produced a logic of Wonderland in which all evidence of co-operation by the Soviets was actually taken as evidence of an even more ruthless urge to dominate. There was fertile ground here for the conspiratorial mentality which saw only the monster it had created, and which reacted, with frighteningly consistent but perverse logic, according to that image. And the response had to be all the more vigilant because the evil monster was seen to have the devious and seductive ability to appear friendly while using proxies or other means to further its goals. It is testament to the power of the image of Soviet communism articulated by Kennan that it should prove so compelling, and of course it was not without a foundation in reality; but the cool and measured manner of this articulation belied the seeds of paranoia contained within it.

If, by creating an implacable foe, Kennan's analysis pushed America to adopt an intransigent policy towards the Soviet Union, this trait was accentuated by another aspect of international relations that goes beyond the particular character of either the USA or the USSR and derives from conventional political explanations of the international behaviour of states. This is the problem of uncertainty. For a state deciding on a policy towards a potential aggressor, let alone the sworn enemy that the Soviets represented, calculations have to be made in terms of the capacity of the aggressor at least as much as of probabilities of aggression actually taking place. Because states are dealing with fundamental interests, indeed with their very survival, it is unwise to take risks based on estimates of the likelihood of being attacked. It is far better to pursue policies, both military and diplomatic, which provide security against all eventualities. While the goal of absolute security is never fully realizable, the pursuit of maximum security in the face of uncertainty as to the intentions of other states provides a basic impetus to the foreign policy of all states. How much more compelling then is this impetus when it is allied to the prospect of an enemy whose intentions are assumed to be aggressive without limit.

The basic problem of uncertainty, added to the image of a hostile Soviet Union, has provided the opportunity for American politicians, not always of the right, to exploit the attendant fears and insecurities for their own electoral purposes. At times they have voiced genuine concerns, but at others they have manipulated fears of the electorate unscrupulously. On all occasions, however, it is the objective facts of international relations combined with the constructed image of the Soviet Union which have given them the basis upon which to act, and which have ensured, together with the strength of the lobby for defence contracts, that this aggressive policy stance will always be taken up in the debates on American foreign policy. Taken together, the analysis of Soviet imperialism, the problem of uncertainty and the political advantages to be gained from an aggressive policy created a straitjacket for American policy towards the Soviet Union and confined it for much of the post-war era to channels which not only were narrow and unimaginative, but also contributed to dangerously high levels of tension in world affairs.

To complete the picture of American response to the Soviet Union, however, we need to go beyond these factors because they retain the view of the USA as a passive actor responding to external threat rather than an active participant in world affairs with designs of its own. When America's own needs are recognized the importance of the Soviet Union is transformed: instead of being the aggressor, it becomes the sole obstacle sufficiently powerful to thwart American designs. The fact that the extreme interpretation of Soviet intentions was so readily adopted in the USA is as much a function of its own expansionist imperative as of the actual Soviet threat. Containment and the analysis of Soviet society underlying it provided a cast-iron rationale to justify what the USA wanted to do anyway in world affairs, which was to extend the hegemonic position it found itself in after the war. Containment was a policy ideally suited to a hegemonic power precisely because its hallmark was the absence of limits on intervention; but it was also a policy which for the same reason invited the hubris of American intervention in Vietnam, brinkmanship on Cuba and elsewhere, a seigneurial posture in Latin America, active involvement in the Middle East and a range of other activities which bore all the signs of a world imperial power. The implementation of an expansionist strategy was governed more by the inevitable limits of US power to dominate the world than by any response from the Soviet Union, as indeed was America's subsequent response to these limits.

Soviet strategy was in fact characterized first by a desire to secure specific goals in limited areas where its vital interests, as it saw them, were affected. The fact that these interventions were deeply unattractive to countries other than those which were directly affected by them does not mean that they were attempts to initiate global domination. On the global scale Soviet policy has been to seek parity with the USA rather than domination. The massive arms build-up of the 1960s and 1970s, which was seen as providing the most convincing evidence of Soviet intentions, was in fact much more a response to the humiliation of the Cuban missile crisis and an attempt to reach the parity with the USA which would prevent its recurrence. When considering the level of Soviet armaments in this period it is important to recognize the Soviets' belief that they were threatened on two fronts: by an aggressive American-led Nato alliance to the West and a potentially enormously powerful China to the East. Their geographical and historical situation alone would have justified a higher level of armaments than that of the USA, which is comparatively privileged in these respects. If the level of intervention overseas by the two superpowers is compared since the war, the USA has been much more active in terms of both quantity and extent, which is hardly consistent with the idea of America as merely the reactive partner in the relationship.

The real problem has been American unwillingness to accept Soviet parity as a world power. Its characterization of unlimited Soviet expansion is more revealing about its own mentality than about the USSR. It is because it is so wedded to its own status as a world power, recognizing no limits on its right to intervene, that it cannot conceive of any other country which had equal power not having a similarly expansionist attitude. In this way American attitudes do confirm the political theory of imperialism, which argues that states which have power will use it up to, and beyond, its limits. It is this belief which underlay American unwillingness to tolerate the Soviet Union as an equal. The characterization of the Soviet Union as ideologically bent on world domination therefore became a necessary fiction to justify the pre-emptive actions that the USA wished to take to preserve its hegemonic position. Carrying sufficient plausibility to convince, it provided the ideal framework for America's own highly pro-active post-war agenda.

The most obvious objection to this view of the relations between the USA and the USSR is to point to the periods of co-operation they have undoubtedly enjoyed in the post-war era.[19] Since they manifestly do co-operate at certain times, this would seem to undermine an argument which stresses the unrelieved antagonism of the relationship. The first such period of co-operation was the era of *détente* in the early 1970s when US foreign policy was guided by Nixon and Kissinger. How could America have taken the initiative in developing a co-operative policy such as *détente* when the whole thrust of its policy up until that point had had the opposite coloration? How in particular could Nixon and Kissinger, neither known as an advocate of any weakness in response to the Soviet threat, indeed both prime exponents of its unlimited dangers, have instigated such a policy? The answer lies in the fact that *détente*, far from being a repudiation of the strategy of containment, was really a policy of containment by other means.[20]

The reason for the apparent transformation of policy was not a change in philosophy but a change in American awareness of the limits of its own power.[21] This was in turn the result of its experience in Vietnam. Even while refusing to accept outright defeat in Vietnam, Nixon and Kissinger were quick to recognize that victory was impossible as well. The strategy they evolved to preserve as much of American prestige and power as possible in the face of this setback was complex, sophisticated and multi-faceted.[22] In relation to the USSR it was not a capitulation to growing Soviet military power around the world, but was always double-handed, involving both carrot and stick in an attempt to neutralize Soviet power. The proposed enhanced economic co-operation between East and West was designed more to increase Soviet dependence on Western technology than to signal any warming in the relationship for its own sake. Nixon and Kissinger recognized that, even if militarily the Soviets had been catching up and America could no longer enjoy unchallenged supremacy, in economic terms the advantages enjoyed by the West remained overwhelming. Indeed, if anything they were increasing because the resources the Soviet Union was forced to devote to military production in pursuit of its goal of military parity had beggared the rest of its economy, particularly the production of consumer goods in which the West was so proficient.

This imbalance provided Nixon and Kissinger with a lever they were determined to exploit. To do so they had to tie the Soviet economy to the West, to give it an interest in continuing economic co-operation. This required use of the carrot of aid and incentives to economic co-operation. But once this had been achieved they were determined to use the resulting dependence of the USSR as a stick to affect Soviet policy in other areas. The concept of linkage, whereby economic power was used to influence non-economic policy, was basic to the strategy of *détente*. And it was supplemented by the opening of relations with China, a move designed to produce another lever by which to restrain Soviet power. The Soviets were to be made to realize that all their actions were linked, and that adventurism in one area would have adverse consequences in another. The economic opening involved in *détente* was simply a way of extending America's range of options in imposing these adverse consequences. A prime example of how this worked occurred with the bombing of Haiphong harbour in 1972.[23] The USA had always been reluctant to take this step, despite its military value, because it feared Soviet retaliation. Nixon was able to do it in 1972 because he had already ensured that the Soviets would not respond, making it clear that the economic agreements that were in prospect as a result of *détente* would be abrogated if they did so. This relied on the USSR putting its own economic well-being, which was now to some extent in America's hands, above its commitments to North Vietnam. Soviet inaction showed this calculation to be sound.

The critical point is that the goal of restraining Soviet expansionism remained unchanged; what did change, and in a creative way, was the means by which this goal was to be attained. With an acute awareness of the shifts in the relative strengths and weaknesses of the two superpowers, Nixon and Kissinger devised the most appropriate way to maximize US interests. They concluded that closer ties with the Soviet Union would gain the USA more than it would lose because such ties would provide more opportunities for manipulation of Soviet behaviour than continuing outright hostility. It was a more subtle strategy than what had gone before, and it needed to be, since the era in which the USA could afford to dispense with subtlety because of its overwhelming strength had passed. And the fact that on the surface this appeared to be an ideological volte-face, for them personally as well as for the USA, mattered less than the effectiveness of their strategy. It presented Nixon in particular with the political problem of how to sell to the American people, who had been fed on a steady diet of anti-communism, the idea that co-operation was now in America's best interests. But he was politician enough to relish the challenge, and his own impeccable anti-communist credentials gave him room for manoeuvre because they effectively pre-empted an attack on the policy from the right.

If *détente* represented as much a creative development of the overall strategy of containment as a repudiation of it, it also suffered from some of the same weaknesses, and these were in part responsible for its short-lived nature. The concept of linkage was intimately connected to a continuing zero-sum view in which all successful challenges to regimes in the non-communist world were seen as gains by the Soviets or their proxies and, equally, as losses for the USA and its allies. This boxed the USA into a position where it could not tolerate any reverses in its area of influence lest they be seen as evidence of weakness in the struggle against communism. The flaw in this was that it required the USA to prop up the status quo everywhere in its sphere of influence, no matter how unsustainable the ally to which it had given its support. The requirement to defend the indefensible inherent in containment was one of its greatest weaknesses, and it ensured that battles were fought on ground not of America's choosing, since the chain of its alliances was always likely, virtually by definition, to be attacked at its weakest link. Unfortunately, *détente* exacerbated the problem rather than resolving it because when attacks inevitably came, and when they were linked, however indirectly, to Soviet aggression, as the continuing containment mentality required, it made it appear that the policy of co-operation with the USSR had failed in its objective of restraint. This in turn gave ammunition to those who saw in *détente* a policy of weakness and capitulation to the 'inevitability' of Soviet power. While Nixon and Kissinger in their prime were able to forestall the development of this contradiction, in other, less experienced hands the problems got out of hand and the policy was discredited as a result.

Carter in particular was vulnerable in this respect because unlike Nixon he did not enjoy immunity from attack by those on the right who had always suspected that *détente* was a sign of weakness. The irony was that the episode which initially discredited both Carter and *détente*, the hostage-taking in Iran, had nothing to do with Soviet expansionism and everything to do with US attempts to prop up an unpopular ruler. But such niceties did not deter those who saw the opportunity to make political capital out of accusations of weakness, especially when the Soviet invasion of Afghanistan gave them much more plausible grounds for such charges. The disgrace of Watergate, and the loss of authority it represented for its most sophisticated exponents, also did not favour a long life for *détente*. And it has to be noted that the manipulation and secretiveness that were an essential component of *détente*, at least in its early stages, were the product of a mentality which, when transposed to the domestic stage, lay at the root of the Watergate tragedy.

The principal reason for the rejection of *détente*, however, was its inherent weakness as a part of the containment strategy. The more complex relation it created with the premises of that strategy meant that it would always be open to attack from those who felt that these premisses more logically implied a strategy of confrontation with the Soviet Union. And when there was political advantage to be derived from a return to basics, it is not surprising that opponents of *détente* became more vociferous and, with the election of Reagan, politically successful.[24] It is not perhaps true to say that *détente* was doomed to failure, but it has to be admitted that the basic US view of the Soviet Union as articulated in the strategy of containment would always have threatened to undermine it. At most, *détente* gave a pendulum character to US policy in which unrestrained hostility was tempered by periods of co-operation which were in turn undermined by the logic of confrontation implicit in the containment perspective upon which it rested.

If the election of Reagan represented the swing back to the old verities, the latter part of his administration witnessed a reverse with a vengeance. The fact that it was prompted by the upheavals of *glasnost* and *perestroika* in the Soviet Union raises the possibility that this phase will be of a much more fundamental character than another swing of the pendulum, and will eventually result in a complete transformation of the basis of USA–Soviet relations.[25] Faced with such momentous events, American policy-makers have necessarily responded with wariness. There is understandable caution because of the fear that the reforms will not prove durable, and that it will become apparent that little has changed. In the more paranoid reaches of the containment mentality there is suspicion that the reforms are merely cosmetic, that the Soviets, far from having given up their goal of world domination, are reforming in order to be able to pursue it more effectively. Both views carry the implication that the USA would be unwise to lower its military guard.

Such views become increasingly hard to maintain, however, as the scale of change in Eastern Europe and the Soviet Union takes on an air of irreversibility which demands new thinking from the USA.[26] The problem is, of course, to formulate a response when the outcome of this Soviet revolution, or indeed the time-frame by which that outcome will be apparent, is so uncertain. The position is further complicated by the fact that the American response can be assumed to have an effect on the outcome. The danger here is that of self-fulfilment: if out of suspicion the USA refuses to co-operate with the Soviet Union in, for example, arms reduction or in giving food and economic aid, then it may contribute to bringing the whole process of liberalization to a halt, and help to recreate the enemy it fears. Far better to respond as generously as is prudent, since a co-operative strategy too could prove self-fulfilling and create a liberal Soviet society that would cease to pose a threat to US interests in the world.[27]

If the assumption of this argument is accepted, that the USA can to some extent choose the kind of Soviet Union it wishes to deal with, then it would seem to follow that the USA should exert its influence on the side of liberalization through co-operation. But this neglects the further argument that *perestroika* itself would not have come about had it not been for the confrontational stance initially adopted by the Reagan administration. Reform in the Soviet Union is basically the product of economic weakness. This in turn is the result of the enormous burden of military expenditure it has had to bear in the service of its ambition to achieve parity as a superpower with the USA. It is this burden which has diverted resources away from production of consumer goods and given the Soviet population the impoverished standard of living that has proved fatal to the legitimacy of the old system. Although high military spending has been a burden on the USA economy, the weight is minimal compared to that placed on the Soviets by their attempts to match it. Not to put too fine a point on it, the argument is that confrontation and military preparedness have been a rational policy for the USA because they have capitalized on the fact that it has the stronger economic system and have forced the Soviet Union to capitulate in the struggle between the superpowers. It follows that, if confrontation has produced the desired result, it should be carried through to its logical conclusion since it might ultimately result in the complete disintegration of the Soviet Union.

It would in fact be presumptuous to credit American policy with the leading role in the transformation of Soviet society, though this has not prevented Western leaders claiming just such a vindication. The weaknesses of the Soviet economy have to a considerable extent been the result of an outmoded planning structure which is directly related to Marxist ideology, and in this respect the influence of the USA is relevant only as an example of a contrasting and more efficient economic system. Moreover, any rejoicing at the victory in the cold war that it is claimed confrontation brought about would have to be tempered by the adverse effect that the policy of beggaring the Soviet Union into submission has had on American competitiveness with other capitalist powers. It would be a Pyrrhic victory indeed if the USA had so

weakened its economy in order to break the power of the Soviets that
it diminished its own position and ceded the leading role in the new
world economy to Japan and a revitalized German–dominated Europe,
and allowed them to reap the benefits of its self-sacrifice. Such has been
the preoccupation with the Soviet threat that tunnel vision of this kind
cannot be ruled out. But the implication must be that, if the USA is
to avoid winning the battle but losing the war, it must reduce its own
military burden, a goal which would make co-operation with the
Soviets imperative.

In sum, the American dilemma as to what stance to adopt towards
the events in the Soviet Union is profound and compounded by
uncertainty. If it co-operates and helps to produce a more open Soviet
society, then a deadly rival may be replaced by a non-threatening
society that can assist in creating stability in international affairs through
its participation in a virtually global economy organized on capitalist
principles. Liberalization of the former communist economies would
therefore provide the USA with enormous opportunities for extending
its economic sway and enhancing its domestic prosperity. On the other
hand, such a strategy also risks helping to create a rival on the world
stage made all the stronger by the revitalization of its economy. A
realist view would suggest that a strong Soviet Union would make this
an inevitability rather than a possibility, and that the American interest
lies in keeping the Soviet Union as weak as possible. Pressure brought
the Soviets to their knees, and a refusal of all aid to the reform process
would be the best way to keep them there. Indeed, the USA should
go further and do all in its power to sow dissension within the Soviet
Union, seeking to promote the break-up of the USSR which the reform
process has made a possibility. The danger here is again that this
strategy may assist the forces of reaction in the Soviet Union and result
not in the break-up of the USSR, but in a military takeover that would
reinstitute repression and produce an even more dangerous and
reactionary adversary.

The range of possibilities would therefore appear to fall into three
categories. The first is the emergence of a reformed Soviet Union
liberated from its communist ideology, and therefore from the imperative
to world revolution, and purged as a threat to American interests. If
incorporated into the capitalist world order, it might eventually become
a rival to the USA, but in the medium term the opportunities for
investment and growth which the opening of the Soviet market would
produce far outweigh any such negative prospect. The second possibility
is that the forces unleashed by *perestroika* will result in the disintegration
of the Soviet Union on the basis of nationalist revolts among its
constituent republics.[28] This too would eliminate the threat that the

Soviet Union has been perceived as mounting to American interests, and would create a world order with greater scope for American leadership as the only remaining country with the combination of economic and military power necessary for superpower status. If this possibility is to transpire, however, it is unlikely to come about without a titanic struggle. There are forces within the Soviet Union, most notably the military, which would not be content to sit back and let disintegration happen. Were they to prove dominant, and this is the third possibility, it would lead to a reversion of the Soviet Union to a dictatorial society in which order was maintained by the internal use of military power. Such a society would not only be internally repressive, however, it would almost certainly project a more reactionary policy abroad and might well revive the cold war, if only to provide itself with the external enemy it would need to maintain its rule at home. Its legitimacy would be severely undermined, but it might prove all the more dangerous and adventurist an adversary for the USA because of that.

American policy should be oriented towards promoting the first possibility for two major reasons. The first is that America's best hope for continuing world leadership lies in the globalization of the capitalist system, and it should grasp all opportunities that present themselves for an extension of capitalism. That has been the animus of much of its post-war policy, but it has had to be pursued on a defensive basis, maintaining the present area open to capital. Now that the opportunity has arisen for taking the offensive and extending the boundaries of the capitalist world, it would be folly not to take advantage. This remains true despite the existence now of other capitalist powers more economically dynamic than the USA, which might benefit from the order that American hegemony has created and even threaten to supplant it. The USA remains the single power possessed of the combination of attributes necessary for leadership, and it should follow policies intended to capitalize on these advantages rather than allow policy to be dictated by fear of other countries' economic prowess.

The second reason that the USA should foster liberalization in the Soviet Union arises from what continues to be the pre-eminent feature of the US–Soviet relationship: its nuclear dimension. This has had a dual character in the post-war years. On the one hand, it has obviously heightened the level of tension between them and raised the stakes of the conflict to previously unimaginable levels. But it has had other effects too. The very possession of massive nuclear capacity distinguishes the superpowers from all other countries and by that token creates a common bond because they become in effect the only active participants in a struggle whose stakes are beyond calculation. The fact that each has the unique capacity to obliterate the other, and indeed everyone else, creates a common interest in survival. This is the rationale underlying the strategic philosophy of mutual assured destruction: behind even so deep-seated a conflict as has existed between the Soviet and American systems, there is a common humanity which shares a basic instinct for self-preservation. The effect of nuclear capacity has also been therefore to restrain conflict between the superpowers. Given the diagnosis of expansionism each has made of the other, it is likely that in the absence of nuclear weapons full-scale military conflict would have erupted between them. In fact nuclear weaponry has not eliminated conflict, rather it has displaced it to areas of the world in which it could be contained, often on to territory where it could be fought out by surrogates. Effectively, the superpowers have been brought by the nuclear factor to temper their analyses of each other's intentions and incorporate a recognition of spheres of influence; this has by no means eliminated conflict, but it has confined it largely to the margins and provided a cap on the extent to which conflict has been allowed to develop.

But there is no guarantee that such displacement will continue, of course, and the reliance on nuclear defence has reduced the level of conflict only at the expense of increasing the dangers inherent in the relationship. In the long run this may prove disastrous, since it is unlikely that these dangers could be displaced for ever if the diagnosis by each of the intentions of the other were to remain so implacably opposed. The most appropriate analogy may be with the man falling from a twenty-storey building who, as he passes the tenth floor, remarks that everything seems fine so far!

In one sense, then, the nuclear dimension has kept the peace and restrained the conflict between the superpowers; in another it has increased the penalties of mishandling or misunderstanding to previously unimaginable levels. The implications for policy are clear: since the nuclear capacity of either side will not simply disappear, any development which helps to alter the balance in favour of the positive aspect of this dimension should be pursued with vigour. The upheavals in the Soviet Union offer just such a prospect. If the USA can respond to them in such a way as to promote the incorporation of the Soviet Union and its former allies into the world capitalist economy, it will have succeeded in eliminating much of the rationale for conflict and the accompanying threat of nuclear destruction. It may even be that such incorporation combined with the facts of a nuclear duopoly would create the conditions for a form of ultra-imperialism undreamt of even in Kautsky's formulation.[29] But even the negative connotations of such an outcome would pale in comparison with the threat of nuclear annihilation that the world has endured for most of the post-war era.

The Soviet–American relationship, then, particularly in its present uncertain phase, reveals a remarkable combination of economic and political opportunities for the USA, and provides a necessary corrective to any economistic approach to America's role in the modern world. Once again we see that the economic aspect provides the substance of the opportunity to advance American interests, while also liberating the world from the threat of nuclear annihilation. But this does not alter the fact that the nuclear aspect of the superpower relationship gives it a fundamentally political character. Important, indeed essential, as the economic aspect provided by the dynamism of the capitalist system is, it is given meaning only in its relationship to the literally vital and therefore primary issues posed by the nuclear aspect. Prosperity matters, but survival matters more. What is remarkable about the present conjuncture is the possibility it raises that the former can contribute to the latter in so critical a sense. The outcome is not under American control by any means, but the challenge of these new developments will, if successfully met, enhance America's role even as it creates a new world order.

Notes

1. N. Graebner (ed.), *The Cold War: Ideological conflict or power struggle?*, London: Heath, 1963; W. Lafeber, *America, Russia and the Cold War 1945–84*, New York: Wiley, 1985, 5th edn.
2. D. Bell, *The End of Ideology: On the exhaustion of political ideas*, New York: Free Press, 1960.
3. D. Horowitz, *From Yalta to Vietnam: American foreign policy in the cold war*, Harmondsworth: Penguin, 1967; W.A. Williams, *The Tragedy of American Diplomacy*, New York: Dell, 1972, 2nd edn; J. Kolko and G. Kolko, *The Limits of Power: The world and US foreign policy 1945–54*, New York: Harper & Row, 1972; J.L. Richardson, 'Cold war revisionism: a critique', *World Politics*, 24, 2, 1972, pp. 579–612.
4. L. Shoup and W. Minter, *Imperial Brain Trust: The Council on Foreign Relations and United States foreign policy*, New York: Monthly Review Press, 1977.
5. G. Alperovitz, *Atomic Diplomacy: Hiroshima and Potsdam*, London: Secker & Warburg, 1966.
6. A.P. Dobson, *The Politics of the Anglo-American Economic Special Relationship 1940–87*, Hemel Hempstead: Harvester Wheatsheaf, 1988.
7. D.C. Watt, 'Rethinking the cold war', *Political Quarterly*, 49, Oct.–Dec. 1978, pp. 446–56.

8. A.M. Schlesinger, 'The cold war revisited', *New York Review of Books*, 10 October 1979; J.L. Gaddis, *The Long Peace: Inquiries into the history of the cold war*, New York: Oxford University Press, 1987.
9. D. Yergin, *Shattered Peace: The origins of the cold war and the national security state*, New York: Houghton Mifflin, 1979.
10. R. Hofstadter, *The Paranoid Style in American Politics and Other Essays*, New York: Knopf, 1965.
11. G.F. Kennan, *American Diplomacy*, Chicago, Ill.: University of Chicago Press, 1984, expanded edn; G.F. Kennan *et al.*, *Encounters with Kennan*, London: Cass, 1979; G.F. Kennan *et al.*, M.F. Hertz (ed.), *Decline of the West: George Kennan and his critics*, Washington, DC: Ethics and Public Policy Center, Georgetown University, 1978.
12. For a discussion of the extent of the differences between Kennan and NSC–68, see J.L. Gaddis, *Strategies of Containment: A critical appraisal of postwar American national security policy*, New York: Oxford University Press, 1982, chapter 4.
13. H. Arendt, *The Origins of Totalitarianism*, London: Allen & Unwin, London, 1958.
14. E. Latham (ed.), *The Meaning of McCarthyism*, London: Heath, 1973, 2nd edn.
15. Kennan, *American Diplomacy, op. cit.*, G.F. Kennan, 'The US and the Soviet Union 1917–76', *Foreign Affairs*, 54, 4, 1976, pp. 670–90.
16. S. Brown, *The Faces of Power: Constancy and change in United States foreign policy from Truman to Reagan*, New York: Columbia University Press, 1983, pp. 50–1.
17. R. Foot, *The Wrong War: American policy and the dimensions of the Korean conflict, 1950–53*, Ithaca, NY: Cornell University Press, 1985.
18. A. Wolfe, 'The irony of anti-communism: ideology and interest in post-war American foreign policy', *Socialist Register*, 1984, pp. 214–29.
19. R.W. Stevenson, *The Rise and Fall of Detente: Relaxations of tension in US–Soviet relations 1953–84*, London: Macmillan, 1985.
20. *ibid.*
21. Gaddis, *op. cit.*
22. Bell, *op. cit.*
23. S. Hersh, *Kissinger: The price of power – Henry Kissinger in the Nixon White House*, London: Faber, 1983.
24. R. Garthoff, *Detente and Confrontation: American–Soviet relations from Nixon to Reagan*, Washington, DC: Brookings Institution, 1985.
25. J.L. Gaddis, *Russia, the Soviet Union and the United States: An interpretive history*, New York: McGraw-Hill, 1990, 2nd edn.
26. S. Bialer and M. Mandelbaum (eds.), *Gorbachev's Russia and American Foreign Policy*, Boulder, Colo.: Westview, 1988.
27. M. Mandelbaum, 'Ending the cold war', *Foreign Affairs*, 68, 2, spring 1989, pp. 16–36.
28. Z. Brzezinski, 'Post-communist nationalism', *Foreign Affairs*, 68, 5, winter 1989/90, pp. 1–25.
29. K. Kautsky, 'Ultra-imperialism', *New Left Review*, 59, Jan.–Feb. 1970, pp. 41–46.

CHAPTER FOUR

THE CAPITALIST POWERS: DISCORD AND HARMONY

The essentially political nature of American–Soviet relations serves, as we have seen, to enhance rather than diminish the importance of the internationalization of the capitalist system which has occurred under American hegemony. This process has now reached the critical juncture in which it raises the prospect of replacing a world system dominated by competing hegemonic blocs – one capitalist, the other communist – with a truly global capitalism. While this offers the hope of reducing fundamental tensions in world politics, it would be naive to assume that it will resolve all difficulties in the relations between the established capitalist powers. On the contrary, globalization has made these relations a good deal more problematic, involving a quite different interaction of economics and politics from that presented by superpower relations.[1]

To investigate this aspect of America's position in the modern world we must take up the theme of decline. There can be no doubt that, in terms of conventional economic indicators, the USA has suffered a decline relative to several other capitalist countries, most notably Germany and Japan.[2] Of course, this is as much a testament to the success of US policies since the war in stimulating economic regeneration in the rest of the capitalist world as it is any sign of weakness on America's part. In this respect 'decline' is not only inevitable but has indeed been desirable. The more important question is whether this will necessarily result in the elimination of American hegemony in a wider political–economic sense.[3] The transformation of the world economy from one in which the USA was thoroughly dominant to a position of multipolarity containing several centres of economic power need not be inimical to American interests. The subject of this chapter is to consider whether it is likely to prove to be so by investigating the implications of the transformation of the world capitalist economy for relations between the capitalist powers.

The hypothesis of American decline presents three possibilities. The first is that, despite the statistical economic trends, the USA has in fact

67

continued to be the dominant force in the capitalist world. There are other sources of domination beyond simple economic growth, and on these it is quite possible that the USA has remained pre-eminent. If this is the case, the economic trends are merely surface phenomena which give a misleading picture by masking what remains essentially the same relation between capitalist countries, and the question then becomes how sustainable this American hegemony is.

The second possibility is that the new system of relations may be essentially co-operative. After the experience of the first half of this century, in which the competitive element predominated and led to two world-wide conflagrations, the common interest in restraining conflict has become apparent. The mechanisms for doing so are not easy to establish in a system in which competition is the driving force. But the object is to bring the influence of politics to bear in a way that keeps conflict within constructive and manageable bounds rather than exacerbating it, even if this requires sacrifices of advantage by individual countries for the greater good of the system as a whole. In this possibility the power of the USA would indeed have been transcended, to be replaced not by another country, but rather by a supra-national network of political institutions. The rapid globalization of the world capitalist economy has posed a massive political challenge to the nation-states involved in it to develop a framework which can regulate the new economy. It may be that the political response is not consistent with the hegemony of any one state, including the USA. This does not mean it will be global in the sense that power will be widely dispersed. More likely is some midpoint where power is shared, but between a few leading capitalist powers who may remain in an exploitative relation to the less developed capitalist world. This would suggest an alternative form of ultra-imperialism to the US–Soviet model discussed in Chapter 3. The US state would obviously have a major role to play in managing this transition, one which would involve recognition of declining power, but which would none the less fulfil its basic function of creating a secure world environment for US-based capital to operate in.

The third possibility is that the challenge posed by the internationalization of the economy will prove too great.[4] In such a massive change some parts of the system, some nation-states, are bound to lose even if the gains for the system as a whole outweigh these. Because of where the process has started from, it is the USA which has the most to lose. The temptation to secure sectional gain through increased rivalry with other capitalist states, even at the expense of the general prosperity, will remain great. At its worst this could produce a vicious spiral of conflict which will carry echoes of the 1930s. It is impossible to tell what the limits of such conflict might be, but the history of this century demonstrates that they do not exclude the possibility of a spillover into military conflict that would be even more devastating with today's weapons than the outcome of such competition was half a century ago.[5] Even if the USA did not take the lead in escalating such conflict in order to protect its position, its loss of hegemonic power might prevent it from stopping others initiating the process or cause it to be dragged into the conflict once begun.

The range of possibilities along which intra-capitalist relations might develop is then very extensive. They are separable only analytically, and the outcome will be a mixture of elements from each of them, but by examining each in turn we will come to a clearer understanding of the direction these relations are most likely to take. The first possibility, continued US dominance, recognizes some element of decline if only in the sense that the immediate post-war situation was an aberration and quite unsustainable. It is in US interests for there to be other healthy capitalist markets around the world, and US policy has been designed to promote these.[6] But this is true only up to a point, and so the question becomes whether that point has been breached and the decline has become substantive and undesirable, as opposed to superficial and intended.

Continued American dominance could have a number of sources: economic, military and cultural factors can all contribute to political strength. The most obvious area where American dominance has been challenged is the economic. This is partly because economic indices of progress are most easily measurable and comparable. On most such indices the USA has not done well in recent years. Its growth rate has been lower over time than other leading capitalist powers; its level of savings and spending on research, which determine future growth, are also relatively low.[7] Lower productivity is reflected in growing import penetration and the development of a massive trade imbalance in the 1980s which has been financed by a huge inflow of capital, principally from Europe and Japan.[8] This may be seen as a sign of confidence in the US economy as a safe and profitable haven for capital; or it may be seen as eating away at US economic power by selling off the capital resources of the country to finance excessive current consumption – selling the family silver, to invoke a phrase used in a different but similar context.[9]

The changing role of the dollar provides a clear illustration of how these changes have affected America's international economic position.[10] Prior to 1971 the general pattern of the US balance of payments was to have a surplus on trade and a substantial capital outflow. The build-up of investment overseas was facilitated by the role of the US dollar as, in effect, the reserve currency for the world economy. From the end of the war until 1971 it was tied to gold at a fixed price of $35 to the ounce. This meant that other countries were willing to accept US dollars as a substitute for gold in settlement of international debts. Without some such international currency the extraordinary growth in world trade which lay at the basis of Western economic resurgence could not have occurred. So the flow of dollars from the USA into the world economy at large was beneficial to the receiving countries. However, it also freed the USA from the usual balance of payments constraints. Rather than having to curb domestic demand in order to bring its external accounts into balance, it was able to finance any overall deficit simply by issuing more dollars. For any other country such a course would simply have led to a devaluation of its currency. But such was the international confidence in the strength of the US economy that its tie to gold, and thus its fixed price, were not threatened.

This meant that in effect the USA was able to act like a banker issuing cheques (dollars) on an account (gold), without the need to ensure that there was anything in the account to cover them, so eager were other countries to use these cheques (dollars) to finance their own trade. This was a remarkably painless way to build up a massive overseas portfolio and the clearest possible illustration of the benefits, as opposed to the burdens, of a dominant position. In this respect, at least, the USA was playing by easier economic rules than all other countries. It was able to do so because, although this system benefited the USA, it was also indispensable to economic growth in the rest of the capitalist world economy. Thus the financial system reinforced America's economic pre-eminence, but because it simultaneously financed the growth of world trade and prosperity, it also contributed to America's more general hegemonic position. It therefore benefited all, but it benefited the USA more than the others. This was indeed benign hegemony.

This situation was dependent both on the strength of the US economy in this period and on confidence in US leadership. As the other capitalist economies began to catch up after post-war rebuilding, the first factor became less pronounced; and, as a result of the Vietnam war, the second too suffered a crisis. The two factors were closely interrelated. For the dollar's reserve role to work effectively the amount of dollars fed into the world economy had to match the increased liquidity necessitated by the growth of world trade: too little and that growth would be restrained, but too much and the dollar would become subject to inflationary pressures, which would fatally undermine its position as the bedrock of world finance. The demands of the Vietnam war, besides alienating many allies from US foreign policy, also pushed this economic balance awry as, in order to finance the war, the USA pumped more dollars into the world economy than were needed for trade. Once confidence was lost other countries began to question US capacity to honour the principle of convertibility.

By 1971 there were approximately six times as many dollars held by foreigners abroad as the USA had gold to convert at the fixed price. The logic of the market now became to develop a rush on the dollar. Since the dollar, by definition, lacked the elasticity of price to respond to this, the pressure increased, which only threatened confidence even more. The elastic snapped in August 1971 when President Nixon was forced to break the fixed link between the dollar and gold. From then on the dollar enjoyed no special status as a world currency and was subject to the same fluctuations as others. This resulted in an immediate substantial devaluation to relieve the pressure, and since then its fortunes have varied considerably.[11] The important point in this context, however, is that loss of economic and political pre-eminence led to the elimination of financial pre-eminence. Just as economic strength and political confidence had been mutually reinforcing and in turn strengthened by the financial system, so when the tide turned the three elements reinforced each other in a negative direction. Financial movements may often seem arcane, but this illustration demonstrates how they actually manifest and accentuate underlying shifts of power.[12]

In statistical economic terms, then, the picture is unequivocal: the USA has experienced a relative decline and this has been accentuated by the concomitant loss of its hegemonic privileges in the world financial system. In the early post-war years the role of politics was how best to capitalize on America's overweening economic strength. The goal was not only to preserve and extend economic power, but also to use it to enlarge the general sway of the USA in the world. In this America was largely successful, but inevitably in ways which ate into its economic pre-eminence. Since the crisis became manifest sometime in the late 1960s, the goal of US policy has altered and focused on the development of strategies to cope with, and if possible reverse, the threat of decline. Each administration since Nixon has employed different strategies in pursuit of this goal, but the common thread is important to grasp.[13] The continuing size of the American economy has given US policy-makers greater flexibility than most, but its responsibilities and the burdens attached to them have also been greater and all the more difficult to manage with the loss of the immunity enjoyed in the halcyon post-war days. In order to cope they have used all dimensions of American influence.

In the cultural sphere, for example, especially in popular culture,

there is a case for continuing and even increasing American influence.[14]
The US popular music industry is unquestionably the most influential
in the world, and the wide distribution of American-made films and
televison programmes has created a world-wide popular imagery. In
more material matters too the continuing penetration of the likes of
Coca-Cola and McDonald's is creating a global culture that is heavily
American-influenced, while the universal appeal of the Disney characters
has provided the leading edge for American domination in the provision
of leisure facilities such as theme parks. These aspects combine to
produce an iconography that is global in its appeal and influence,
especially for the young. Rather than the dry abstractions of freedom,
justice and democracy, it is a *mélange* of imagery centred around Levis,
hamburgers, soft drinks and rock music that has come to symbolize
the desirability of the American way of life to youth across the world.
The success of the United States in creating such powerful imagery
centres on the influence of its language. Here the USA has benefited
from its position of pre-eminence at a time when the development of
communications has increased the pressures for a global language; it
has also benefited, of course, from having inherited world leadership
from another country, Britain, which spread the influence of the
language through empire.

The importance of American influence in the communications
industry around the world as a transmitter of values should not be
underestimated.[15] The growing relative size of this sector domestically
is evidence of the fact that the USA continues to be in the vanguard
of economic development, since it is in this post-industrial direction
that mature capitalist economies must all move. So the USA retains its
advanced status in the most dynamic sector of the economy and has
built upon this a range of post-modern imagery that establishes it as
the leading element of the emerging global consumer culture, a culture
whose values of individualism and consumerism serve to buttress
American hegemony.[16] The implications of such a role are, however,
much harder to pin down. In the first place the ubiquity of the symbols
of American culture leaves open the meaning of those symbols when
transposed to the receiving cultures. It should not be assumed that they
carry the same meaning when set in other cultures as they do in the
USA. In particular it is not evident that, even though their penetration
is accepted, they carry such unequivocally positive connotations in the
rest of the world as they do in their own culture. The meaning of such
symbols is extremely flexible, and while other cultures absorb American
influence they also transform it. The transformations they undergo once
they are detached from their origins may mean that they do not enhance
the influence of the USA to the extent that might be apparent from

the American perspective. On the other hand, the fact that it is values rather than interests which are involved may make the effect more insidious: less visible perhaps, less quantifiable, but none the less important for that.

The interconnectedness of culture with economics is vital in this context. The extensive distribution of American television programmes owes as much to the cheapness of their production, derived from economies of scale, as to their intrinsic quality, and the market penetration of many consumer products is more a testament to the power of advertising and effective distribution networks than to their inherent superiority. It may be that, to the extent that this cultural influence does rest on an economic base, the American lead in the tertiary sector of the economy will be eroded just as it has been in the manufacturing sector, and the ubiquity of American cultural influence will prove to be similarly transient. The takeover of major American companies such as CBS by Japanese capital may presage the way in which the shifting balance of power becomes manifest in this area. Cultural production could remain in the hands of those who have established global success in this sphere, but ultimate, financial control will come to be held by representatives of the rising economic power. Any such hierarchy is a long way off, however, and up to the present the cultural dimension continues to lend weight to the argument that to describe America's role in the world as one simply of decline is less accurate than to view it as undergoing a process of transformation in which its influence has shifted as between different spheres of activity. The USA may not dominate the world economy as before in manufacturing output, but its cultural influence and the domination of the rapidly expanding communications industry upon which it rests appear to be stronger than ever.

The interaction between America's economic position and its military power is a good deal more problematic. The growing demands in Congress for 'burden sharing' are evidence that in recent years the costs of maintaining its military establishment have become a drain on the American economy. The argument made in Chapter 2 that military production, while it may boost a flagging economy in the short run, eventually diverts resources from more productive economic activity seems apposite. The military expenditure required to build up the American sphere of influence was made possible by a thriving economy. Its maintenance is at least as expensive, but the economic basis no longer exists, not least because other countries have been able to develop their economies more rapidly since they have been freed of the necessity to provide their own military protection. Like other imperial powers before it,[17] the USA has had to confront the problem of economic decline accentuated by military spending that is the product of commitments undertaken in an earlier, more prosperous period. The dilemma arises because reduction of military commitments, while cutting the economic burden, also threatens to reduce American political influence. In so far as this in turn contributes to international economic influence, the reduction of military spending for economic reasons becomes self-defeating. The twin possibilities, therefore, are either to maintain military spending and risk crippling the competitiveness of the economy, or to cut it and risk undermining American influence in world affairs on both the economic and political planes.

The complicating factor in these calculations, however, is the nuclear pre-eminence that the USA enjoys among the allies. Notwithstanding the independent nuclear forces of the UK and France and the framework of the Nato alliance, it has been US nuclear power which has provided the guarantee of security for all capitalist countries in the post-war period.[18] Whether it will provide the basis for continuing USA dominance within the alliance depends on two factors. The first is the willingness of other countries to take responsibility for their own nuclear defence. The position in Europe is complicated by the historical position of Germany which would appear to preclude it from adopting such a role. In addition, the costs involved make it difficult for other countries presently without nuclear capacity to enter this arena, and for those which do have it to expand significantly. The solution would appear to be a joint acceptance of this burden, presumably through the agency of the European Community. However, the degree of social and economic integration needed to make the sharing of responsibility in such a sensitive area acceptable to the nation-states of Europe is still far from realized. On the eastern flank of the alliance the possibility of Japan taking on an enhanced role in this area is not precluded either by the economic and technical constraints or by those of federalism. But again historical factors would lead the other alliance powers to view rapid development in this direction, particularly in the nuclear sphere, with great suspicion. The fear of a revival of Japanese militarism and its own experience of nuclear war would seem to make unlikely a type of burden-sharing that would alter the strategic balance of power. While feasible, therefore, the idea of nuclear burden-sharing as a mechanism by which US economic decline is translated into military and therefore political decline does not appear to be an immediate prospect.

Of much greater significance for the relations between the USA and its capitalist allies are the developments in the socialist world, and particularly in the Soviet Union. The need for the USA security umbrella has been predicated on the existence of a hostile and powerful enemy capable of threatening the existence of the allied states. Without this external threat the need for protection, and thus the basis of US domination, ceases to exist.[19] It is possible that *perestroika* and *glasnost* in the Soviet Union will lead to the abolition of just such a threat. One aspect of *perestroika* is that the USSR seeks much greater economic co-operation with the West, and the allied powers have been competing for entry into this potentially enormous market. If the economic ties between the USSR and the Western powers develop as the Soviet Union appears to want, economic relations will gradually take precedence over strategic considerations. The issue therefore becomes not whether the USA continues to enjoy a nuclear monopoly, but whether that monopoly would retain any significance in the face of a level of economic co-operation between East and West which made the employment of nuclear forces as unthinkable against the countries of what was the Soviet bloc as it would be in intra-capitalist disputes.

These possibilities may be viewed as a reverse form of *détente*. As explained in Chapter 3, the closer economic co-operation pursued by Nixon and Kissinger in the 1970s was intended to weaken Soviet power. Similarly, whether by intention or not, the new Soviet openness may have the effect of sowing seeds of division between the Western powers as they compete for closer economic ties with the USSR; and by obviating the need for American military protection, such ties may in turn weaken the power of the USA. The dilemma these developments pose for the USA is acute. Its vested interest in continuing confrontation with the traditional communist monolith becomes more apparent as the idea of the total threat posed by communism becomes more difficult to sustain. To embrace the disintegration of the threat to peace caused by the transformation of socialism and to term it a victory could become a triumphant fulfilment of US policy. But if to do so would be to collude with its own decline as a world power, then the attitudes of American policy-makers are bound to be much more circumspect.

In view of the ever-present factor of uncertainty, in this case both as to the ultimate intentions of those advocating *perestroika* and as to their capacity to retain power, and therefore of the possibility of reversal to the status quo ante, it is not surprising that caution has been the watchword of the American response. Clearly the weakening of the traditional basis for US dominance, the nuclear umbrella, makes it highly unlikely that the USA will be able to maintain its pre-eminence as of old. But perhaps it is wrong to ask whether it can. If we recognize that the possibility of continuing with the old forms of dominance has been overtaken by events, then the issue becomes whether new forms are emerging which will permit the USA to continue to play the leading role in the modern world, and whether US policy has sought such forms. The answer to this question raises the second possibility outlined for the development of intra-capitalist relations, that of ultra-imperialism.

The concept of ultra-imperialism in the contemporary context involves less the issue of collaboration between capitalist states to exploit less developed regions of the world economy, as was the case in its original formulation,[20] than the idea that the globalization of the world economy has made employment of the nation-state as the governing agent of economic development obsolete.[21] Following Marxist theory, it is the drive for the accumulation of capital which is seen as the dynamic of economic and social change. This is a process which in itself recognizes no national boundaries, and when combined with a level of technological development which is easily able to transcend boundaries established in quite different historical conditions, then the effect is for the economic power embodied in these forces to transcend that of any state. The example of the UK demonstrates how macroeconomic policy is heavily constrained by the imperatives of international capital.[22] The British economy seems incapable of generating sufficient development capital to fund the investment needed for rapid economic growth, not least because indigenous capital has been quick to find more profitable overseas outlets in the 1980s. The government therefore has to compete with other countries to retain its 'own' – that is, British – capital at home. It is also forced to compete for overseas capital to develop the home economy. The need to attract American, Japanese and French capital to build a motor industry on its soil at the same time that British capital has been investing heavily in all these countries demonstrates the internationalization of the movement of capital.

Government success in the competition for capital can only be achieved by providing economic conditions in which this capital finds it congenial to operate, such as tax and other financial incentives, together with low inflation, relatively low wages and an amenable workforce. Social and economic policy is therefore heavily constrained by the need to create this environment. The vulnerability of the value of the currency to speculative movements of capital is also well documented, as indeed is the constraining effect this has had on both monetary and fiscal policy.[23] The extent of this problem has not been so apparent in the UK in the 1980s because the disposition of the government has been to embrace these constraints on its policies as a spur to economic growth. The power of capital to alter government policy would become much more visible with a government which had other priorities than the provision of a congenial environment for capital.[24] The capital flight that has occurred in a number of countries at the prospect of left-wing governments illustrates the point. The very mobility of international capital as compared to the rootedness of nation-states gives its agents, whether in the form of multinational corporations, fund managers or indeed currency speculators, enormous leverage over nominally sovereign governments, leverage that can be used to play them off against each other in pursuit of policies that, although implemented by governments, are in effect dictated by the power of capital.

If a country such as the UK is evidently subject to these forces in its policy making, the question arises as to whether even as large an economy as the USA can be immune from them. Because the internationalization of capital developed with such speed during the era of American hegemony, it has been easy to conflate the two factors and assume that internationalization was an aspect of US domination. The fact that the majority of multinational corporations and banks which were instrumental in this process were based in the USA reinforced this perspective. The rise to prominence of European- and Japanese-based multinational corporations and banks has made it increasingly clear that American pre-eminence can no longer be taken for granted. However, this does not necessarily mean that the world economy has simply moved to a more pluralistic position in which there operate a series of corporations each allied to its own nation-state. The more radical possibility is that we are witnessing a realignment in which international capital has become independent of all states, including even what remains the biggest single one, the USA.[25] Thus it may be irrelevant whether a corporation is 'based' in any given country, since its interests are global and its behaviour will be dictated by this fact. In deciding where to locate its plant, for example, the idea that it should owe allegiance to its home country, and should give priority to creating jobs there even if economic conditions are more favourable elsewhere, has become increasingly *passé*. The importance of such developments is that they are creating a separation of interests between every individual state and international capital. In other words, the bifurcation is not a benign one but involves potentially serious conflicts of interest. And again, the real innovation is that in such conflicts the mobility of capital and the essential and scarce nature of the resource it controls give it the upper hand against even the biggest nation-state.

While the growth of multinational corporations, the increased mobility of vast quantities of financial capital and the other aspects of globalization which have become familiar are of great significance, it is a fallacy to presume that these developments in themselves can ever allow economics to dictate or to operate independently of political conditions. The economic internationalization that has gathered pace in recent years has not been solely the result of a combination of technological, transportation and cost factors; it has only been able to occur because of the liberal international environment that American hegemony has done so much to create. At the very least a steering mechanism will continue to be required which will guarantee this open political environment, if only to save the market from itself. For example, markets by their nature tend to exaggerate fluctuations, and the destabilizing potential of the rapid flows of financial capital across the world in this context is obvious. Such regulatory mechanisms cannot be plucked fully formed out of thin global air; they have to develop out of current political realities and the distribution of power these presume.

Realism tells us that the component units of the international system, nation-states, have interests of their own and the power to protect those interests. The idea that they will allow themselves to be made redundant *en masse* by faceless and nebulous economic forces is not credible. Their function is too basic and their power too great for this to happen. Much more likely is that the hierachy of power between nation-states will dictate the extent to which globalization will proceed. The point is that because America remains at the apex of this hierarchy its influence will remain critical. Since American interests, in the future as in the past, favour economic globalization, this places it on the side of the representatives of internationally mobile capital, as embodied for example in multinational corporations, and creates a formidable alliance that could well increase the power of both its economic and political components. There is, of course, the danger of America's relative position being weakened by a host of factors, and it must be the aim of policy to minimize the effect of these, but the dynamic of globalization and the political–economic interaction underlying it will not make the USA irrelevant, any more than it will represent the triumph of economics over politics. On the contrary, it will present America with opportunities for even greater influence in constructing a new world order which will produce an unprecedented configuration of the relationship between economics and politics.

This new order will require increased international co-operation between nation-states. The development of supranational co-operation has grown apace as the political dimension of world affairs has attempted to keep pace with the extraordinary dynamism of the economic. Institutions such as the International Monetary Fund, the World Bank, GATT and the OECD have all in different ways addressed the task of reconciling competing interests between nation-states. Of these perhaps GATT and the IMF have had the greatest impact on creating a liberal international economic order, the former by being the forum for an extraordinary reduction in trade barriers and the latter by bringing domestic economic policies into line with the requirements of the

international system. The World Bank[26] has been more concerned with
Third World development, which in this context has been relatively
marginal, although it will not be so in future, while the OECD has
suffered from too diffuse a political identity and has therefore made its
principal contribution through the provision of excellent technical
analysis and other support work for national governments.[27] They have
all affected nation-states, however, by imposing on them an economic
orthodoxy which is congenial to capitalist development, and they may
be seen therefore as agents of both American interests and those of
international capital.

While 'advanced' economies have been subject to this treatment as
well as less developed ones,[28] the development of regular economic
summits between the political leaders of the leading Western powers[29]
have been the more visible response to the power of international
capital. By trying to synchronize the economic cycle in their respective
economies, and by attempting to stabilize currency movements through
mutual support arrangements, political leaders have attempted to
counteract the disruptive effects of capital movement and present a
united front so as to increase their ability to deal with the power of
international capital. The levels of co-ordination implicit in this have
meant that they have sacrificed some national autonomy, but in this
case it has been done voluntarily in order to protect their common
interest as political entities. The alternative would have been to ally
with international capital against other nation-states in an attempt to
gain advantage over them. While such competition is a continuing
feature of international relations, the temptation to indulge in it has
been tempered by the recognition that to go too far in this direction
would be a short-sighted response to the globalization trend, and one
which would in the long run only enhance the capacity of capital to
play nation-states off against each other.

Some developments embody these dual pressures in their character,
since they contain the potential both for increased co-operation and for
enhanced competition. The European Community is a case in point,
where harmonization within the Community strengthens its political
efficacy on the world stage but does not guarantee that this will not
be employed in a divisive fashion against other power blocs. In fact it
seems to have acted in both ways, increasing tension with America and
Japan in respects of terms of trade, but simultaneously facilitating co-
operation by reducing the diversity of interests that have to be
accommodated at summit conferences. The political authorities of
Europe were faced with the choice of either attempting to halt this
economic dynamic, a prospect which could only have revived the
conflicts of a recent dark age, or going along with it in a way which

maintained as far as possible the scope of political authority as well as economic prosperity. The speed with which past conflicts between the member states of the Community have been transcended and new institutions created is salutary, and is undoubtedly due in part to the need to match politically the economic transformation of the European land mass, and to create the ability to compete on a global scale with other power blocs.

In addition to these formal mechanisms for increased co-operation, a parallel informal network has grown up which is even more revealing of the relationship between economics and politics at the international level.[30] The most recent and most imaginative manifestation of this is the Trilateral Commission.[31] This was founded in the 1970s in recognition of the transformations that were gathering pace in the world economy. Its premisses were to recognize, first, that America needed to co-operate rather than compete with the emerging powers of Europe and Japan; and, second, that political leaders needed to co-operate rather than compete with the leaders of the emerging global business network. The Commission therefore assembled business and political leaders from all three areas, together with academics, in a forum in which potential conflicts of interest could be discussed and perspectives harmonized. Sponsored as it was by international business,[32] the object of the Commission was to prevent global competition deteriorating into a restrictive regime which hindered the free flow of goods and capital across national boundaries. It has been an attempt to create an international consensus by which political leaders recognize the advantages for all of a free economic environment, while corporations correspondingly accept their responsibility to the stability of those countries in which they wish to do business.

In attempting to manage conflict on a world scale the Trilateral Commission has brought about a fusing of economics and politics at an informal but none the less influential level, and has perhaps begun the creation of a transnational capitalist class including not only business leaders but also a sympathetic political and intellectual element.[33] Its corporatist approach implies a limiting of rivalry between states, if not its abolition, and is consistent with a mentality which recognizes the value of both competition and consensus in politics as in business. The success of the Commission in building a world-wide network of communication at the élite level is indicative of the fact that one element at least of the American establishment is willing to share power in order to preserve it in the face of a period of rapid and threatening change, and that it finds willing partners in this approach in other capitalist powers. The type of co-operation symbolized by the Trilateral Commission is vital in managing the transition from hegemony to complex interdependence, but it is equally important to America in forestalling its decline by fusing its national interests with those of the emerging forces of international capital. In thus marrying liberal and realist perspective, it also reinforces the argument that it is too simple to see the globalization of business as transcending the power of nation-states.

Internationalization, then, far from dispensing with politics has prompted its reorganization on a global scale. What shape this will give to international affairs remains to be seen, since the pressures for mercantilism are strong; but that economic globalization has increased co-operation between nation-states and between them and transnational business seems undeniable. To this extent the concept of ultra-imperialism has developed a new and higher relevance. To this extent also the power of the USA has been not so much diminished as transformed by incorporation into this newly emergent pattern of economic/political relationships. But the pattern remains embryonic, and before we can conclude that co-operation has indeed become the dominant theme of intra-capitalist relationships, and that the USA has participated willingly in this process, we need to consider more fully those pressures which might push events in the opposite direction of capitalist competition, and the implications of this for America's role in the world.

The theoretical basis for competition between capitalist countries is the same as for that between corporations, access to overseas investment and markets, but with the additional element of preventing access to the home market for firms from competitor countries. It is the relation between access to overseas markets and protection of the home market which creates the free-rider problem that characterizes national competition.[34] All countries may recognize that, as demonstrated by the principle of comparative advantage, free trade is economically beneficial in the sense that it creates greater prosperity for all. It is equally the case, however, that protection of key industries from competition can be beneficial to a given country, even though it may diminish output for the world economy as a whole. The temptation for any country, therefore, is to try to reconcile these facts by obtaining free access for its goods and capital in other markets, while restricting access to its own economy. In other words, countries will seek protection for themselves and free trade for everyone else; they will seek to take advantage of free trade, accepting the rewards it brings but avoiding the sacrifices it entails.

Clearly, there are constraints on how far this policy can be taken through simple tariffs, since they invite retaliation in kind. Other less blatant tactics to achieve the same competitive advantage are therefore employed. One is to dump products in overseas markets at prices below their true production costs. This is done to gain access to the market and then to eliminate home competition, at which point prices can be raised and monopoly profit taken. An alternative is currency devaluation, which uses the price mechanism to increase access to overseas markets by making home goods cheaper, while restricting access to the home market by making overseas goods relatively more expensive. A further tactic is to impose other forms of import restriction that are not simple tariffs, but that have the same effect. The use of technical specifications or bureaucratic delay are examples here. Finally there is, in the case of Japan particularly, a cultural solution which obviates the need for formal restrictions since the preference for home-produced goods is embedded deeply in the culture.

The problem underlying all such tactics is that of the relation between individual rationality and collective rationality. While such competitive methods are rational for each individual country, they are irrational for the collectivity of capitalist nations in the sense that they will reduce overall output. Since each state has both individual and collective interests, it is impossible to determine which will be paramount in the absence of a single, governing political authority; it is possible to say that these centrifugal pressures will always exist, however, and that the pressure for destructive competition is likely to be a function, first, of whether any single country is powerful enough to control the others and, second, of the degree of economic crisis in each country. If a power is sufficiently strong economically to withstand all free competition, and politically to impose its interests on the other countries, free trade will result. This was the position that America enjoyed in the early part of the post-war era. However, once this pre-eminence declined the pressures revolved around the level of general prosperity. When this is high, countries can afford to give the collective good priority and take their 'fair' share of the gains. In times of crisis the tendency to try to gain advantage, even if only temporarily, becomes irresistible. The danger is that such attempts are not self-correcting because they produce an equivalent reaction in other countries and thus set off a vicious spiral of destructive competition which leaves all worse off.[35] This can only be avoided by an act of political will which recognizes the collective interest and imposes it on all equally.

Economic tensions can also be exacerbated by differences in perspective on political issues.[36] The gap in attitude between Europe and the USA on the stance to be adopted to Eastern Europe and the Soviet Union is a case in point. After the Soviet invasion of Afghanistan, for example, the USA took a more hostile line than Europe. This reflected not only greater European pragmatism born of a history which made the certainties of the US approach to international affairs unpalatable, but also the greater economic interest of Europe in dealing with the Soviet Union. This interest was itself a result of geographical proximity, which produced greater opportunity for economic interaction with the East than was available to the USA. Once established such differences of perspective spill over into other areas such as the Middle East and Central America, and help to create fissures in the alliance in which economic and political factors reinforce each other.

If tension is endemic to the economic relations between capitalist countries, and if political factors can easily exacerbate it, we have to ask what restrains this centrifugal pressure. Military alliances and the US nuclear umbrella underpinning them clearly provide a significant restraint on destructive competition. The fundamental doctrine of the Nato alliance, for example, is that an attack on one ally will be perceived as an attack on all, and that each country will therefore defend the others as itself.[37] In practice, since the war this has meant that the USA has undertaken to defend Europe because it was assumed that the enemy was the Warsaw Pact and that any attack by it would be initiated in the European theatre. The ultimate guarantee against attack lay in the concept of mutual assured destruction, by which Nato insisted on its willingness to use nuclear weapons and obliterate its attacker rather than permit defeat. This commitment was made in the equally certain knowledge that it would produce an equivalent response from its adversary, the point being that no power would rationally instigate armed conflict if it was convinced that the outcome would include its own destruction.[38] The confidence placed in this doctrine was manifested by the fact that Nato largely ceded superiority in conventional weapons in Europe to the Warsaw Pact on the grounds that the willingness to engage in nuclear escalation made such superiority worthless. But of course the whole strategy depended on the threat to escalate not being an empty one. And since it was the USA which largely controlled the nuclear forces, but it is in Europe that the conflict was assumed to take place, this translates into the idea that it was America's willingness to risk its own survival in order to defend Europe which had to be seen to be credible.[39]

It is hardly surprising that European members of the Nato alliance have at times since the war doubted this guarantee; nor indeed is it any reflection on the good faith of the USA. Rather it is a natural suspicion of the idea that one country would so identify with its allies that it would destroy itself rather than allow their defeat. The lack of credibility of the idea that the USA would initiate the destruction of the globe rather than allow the Warsaw Pact to make gains in Europe contributed to the refinement of the basic doctrine by what came to be known as the concept of flexible response.[40] This was applied to other theatres by the USA, but its purpose in Europe was to enhance the credibility of the deterrent by creating more steps to the ladder of escalation. Since it was the idea that even a small setback in conventional conflict could only be met by immediate reversion to total nuclear war that had been seen as the least convincing element of the strategy, the solution was to provide the allied forces with a range of arms that would permit sufficient flexibility to match an attack at whatever level it occurred. The onus for escalation would then be placed on the enemy, while retaining the basic guarantee that, whatever level the enemy chose to fight on, it could not win. In addition, if there were more steps by which the conflict could be mediated, it would give the attacker more time to reconsider the consequences of its actions, and it would mean that the USA would not have to threaten to activate its (suicidal) commitment until it became evident that there really was no alternative.

However, the concept of flexible response was double-edged in its implications for alliance solidarity.[41] If its positive side was to make the deterrent more credible, its negative aspect was to create pressures for division between Europe and America. Another way of looking at the concept of intermediate stages to conflict was to see that this permitted wars fought out entirely on European soil. At least with massive retaliation the USA itself would become vulnerable very quickly. In a conflict which envisaged a number of small steps in escalation, all of which would be confined to the European theatre, it became possible to imagine an American strategy in which Europe would be sacrificed to American goals. The USA could cut off the escalation after Europe was devastated, but before its own territory became directly threatened. Even more disturbing to European eyes was the fact that some of the intermediate weapons developed to meet their anxieties, notably Cruise missiles, gave the USA a first-strike capacity which permitted it to initiate a conflict that could be contained in the European theatre, so that *in extremis* Europe could be sacrificed to American policy goals.[42]

The fear underlying the European perspective was enhanced by the development of intermediate and theatre nuclear weapons because these gave the USA the capacity to pursue limited nuclear superiority consistent with the concept of limited nuclear war. The nightmare was of the USA becoming the aggressor at Europe's expense in a scenario in which Cruise missiles could be used to launch a first-strike in a war fought entirely on the European landmass.[43] These fears were fuelled by the bellicose attitude of the Reagan administration towards the Soviet Union in its early years, and its strong advocacy of the development of intermediate nuclear weaponry.[44] The Strategic Defense Initiative, or Star Wars project, only reinforced fears that this was indeed the direction in which American thinking was moving. Whatever its avowedly peaceful purpose, to European, and indeed Soviet, eyes it could give the USA a degree of survivability from nuclear retaliation which might destabilize the balance of terror that had kept the peace.[45]

The irony of the situation was that European efforts to increase the credibility of the US deterrent and thereby tie the USA more closely to Europe had the effect of increasing the likelihood of nuclear conflict in Europe, an outcome which could only increase the divisions within the alliance. The development of intermediate nuclear weapons had in effect reinstated the logic of conventional warfare in which battlefield losses were limited and so could be judged as a price to be paid for the political gains which might accrue from them. Such cost–benefit analysis had become redundant when the only form of nuclear conflict was total and when any conventional reverse led directly into this total conflict. It was the absolute nature of nuclear conflict which had prevented war in Europe, even while it had made the Europeans mistrustful of American guarantees. Attempts to remedy this mistrust had only opened a greater chasm between Europe and America because they gave the USA the option of sacrificing Europe to its own goals. The position was, in the final analysis, that the alliance was based either on an incredible deterrent (mutual assured destruction) or on a divisive one (flexible response). The shaky basis of the security umbrella provided by the USA had thus become much more apparent because it had become clear that there could be no guarantee of security for Europe except trust in its ally, the very quality that was lacking in the first place.

The conclusion therefore has to be that the military alliance does not unequivocally counteract economic pressures for divisions between the capitalist powers. Its effective nuclear monopoly is therefore a wasting asset for the USA: it is no longer the trump card it can play to discipline its partners when conflict arises in other fields. This becomes all the more true when combined with the decline of the external threat which had previously provided the unifying force upon which US domination rested. In the absence of a clear-cut external enemy, the economic fissures threaten to become wider and more destructive. The real counterweight to this tendency, however, also follows from the demise of the Soviet or communist threat. This demise has given massive new impetus to the prospect of a truly global capitalism, which provides enormous opportunities for increased prosperity for all the existing capitalist powers. It is the common interest in taking advantage of this which will ensure that the consensual element of the post-war order will prevail over the competitive aspect.

This does not imply that nation-states and indeed multinational corporations will not compete vigorously to take a bigger share of the opportunities; they could do no other in a market system. But it does suggest that such conflict will have a constructive role in providing the dynamic of capitalist expansion rather than becoming destructive to the system as a whole. Profit will prove the cement which holds the capitalist world together as it expands into new territory, and the increased economic interdependence resulting from globalization will help keep the structure solid. But the final element necessary to maintain this structure will continue to be political leadership which can promote its benign potential and restrain its destructive aspect. This will clearly be more collective than was necessary in the period of unquestioned American pre-eminence. But it remains the case that it is the USA, as still the biggest single economic actor, as the country with the greatest military capacity, as the most culturally influential society in the modern world, as the most ideologically aggressive nation, and as the state with the greatest political coherence and will in the exercise of power in the world, as, in short, the single remaining superpower, which has the potential to sit at the apex of this new co-operative political leadership of world capitalism as the first among equals.

America will undoubtedly have to put its own economic house in order if it is to realize its potential in developing a new world system and not be supplanted by other more vigorous economic powers.[46] But the decline of the Soviet threat will assist in this by permitting it to avoid the danger of overextension that was one of the products of a bipolar world.[47] It will also have to demonstrate political and diplomatic skill if it is to strike the balance between taking the leading role and sharing power that the emerging post-communist world demands. The responsibility of helping to create a more prosperous global society while maintaining its own leading role is great, but so too is the opportunity. Many factors have combined to produce this opportunity, but it is the dynamic of capitalist expansion which is its best hope of success and upon which the USA must seek to build. Capitalism is entering a new global phase and it is one for which the United States has prepared it. The USA may yet prove to be the main beneficiary.

Notes

1. G. Treverton, *Making the Alliance Work: The US and Western Europe*, London: Macmillan, 1985; R. Barnet, *Allies: America, Europe and Japan since the war*, London: Cape, 1983.

2. A. Szymanski, *The Logic of Imperialism*, New York: Praeger, 1981, chapter 15.
3. S. Gill, *American Hegemony and the Trilateral Commission*, Cambridge: Cambridge University Press, 1990.
4. E. Mandel, *Europe vs America: Contradictions of imperialism*, London: New Left Books, 1970.
5. M. Kaldor, *The Disintegrating West*, London: Allen Lane, 1978.
6. L. Shoup and W. Minter, *Imperial Brain Trust: The Council on Foreign Relations and American foreign policy*, New York: Monthly Review Press, 1977; D. Calleo and B. Rowland, *America and the World Political Economy: Atlantic dreams and national realities*, Bloomington, Ind.: Indiana University Press, 1973; R. Keohane, 'US foreign economic policy towards other advanced capitalist states', in K. Oye (ed.), *Eagle Entangled: US foreign policy in a complex world*, New York: Longman, 1979.
7. Szymanski, *op. cit..*
8. IMF, *Balance of Payments Statistics, Yearbook*, Washington, DC: IMF, vol. 32, 1981 onwards.
9. Harold Macmillan, Lord Stockton, describing the policies of the Thatcher government in the UK. The alternative idea, that balance of payments deficits were an overrated problem because the inward flow of capital which financed them indicated international confidence in the domestic economy, was frequently expressed by Nigel Lawson about the UK economy in the late 1980s when he was Chancellor of the Exchequer. See P. Riddell, *The Thatcher Decade: How Britain has changed in the 1980s*, Oxford: Blackwell, 1989.
10. R. Parboni, *The Dollar and Its Rivals: Recession, inflation and international finance*, London: New Left Books, 1981.
11. R. Parboni, 'The dollar weapon: from Nixon to Regan', *New Left Review*, 158, July–Aug. 1986, pp. 5–18.
12. D.P. Calleo, *The Imperious Economy*, Cambridge: Harvard University Press, 1982.
13. *ibid.*
14. A Mattelart, *Multinational Corporations and the Control of Culture: The ideological apparatuses of imperialism*, Hemel Hempstead: Harvester Wheatsheaf, 1979.
15. Gill, *op. cit.*, pp. 206–8.
16. *ibid.*
17. P. Kennedy, *The Rise and Fall of the Great Powers: Economic change and military conflict 1500–2000*, London: Unwin Hyman, 1988.
18. P. Bobbitt, L. Freedman and G. Treverton, *US Nuclear Strategy: A reader*, London: Macmillan, 1989.
19. McG. Bundy, G.F. Kennan, R.S. McNamara and G. Smith, 'Nuclear weapons and the Atlantic alliance', *Foreign Affairs*, 60, 4, winter 1982, pp. 753–68.
20. K. Kautsky, 'Ultra-imperialism', *New Left Review*, 59, Jan.–Feb. 1970, pp. 41–46.
21. S. Gill and D. Law, *The Global Political Economy*, Hemel Hempstead: Harvester Wheatsheaf, 1988.
22. W. Keegan, *Mrs Thatcher's Economic Experiment*, Harmondsworth: Penguin, 1985.
23. *ibid.*

24. The experience of the Socialist government in France in the early 1980s is a case in point.
25. R. Vernon, *Sovereignty at Bay*, New York: Basic Books, 1971.
26. More properly the International Bank for Reconstruction and Development.
27. M. Camps, '"First World" relationships: the role of the OECD', Atlantic Paper no. 2, Paris: Atlantic Institute for International Affairs, 1975.
28. The most notable case being that of the UK in the mid-1970s.
29. Notably in the so-called G7 group of leading economic powers.
30. K. Van der Pijl, *The Making of an Atlantic Ruling Class*, London: Verso, 1984.
31. Gill, *op. cit.*, H. Sklar (ed.), *Trilateralism: Elite planning for world management*, Boston, Mass.: South End Press, 1980.
32. David Rockefeller, Chairman of Chase Manhattan Bank, was the Commission's founding spirit.
33. Gill, *op. cit.*
34. C. Kindleberger, 'Dominance and leadership in the international economy: exploitation, public goods and free rides', *International Studies Quarterly*, xxv, 1981, pp. 242–54.
35. R. Rowthorn, 'Imperialism in the 1970s', in H. Radice, (ed.), *International Firms and Modern Imperialism*, Harmondsworth: Penguin, 1975.
36. L. Freedman (ed.), *The Troubled Alliance: Atlantic relations in the 1980s*, London: Heinemann, 1983; J. Godson (ed.), *Challenges to the Western Alliance*, London: Times Books, 1984.
37. W. Park, *Defending the West: A history of NATO*, Hemel Hempstead: Harvester Wheatsheaf, 1986.
38. R. Jervis, *The Illogic of American Nuclear Strategy*, Ithaca, NY: Cornell University Press, 1984.
39. J. Joffe, 'Europe's American pacifier', *Foreign Policy*, 54, spring 1984, pp. 64–82.
40. J.L. Gaddis, *Strategies of Containment: A critical appraisal of postwar American national security policy*, New York: Oxford University Press, 1982, chapters 7 and 8.
41. C. Bertram, 'The implications of theatre nuclear weapons in Europe', *Foreign Affairs*, 60, 2, winter 1981–2, pp. 305–26.
42. R. Kolkowicz (ed.), *Dilemmas of Nuclear Strategy*, London: Cass, 1987.
43. R. Scheer, *With Enough Shovels: Reagan, Bush and nuclear war*, London: Secker, 1983.
44. R. McNamara, *Blundering into Disaster: Surviving the first century of the nuclear age*, London: Bloomsbury, 1987.
45. L. Deschamps, 'The SDI and European security interests', Atlantic Paper, no. 62, London: Croom Helm, 1987.
46. F. Rohatyn, 'America's economic dependence', *Foreign Affairs*, 68, 1, 1988/89, pp. 53–65; M. Porter, *The Competitive Advantage of Nations*, London: Macmillan, 1990.
47. D. Calleo, *Beyond American Hegemony: The future of the Western alliance*, New York: Basic Books, 1987.

CHAPTER FIVE

AMERICA AND THE THIRD WORLD

The globalization of capitalism necessarily implies a process which extends beyond advanced capitalist societies and into those less developed societies described collectively as the Third World. The relationship between the First and Third Worlds remains problematic, however. It cannot be assumed that the extension of capitalism is achieved through a simple or linear progression which marries economic growth with liberal democracy as has happened in the USA.[1] The relationship of advanced capitalist countries to the Third World has long been seen as exploitative, and even if the capitalist mode of production is being extended to the latter, we cannot assume that this exploitative element is therefore being eliminated. The opportunity with which the globalization of capitalism presents America may, when seen from a Third World perspective, leave it tainted with the darker connotations of imperialism. This relationship will certainly reveal a different aspect of the interaction of economics and politics in America's role in the modern world; the question to be addressed in this chapter is whether in doing so it substantiates or contradicts the thesis of the essentially benign implications of globalization and of America's role in it that we have advanced thus far.

The fact that Third World countries are developing in a world context which is dominated by an advanced capitalist sector will cause their experience to assume a distinctive shape, and this precludes any assumption that development in the Third World will replicate the model by which capitalism has matured in the advanced economies. It may even mean that this experience cannot reasonably be termed development at all, so constrained will it be by the relationship to the First World. And it is also unlikely that all the countries of what is termed the Third World will experience the same pattern. As the dynamic of world capitalism touches them, it is probable that their experience will become much less homogeneous. Consequently, although the issue in this chapter is what role the USA as the leading capitalist power is playing in shaping this process of development, prior to assessing it directly we must consider more fully the nature of the development of capitalism in the Third World.

There are two schools of thought on this question, whose conceptions of development derive from differing definitions of capitalism.[2] The first sees the essence of capitalism as production for profit and exchange in the market; the second defines it as the accumulation of surplus via a process of class conflict. This derives in turn from the system of wage labour which permits the private appropriation of surplus value created by labour power and its subsequent reinvestment as the means of survival in the face of the pressure of competition. These differing definitions form the basis of the contemporary debate on the Third World, but they are just as applicable to the debate on the origins of capitalism.[3] They are important precisely because of their generality, they govern the perspective adopted on the whole of capitalism from its origins to the present day, and they have widely differing implications for how the Third World is likely to develop. They go to the heart of the nature of capitalism, and we must consider each more fully to understand these implications.

The first school argues that the growth of capitalism lies in the process of trade and exchange. It was the growth of trade which generated the original surplus from which the accumulation process began.[4] Merchants who engaged in trade appropriated this surplus and were transformed into bourgeois when they began to invest it to create more surplus value rather than simply consuming it. Once initiated, the accumulation process continued by virtue of the stimulus of competition. There is no dispute between the two schools on the importance of competition: it is its rigours which provide the iron discipline that forces capitalists to maximize profit, invest it and thereby accumulate more surplus if they are to survive. The critical point of this perspective, however, is to see the dynamic of capitalism as stemming from a factor, trade and exchange, that is exogenous to the class structure of a capitalist society. This is in fact generally true and applies equally to feudal society and to the post-industrial stage. There are echoes here of the principle of comparative advantage, which also focuses on trade as the spur to increased prosperity.

The essence of capitalist development on this view is the transfer of surplus between parts of the system, a transfer which is effected by unequal exchange between the core and the periphery of the system. The location of the core and the periphery may shift over time, since they are defined by their function rather than by their geographical location. In the early stages of capitalism the core was centred on north-west Europe, with Britain coming to centrality in the late nineteenth century and its empire forming a considerable part of the periphery of the system. In the twentieth century, while Western Europe has remained part of the core, its centre has perhaps moved to the USA, with its sphere of influence across the Third World, notably in Latin America and Asia, constituting the periphery. In the next stage it is quite possible that the USA will be supplanted by Japan. The point is that, for the purposes of systemic development, it is the two poles which are necessary; their physical location is immaterial because the essence lies in the process of extracting and transferring surplus via trade and investment, not in territories or states.

The implication of this school of thought is that the core and the periphery, in concrete terms the USA and the Third World, are bound together in one world-economic system, and that this has been true, with varying locations, since the beginning of capitalism.[5] The relationship is not necessarily, or indeed typically, that of empire. Nor is it purely economic, since the economic relationship must invariably be buttressed by political arrangements. While formal colonies provide one such framework, the unified political structure they represent is difficult both to achieve and to maintain. Contemporary equivalents in the form of international institutions such as the International Monetary Fund and the World Bank can readily perform the same function without incurring the costs to the metropolis of maintaining direct colonial control.

The position is complicated by the existence of intermediate or semi-peripheral elements. In the contemporary world the principal element of the semi-periphery is the socialist block which contains elements of both poles in its character.[6] Similarly, within countries there may be both core and peripheral regions; in a Third World country a particular region may act as core in relation to its own hinterland, extracting surplus from it, while simultaneously being in a peripheral position in relation to the metropolitan powers, contributing surplus to them. If we add to this the idea that countries can move over time between the core and the periphery, we see that a relationship which may appear quite simple conceptually is in practice enormously complex. This is particularly true in respect of the political relationships it implies. While the two economic poles may remain constant in an abstract sense, the struggles between nations to occupy a more favourable place on the continuum connecting them are never-ending. The constancy of the abstract model is therefore in direct contrast to the flux at the surface, and its chief strength is to allow us to see past the daily struggle to the continuing essence beneath it.

Despite this complexity the principal lesson of this approach remains straightforward. It is that development and underdevelopment are part of the same process, that the prosperity of the USA and the poverty of Latin America, for example, are not separate phenomena engendered by factors indigenous to each area; rather they are two sides of the same coin, produced in a symbiotic relationship out of the development of the capitalist world system.[7] In other words, the prosperity of the core is the direct result of the poverty of the periphery: the rich are rich *because* the poor are poor. If the wealth of the core is derived from the surplus generated in the periphery and extracted from it in an exploitative manner, then it follows that the inhabitants of the First World live off the labour of those in the Third World. And this includes the members of the working class in the core countries, who in world terms are part of the bourgeoisie because they share in the spoils of imperialism and rely on them to maintain a standard of living beyond that which their labour power generates. It is because this relationship is so essential to the wealth of the First World, and because it is in its nature exploitative, that the network of political institutions supporting it, whether formally colonial or not, are vital. Without them the relationship would quickly become unstable, with catastrophic consequences for the standard of living, and therefore for the stability, of the core countries. The methods of controlling the Third World may range from the crudely direct in the shape of military coercion, through the manipulative in the form of comprador élites and stolen elections, to the more subtle and indirect methods of imposing financial orthodoxy through the IMF and the banks; but whatever the form, the function remains constant.

This perspective amounts to a modified restatement of the necessity argument encountered in Chapter 2. Again the USA is seen to depend on imperialism, in this case in the form of the transfer of surplus from the Third World, for its own economic development. But more than indicating the effect of the relationship on the advanced economies, it also suggests that the needs of these economies shape the less advanced ones by producing an economic structure in them that is incapable of self-sustained growth. Because Third World economies are oriented to the extraction of surplus which can be transferred to the metropolis, through, for example, the production of cheap primary goods, their underdevelopment is perpetuated to the point of permanency. Since their whole economy is oriented towards the satisfaction of external rather than indigenous needs, it is structured in favour of consumption of resources, albeit externally, rather than investment to produce enhanced future growth. This amounts to plunder rather than development and it is therefore unsurprising that the relationship with the core countries is one of growing inequality as the underdeveloped economies stagnate and the advanced ones grow richer from their plunder.

This model carries quite the opposite implication to modernization theories which conceive of development in terms of gradual improvement through stages of increasing complexity in essentially the same pattern as that adopted by currently advanced economies.[8] From their very origins the growth of the advanced capitalist economies has depended on unequal exchange with the underdeveloped regions, and this fact in itself precludes the latter from following the same path. Development and underdevelopment are therefore not recent phenomena: what we now term Third World economies have always been 'underdeveloped' in the sense that they have always been exploited for the benefit of the metropolis. The relationship goes back to the origins of capitalism and has long been the basis of the world economic system, and it is only by changing it that genuine economic development will become possible for the Third World. The implication for America's role in the modern world is clear: as the primary part of the core of this system, it must bear the major responsibility for the continuing poverty and lack of development of the Third World. It is not a benefactor which through economic aid and constructive political intervention seeks to promote the well-being of the less developed world; it is, by virtue of its economic structure, the principal agent of the latter's continuing poverty.[9]

The argument has been drawn very starkly, and there are few today who would advocate it in quite this unmodified form. Its strength, however, is to explain why it is that the Third World has not simply followed the path established by Western Europe and North America and remains in what certainly appears to be continuing and often increasing poverty. It exposes the comfortable myth that it is the cultural, moral or political inadequacy of these countries which blocks their economic development: the syndrome of blaming the victim for the crime. It also explains the conservatism of the working class in advanced countries. The absence of a socialist challenge from this class historically in the USA has been widely remarked upon.[10] Explanations have tended to focus entirely on domestic factors such as America's immigrant heritage and ethnic mixture, its distinctive anti-communist ideology, or its flexible and pragmatic political structure. Where explanations have been couched in terms of the effect of relatively high levels of prosperity in its recent history, this prosperity has in turn been explained by America's good fortune in domestic economic resources rather than by reference to its relationship with overseas economies.

This argument suggests that it is quite rational for the working class in America and other Western countries to display a relatively conservative political orientation because their standard of living is high as a result of the exploitation of the Third World. In world terms they are not a proletariat living only off the product of their labour power, with their standard of living driven down to subsistence levels by capitalist competition; instead they are partners, along with the metropolitan capitalist class, in the plunder of the Third World, in whose exploitation they therefore have a vested interest. It would be unrealistic to expect them to rebel against a domestic and international social structure which provides them with such a high standard of living. The key to stability in the advanced economies is therefore that the surplus extracted from the Third World should be distributed widely enough to ensure that all sections of society share in its benefits and have an interest in perpetuating the system which produces them. This perspective provides not only an explanation of underdevelopment in the Third World, but also an insight into its intimate connection with the conservatism and stability of the American social structure.[11]

The drift of this analysis is, from a radical perspective, extremely pessimistic because it suggests that there is little or no potential for revolutionary change in the First World. The proletariat has been neutralized as the agent of such change, the role envisaged for it in the traditional Marxist view of history. The logical conclusion of this analysis is that the new agent of change must be the peasantry of the Third World, since it is the appropriation of their labour power which has created the surplus upon which the world economic system rests. However, the abandonment of the Western working class and the transference of faith to the Third World peasantry seem to diminish the prospects for change further. Whatever the limitations of the former, the latter would seem to have a much smaller capacity for generating such change, however great their interest in doing so might be. Faced with the full might of their own, often brutal, regimes, and the support these receive from the core countries, and burdened with all the inherent organizational weaknesses of a peasantry so acutely analysed by Marx himself,[12] this transference of belief to the peasantry appears naive.

It is perhaps explicable only in terms of the historical origins of the theory itself. It was developed, or at least came to prominence, in the political culture of the 1960s. This was a time when post-war enthusiasm for Third World development seemed to be undermined by the apparent stagnation of these countries, and when Western working-class conservatism seemed to be in striking contrast to the radicalism of so many disaffected but largely middle-class young people in the West.[13] The development of Third World liberation movements, notably in Cuba and Vietnam, as well as the example of the Chinese revolution also appeared to demonstrate that the peasantry did have the capacity to take on and defeat the forces of world capitalism, even if on a basis that was as much nationalist as socialist. This combination of forces required theoretical articulation, and the dependency school, as this perspective came to be known, provided just that. Today, however, the historical specificity of this conjuncture is apparent, and the analysis accompanying it appears correspondingly dated.

What has to be explained now is less the apparently permanent state of underdevelopment of the Third World than the rapid industrialization of parts of it. Perhaps the most striking example is the extraordinary rate of growth in some Asian economies, notably those of Hong Kong, Taiwan, Singapore and South Korea. Rapid growth is far from universal in the less developed world, but it has become sufficiently widespread to cast doubt on the suitability of the very term as a general category. The disparities between countries which were formerly considered together under the rubric of the Third World are now so great as to make the term positively misleading. The growth of previously underdeveloped parts of the world economy appears directly to contradict the prediction of permanent underdevelopment associated with the dependency school. This casts doubt in turn on its perspective on the core economies as crushing development in their own interests. If the relations between the First and Third Worlds are as strong as the dependency view holds, and if some parts of the Third World are developing rapidly, it is at least possible that the core economies are actually promoting this development. Even if such development is not universal, this opens up the possibility that the core economies, and specifically the USA, do in fact play a benign role in respect of development. It is, of course, equally possible in principle that the newly developed regions are progressing in spite of the influence of the core countries. And it is to this issue that the alternative school of thought on development and its relation to the advanced economies has been addressed.

Once again the explanation offered by this school is part of a comprehensive view of capitalist development. It begins from a distinctive definition of the essence of capitalism. In direct contrast to the idea that transfer of surplus constitutes this essence, this argument suggests that accumulation of surplus through class struggle is the basic characteristic of capitalism. The contrast is apparent in the differing explanations of the origins of capitalism.[14] Where the first school sees merchants as the prototypical capitalists because they controlled the source of the surplus and were thus in a position to invest it in a capitalist formation, in this second view it is rich peasants who play this role because they were the first to employ others on the basis of wage labour. The importance of wage labour is that it generated surplus value and was thus the essential precondition for the emergence of capitalism. By acting as employers, rich peasants gained control of this surplus and so were transformed into the first capitalists.

The critical difference is that, on this second view, capitalism developed internally from the feudal system and not externally through the impulse of trade. It is only by making the emergence of capitalism the consequence of the internal contradictions of the preceding mode of production, as opposed to the happenstance of exogenous factors, that the analysis of capitalist development can be placed on a systematic rather than simply a contingent basis. It is only this view, therefore, that can reveal the dynamic of the capitalist mode of production. This derives from its internal contradictions rather than from historical accidents which may help or hinder that development, and which can themselves be only the object of historical description as opposed to systematic analysis and explanation.

The classic sequence of events which underlies the process of class struggle starts with the premiss that all value is created by labour power: capital does not create value, since it is in fact only accumulated labour from previous time periods.[15] The significance of wage labour is that it permits the labourers to be paid less than the total value of the output their labour power produces. The difference between total value and wages is surplus value, and it is this which, though created by workers, is appropriated by capitalists as their own. It is the system of private property which permits this appropriation, and so this, together with wage labour, is a necessary element of the capitalist system. Once appropriated, however, what distinguishes capitalism is that the surplus is reinvested in the production process rather than simply consumed. Surplus value may exist under other social systems and may be appropriated by the ruling class, but it is only under capitalism that they are compelled to reinvest it with the purpose of accumulating more capital.

The reason for this compulsion stems from the existence of a market economy, a further distinguishing feature of capitalism. The market is defined as a competitive framework within which goods and services are exchanged. The fact that it is competitive means that the more efficient producers will be able to undercut the prices of the less efficient to the point where they put them out of existence. If we assume that the reinvestment of surplus value or capital is the principal means by which the production process can be made more efficient, it follows that the capitalist who reinvests the most, and most effectively, will be able to charge the lowest prices and will therefore be in a position to undercut his competitors and put them out of business. It is in order to avoid this threat that all capitalists are compelled not only to reinvest surplus value or profit, but to seek to maximize it in the first place.

Profit maximization is then a matter of survival in a competitive environment and not a matter of choice. By this process a cycle of permanent expansion of capital is established: accumulation of capital becomes the driving force of the system, indeed its *raison d'être*, and something which cannot be abandoned if the system is to remain capitalist.

This is the key to the enormous economic dynamism that has historically characterized capitalist societies. The imperatives to both maximum efficiency and maximum expansion via the agency of maximum profit generate a formidable and historically unmatched economic energy. But there are also consequences in this sequence for the relations between capitalists and workers that are not always so palatable. One of the ways to maximize profit, besides reinvestment, is to reduce the other costs of production. Since wages invariably constitute an important element of production costs, it follows that this system also places an imperative on capitalists to reduce wages to their lowest possible level. But since, by definition, workers live only by selling their labour power, this amounts to an attack on their very right to survival. The relationship is a zero–sum one: the more surplus that capitalists appropriate, the less is left for workers to live on. There is thus a direct conflict of interest between capitalists and workers, and it is this which forms the basis of the class struggle.

This perspective reveals that there is a contradiction between the appearance and the essence of a capitalist system. The appearance is of an open market in which labour and capital meet and exchange labour power for wages in a freely arrived at contract. The reality is that capital exploits labour by appropriating some of the value labour creates, and coerces labour into this relationship. It is able to do this because ownership of capital, itself derived from previous surpluses, permits the capitalist class to monopolize employment opportunities and thus forces the working class, which lacks any other resource but its labour power, to enter into this arrangement on pain of starvation. The class struggle thus instituted is the social counterpart to the economic dynamism of capitalism because it is the struggle for maximum profit and expansion which produces it. It is also the basis for a transcendence of the system. Since it is the labour power of the proletariat which creates value, the proletariat has the ultimate power over its development. The problem is for the proletariat to reach a level of awareness and organization which enables it to see through the appearance of the free market to its exploitative essence, and to expropriate the capitalist class by overturning the system of private property which is the basis of its power. This is a formidable task, but it is the only basis for a true revolution which transcends class divisions and creates a truly co-operative society, as opposed to simply replacing one ruling group with another.

This revolutionary transcendence of capitalism will only be achieved, if at all, when the capitalist system has expanded up to its limit. Up to that point the forces of capital will always be able to find new sources of labour and sites of production and new markets to strengthen their hand in the class struggle. It is expansion which enables the capitalist class to maintain the profit rate, and which thus allows the system to continue to reproduce itself. Hence it is expansion itself which keeps the system viable. And this is the key to the relevance of this rather abstract characterization of the essentials of capitalism to the relationship of advanced and less developed economies. To understand the implications for Third World development we must recognize that these essentials mean that the capitalist system survives only by reproducing itself, but in a mode of expansion rather than a steady state. The system replicates itself in both its social and economic aspects as it expands, so that it reproduces the class struggle in the new arenas it expands into, just as it maintains the rate of profit by doing so.

This must mean that as capitalism develops it will expand into the Third World, but will do so in ways that replicate the system both socially and economically as it has developed in the advanced economies. The constant and ineluctable process of expansion will require penetration of Third World economies, but once established it can do no other than develop them along the same lines as in the metropolis. In direct contrast to the first school, then, this line of argument suggests that capitalism will indeed develop the Third World, and that the advanced economies will facilitate this process through the export of capital and not hinder it through the extraction of surplus via trade.

In this context it is important to bear in mind the double-edged nature of capitalism, even when seen from a Marxist perspective. In its initial stages it is liberating, freeing the economy from the fetters imposed by a feudal social structure and allowing an unprecedented growth of productivity. This is valuable not for its own sake, but because it lays the groundwork for increased standards of living and greater freedom, even though it is produced by a system which rests on the exploitation of labour. Private property, wage labour and the market system are thus necessary evils in the long march of historical progression towards human emancipation. They will only be eliminated when the imperative to expansion has worked itself out and reached the ultimate limit in which the whole of the world economy has been incorporated into its orbit. At this point the liberating aspects will themselves, in a dialectical inversion, become fetters on further progress, economic productivity will falter, the class struggle will intensify and a point will be reached where the system is no longer sustainable.

The essential point in this context, however, is that this transformation cannot take place until all the underdeveloped regions of the world economy have been penetrated by capitalism. Eventually they, together with the advanced economies, will succumb to its contradictions in a process of world revolution. But this will not happen before they have shared in its economic productivity and developed their own version of the corresponding class structure. The conclusion, therefore, has to be that imperialism in its various guises remains essentially a mechanism for effecting the world-wide expansion of capitalism, and as such its impact is progressive in the long run because it develops the economies that it penetrates. This remains true notwithstanding its exploitative nature. Capitalism is in its nature both exploitative and productive, and this is as true in the Third World as it has been in the metropolitan economies. Development will occur not out of some charitable instinct emanating from countries with advanced economies, but out of the deep logic of their economic systems. In the long run, by promoting this development capitalism may, as Marx suggested,[16] only be digging its own grave because it is laying the groundwork for the basis of true socialism, the globalization of capitalism. Even if true, this is certainly far in the future. In the shorter term it is the progressive aspect of capitalist expansion which will be paramount. Even if development is achieved through exploitation and as a by-product of the search for maximum profit, it will nevertheless be development.

It is precisely this process that we are now witnessing in the newly industrialized economies. It is only to be expected that some Third World economies will be subjected to this progressive impulse before others and will respond more positively. Differentiation will therefore increase, and it may be that in some of these economies circumstances will be so favourable that they will be able to move along the continuum and join the advanced sector while others lag behind. But taken overall, such differentiation, even with the competitive and exploitative character it must inevitably possess, only confirms the thesis of the progressive nature of globalization. In sum, we arrive at the explanation of the issues posed at the outset. America's role in the modern world, as the leading representative of the capitalist system, is to contribute to the globalization of that system and to its extension into the Third World. This will not occur evenly, nor without harsh consequences for newly created proletariats in the Third World. And in promoting it America too may be digging its own grave in the sense that it is helping to create a world economy that transcends the power of even the most powerful nation-state. But none of this alters the fact that, at this stage of history, its influence as the agent of the replication of capitalism in the Third World has been and is on balance progressive.

We must bear in mind that the accounts of these two schools have been given as ideal types, drawn starkly in order to reveal the underlying questions at issue and not intended to be accurate descriptions of the reality. It is likely, therefore, that elements of both models will be relevant to the reality of Third World development. We should also note the possibility that factors quite outside the scope of either school will have the greatest determining effect. Both focus on the effect of capitalism on development, and both are preoccupied with the issue of economic growth. It is becoming ever more apparent, however, that growth is likely to have a feedback effect on the global environment which will seriously alter its path. The environment may therefore become the predominant factor affecting economic development rather than the imperatives of capitalism or the challenge from socialism. The consequences of growth for the environment are as yet unclear. It would be unwise to underestimate the flexibility of a market system in coping with this problem because there will be profits to be made from protecting the environment, just as there have been from pillaging it. But the increasing importance of this dimension of development seems undeniable.

As between the two ideal types, it would seem that the second school of thought has a sounder basis inasmuch as its grasp of the essential dynamic of capitalism, locating it in class struggle rather than trade, is superior. The first school is also undermined by the problem of magnitude addressed in Chapter 2. Even if its analysis of the nature of the transfer of surplus from the periphery to the core is correct, it does not seem to be of a size that would make the core dependent on it for its economic well-being. It may be that in the colonial period the spoils of empire – for Britain, for example – were of sufficient size to underpin the whole of the metropolitan class structure. British imperialism may well have helped to create a more stable domestic social structure, but it may also have had detrimental effects on the economy, making it less flexible and vigorous and less able to compete in the post-imperial world, and so hastening Britain's decline as a world power after the prop of empire was removed.[17] Again it is unlikely that the American economy has ever been so dependent on its overseas economic relations as to invite the same fate.

The key to this issue, however, lies in the extent of development that is actually taking place in what has been known as the Third World. Warren has persuasively argued that, contrary to widespread opinion, the era since 1945 has been one of historically unprecedented levels of growth in the less developed parts of the world economy, just as it has been the longest period of sustained expansion for the advanced economies.[18] The reason this has not been more widely appreciated is that the effect of growth on living standards in poorer countries has been mitigated, and in some cases eliminated entirely, by growth in population. In its nature this population growth has been a drain on living standards rather than a spur to increased output, since the additional population is not proportionately represented in the labour force, being either too young or too old. In some of the more dynamic of the newly industrialized economies the increase in living standards has been manifest, but if we take this population factor into account the infusion of economic energy brought about by incorporation into the world economy has been much more widespread than the evidence solely of living standards would allow. The fact that many countries have to run hard even to stand still should not obscure the great strides that have been made in both agricultural transformation and industrial development.

If the empirical evidence does confirm the theoretical superiority of the approach which suggests that replication rather than permanent underdevelopment is the predominant trend among less developed economies, it is clearly not the case that advanced economies are simply being reproduced even in the most successful parts of the newly industrialized sector. Some element of dependency on the core continues to exist, and the dual nature of this phenomenon is perhaps best captured by the description of it as dependent development.[19] This concept implies that, although the relationship of the core to the periphery is not simply one of plunder, it is based on a desire to exploit the cheaper labour of the periphery. Largely channelled through multinational corporations, the influence of the core does indeed structure the less developed economies, but not in a way that produces stagnation. Rather than simply extracting surplus from the primary sector, it takes advantage of cheap labour by locating the production of manufactured goods in these economies. The goods produced are intended largely for consumption in the core economies, often, it should be noted, at the expense of jobs in those economies. This implies a form of development, since indigenous industrial and consumer markets do grow up on the back of this manufacturing base. The role of multinational corporations is more one of providing technical know-how and a ready consumer outlet than of injecting capital. Capital tends to be raised locally, and while much is reinvested, some of it is siphoned off as repatriated profit. This is indeed a process of surplus extraction, but it is one which develops the local economy even as it plunders it.[20]

In sum, there is a strong connection between First and Third World economies, but it is of this dual character which results in a distortion of the pattern of development rather than its elimination. Third World

economies are indeed structured to a significant extent to satisfy the
needs of the First World, and the costs to themselves, for example in
the deterioration of their environment, are often neglected in the process
because they are of little concern to the First World paymasters. But
this does not preclude their increased involvement in the world economy
from generating a capacity for development. The autonomy of all
countries is now constrained by their participation in the world
economy. The constraints may be greater on Third World countries
than on advanced economies like that of the USA, but increasingly the
difference is one of degree rather than kind. The benefits and costs
associated with these constraints are also becoming more widely spread,
with only the balance between the two elements varying between
countries.

The social and political implications of this emerging economic
pattern are also of considerable importance for America's role in it.
The first effect is to create an alliance of interest between the
representatives of international capital and the indigenous bourgeoisie
which is overseeing economic development. This takes the form of a
comprador relationship in which the local bourgeoisie is tied more to
the interests of the core than to its own country. The danger is that,
because it is less rooted in its own community and less dependent on
its community's economic development for its standard of living, this
local bourgeoisie tends to place more emphasis on consumption than
investment as the key to its standard of living. If it is the classic function
of the bourgeoisie to be the channel for reinvestment which promotes
development, this external tie weakens its performance of that function
and cedes control of much of it to external representatives of capital.
In return it is granted a generous lifestyle by the agents of capital, for
whom this is a small price to pay for effective control of economic
development.

Instead of taking a nationalist position which might threaten the
access of international capital in favour of self-generated growth, the
comprador bourgeoisie acts as an agent of social control for the First
World, working to maintain stability in return for a comfortable way
of life. And stability is the key factor, since the very pace of change
involved in economic development has rapidly undermined traditional
patterns of life, as, for example, with the mass migration of the rural
poor from the countryside to the urban *favelas*. Migration is necessary
to provide the workers for the new industries, and an excess supply of
labour is required if it is to remain cheap enough to maintain its
competitive advantage in the world market. But the threat to social
stability posed by this massive dislocation, and the inequality it involves
between the impoverished new proletariat and the cosseted and externally
supported comprador bourgeoisie, is enormous.

It follows that the political role of this alliance is as important as its economic function. In so far as this form of development is a revolution inspired from above, or rather from without, by capital in the core countries, it is a process which does not carry any inbuilt social and political legitimacy. This has to be created to cope with the rapid dislocation and massive inequality involved. It must also deal with the rapidly rising expectations that industrialization and increased awareness of living standards across the world generate throughout society. These changes are in themselves a recipe for instability, and they must have a political counterweight if the whole situation is not to explode. The solution to the problem has often been the establishment of an authoritarian regime to manage this tension. This reflects the fact that a fully democratic political system, with all the scope for dissent it embodies, is not easily reconcilable with stability in such volatile circumstances. In the advanced economies, the historical trajectory has been for the development of the market economy to be associated with a democratic polity. The individualist economic basis of capitalism helped to undermine political participation based on traditional criteria of eligibility, and ushered in an era of equal participation for all in the political process. The introduction of democracy was not always gradual or peaceful, but the historical association between market economics and a liberal democratic polity has become strong. The United States represents a particularly effective form of this association, since the pluralist nature of its polity operates as what amounts to a political marketplace in which the rules governing the behaviour of participating groups and individuals are very similar to those governing economic market transactions.[21]

The point is of some importance, not because the liberal democracies provide a model for Third World societies in this respect, but because they do not. The traditional association of the market economy and liberal polity is being broken under the strains of rapid development. It is becoming apparent that the connection was the product of a particular set of historical circumstances in Europe and North America rather than being a necessary one. If the First World is indeed exporting its economic system to the Third, it does not follow that it is also exporting its liberal politics. On the contrary, under the circumstances prevailing in the contemporary Third World, the advantage of authoritarian, even military, regimes in promoting development become ever more obvious. In their circumstances democracy can easily be seen as a wasteful distraction, equivalent to shifting the deckchairs on the *Titanic*.

This presents the USA with a considerable dilemma in its dealings with Third World countries. In so far as American capital is helping to develop Third World economies by investing in them, it becomes the role of the American state to help secure a political environment where the integrity of that investment is assured; and in so far as this investment is creating profit for American-based firms and lowering production costs of consumer goods sold in the USA, the interest of the state in performing this protective function is enhanced. If, however, this goal can only be achieved by means of an authoritarian regime, the USA is faced with the prospect that it can only fulfil its role of protecting capital by sacrificing its political commitment to liberal democracy. Ideally it would wish to promote both the market economy and democratic politics, to replicate its own institutional framework in effect; but in practice it has to choose whether to sacrifice its political principles or its economic interests. Perhaps the most notable recent examples of this dilemma have occurred in Latin America. The election of Allende in Chile and American reaction to it is a case in point.[22]

Here the sequence of events was that after the war the Chilean economy, like many others in Latin America, embarked upon an import substitution strategy as a way of reducing its dependence on trade in primary goods.[23] This failed due to excessive consumption and the importation of too many capital goods. The consequence was a growth of international indebtedness, the interest payments on which were consuming a high proportion of new foreign earnings, thus trapping the economy in a vicious circle from which it could never take off into independent development. Allende attempted to break out of this by renegotiating interest payments, restricting repatriation of profits and nationalizing American-owned parts of the economy: in other words, as seen from the American perspective, by threatening the integrity of the investment it was the American state's responsibility to protect. Consequently, although Allende had been democratically elected, the USA embarked on a campaign to undermine his administration.[24] At a visible level this involved using its influence to deny Chile credit, debt rescheduling facilities and so on. There is also evidence of direct intervention in the Chilean political process. Whether this extended to support, tacit or otherwise, of the coup which overthrew him will perhaps never be known.

The success of the coup was not entirely due to the effectiveness of this American response, since Allende's own domestic economic strategy was fatally flawed.[25] Having been elected with the support largely of the poor, he was obliged to meet their expectations by increasing consumption in the economy when what was needed was increased investment. The consequence was rising inflation and a squeeze on the living standards of the middle class, which turned violently against him. None the less, there is no doubt that his task, already difficult, was made impossible by the American-inspired international financial blockade of the Chilean economy.[26] The result was the Pinochet coup.

Whether or not the USA played any part in instigating the coup, its attitude to it soon became apparent when it lifted the economic blockade and restored economic assistance to the Chilean government, including economic advisers who helped to formulate plans for the free-market system by which the Chilean economy was run under Pinochet. The actions of the United States were therefore clear-cut: it undermined a democratically elected government and then gave support to one which was not only undemocratic but also particularly brutal, murderous and inhumane. The justification offered for this was that the action was necessary to prevent Chile falling to communism. Even if we accept this at face value, it shows a preference for undemocratic regimes of the right over those of the left. And the most plausible reason for such a preference, given that each should be equally unpalatable to a democratic society, is that the former combine authoritarianism with access for US capital and the latter do not.[27] We should be wary of generalizing from this case, but the experience of both Brazil and Argentina in the same period, and the American involvement with them, was not dissimilar. In the case of Mexico the ruling party, the PRI, has remained sufficiently strong that a coup has never been necessary, but here too the fact that its democratic credentials have long been suspect has not prevented the USA from dealing with it, especially since it too has adopted a free-market orientation.

It appears clearly to be the case that America has responded to its dilemma by choosing economic interests over political principles.[28] This is not to say that it has not tried to re-establish greater democracy in these countries once the threat to free movement of capital has been removed. Brazil, Argentina and even Chile have moved away from their military regimes.[29] Though they remain plagued by problems of international debt and inflation, they have chosen to try to extricate themselves through the mechanism of the free market and have thus met the essential qualification for US support. America's preferred option undoubtedly remains a combination of the free market and political democracy. But the rapid change driven by the world-wide expansion of capitalism has in Third World circumstances frequently distorted development in the direction of authoritarianism, and when the choice has had to be made between democracy and capitalism under the pressures created by this pattern of development, the direction of American influence has been clear.

The form of development that has occurred in Asia in recent years has been somewhat different from that of Latin America. In the first place, economic development has in a number of countries been much more successfully achieved.[30] The economies of Hong Kong, Taiwan, South Korea and Singapore, not to mention that of Japan, have made

strides that were unimaginable until recently, and have contributed to
making the dependency model appear very dated. But they too have
had to wrestle with the dilemmas posed by the relationship between
rapid economic development and political democracy. Japan is a special
case since, although it started from a low ebb in the aftermath of war,
its economy could hardly be described as underdeveloped, and it has
now regained its place among the advanced economies. Even here,
however, the façade of Western-style democracy has been largely that,
with many indigenous mechanisms working to maintain the same
party in power throughout the whole post-war period, though without
the repression seen in Latin America. The story is somewhat different
in the newly industrializing Asian economies. For a variety of reasons
they have not been burdened with the legacy of a democratic framework
within which to try to manage rapid economic growth. They have
employed the trappings of democracy in varying degrees, but in essence
each has been governed by an authoritarian regime that has been able
to mobilize the population in pursuit of economic growth without the
need to resort to repression on the scale seen in Latin America.

It is important to stress that authoritarianism in itself is not sufficient
to guarantee economic development, as the examples of the Philippines
under Marcos and to some extent of Indonesia amply demonstrate.
What does appear necessary, in addition to a political structure that is
able to mobilize resources ruthlessly, is a degree of cultural cohesion
which helps to create a consensus around the pursuit of economic
growth, and which therefore prevents that ruthlessness from having to
manifest itself in overt oppression, even though the threat of it remains
always near the surface. This cultural nationalism strengthens the
indigenous bourgeoisie in its relations with international capital and
ensures that more of the benefits of growth are retained, and this in
turn helps to reinforce the nationalism of the proletariat and ensure its
co-operation.

The corporatist system that these Asian economies have evolved
shows a creative mix both economically and politically: in the economic
sphere, the reliance on free-market incentives is not allowed to preclude
a thoroughly interventionist strategic and supportive role for the state;
while in the political sphere, the benefits of democratic procedures are
never allowed to degenerate into unproductive wrangling over the
division of the spoils and to divert attention from creating them in the
first place. This new hybrid presents a formidable challenge to the
combination of the free market and liberal democracy characteristic
particularly of the Anglo-American world, as is evident from the
Japanese example. If the problem for the USA in reconciling its
economic and political goals has been less acute in Asia, it may come

to be replaced by the much more taxing one of how to compete with countries which have adopted such an effective model.[31]

The general model of the relationship between the First and Third Worlds is, in conclusion, that economic expansionism, or the globalization of capitalism, is the driving force behind it. The impact of this is in broad terms to replicate the capitalist system in the Third World and therefore to promote development. However, it is apparent once again that the economic dimension cannot be seen in isolation. Its impact is modified by the political framework in which it operates, and varies also with the cultural response that the possibilities of development prompt. The combination of these elements has produced very different outcomes, in terms of both the extent of economic development and the form of political regime associated with it. The role of the USA in this process is that, while it has, on balance, acted to promote economic development rather than simply to perpetuate dependence, its political involvement has been less progressive. It has shown no lack of willingness to intervene in the affairs of sovereign nations where it has felt its interests to be at stake, and has responded to the tensions inherent in rapid development by supporting political stability and the protection of the rights of capital at the expense of democracy when the choice has had to be made. The murderous regimes this has led it to be associated with have not lent credibility to protestations that its purpose is to promote democracy and resist communism. The contradiction between its professed commitment to democratic principles and its support for authoritarian regimes abroad has made it clear that the USA has put the defence of capital above political principle, and this accounts for its imperialist image in the Third World in the post-war era.[32]

This negative dimension of American involvement in the Third World has been particularly apparent in Latin America. However, it is from Asia that the real challenge to the American position comes.[33] Several Asian countries are developing a system which mixes capitalism and nationalism in a fashion calculated to make them formidable competitors in the world economy. In helping to promote world-wide development during its hegemonic period, the danger for America is that it will have fostered a child that is capable of bettering its parent and promoting American decline. The functional superiority of the corporatist model that has evolved principally in Asia is the greatest challenge that the USA faces in today's world, for it poses fundamental questions about the effectiveness of its own domestic economic, social and political structures. America's period of unquestioned pre-eminence cushioned it for more than a generation from having to face the difficult choices posed by this challenge, and it is not clear that it is a society well equipped to meet it.

Promoting the continued development of Third World economies provides the USA with a substantial opportunity to achieve both domestic prosperity and leadership in world affairs. But it does put an even greater premium on re-establishing the appropriate structural balance in its economy between consumption and investment if it is to be able to compete to a degree appropriate to a world power.[34] The critical point is that, as is the case in its relations with other advanced capitalist powers, it is open competition with the newly emerging industrial countries that is likely to provide the best incentive to the USA to make the necessary changes. It is the vested interests entrenched in its domestic social structure and the checks and balances of its pluralist political system that threaten America's ability to maintain its position in a post-hegemonic world.[35] If they are allowed to block the necessary readjustments, then American policy will descend into a brand of mercantilism which, in attempting to cushion it from the realities of global capitalism, will forsake America's leadership potential and make threatened decline actual.

If, however, the USA can make the necessary structural economic reforms and resist the growth of mercantilism both at home and abroad, then the open world-economic system it has sponsored will have a bracing effect on its own economic development and thus provide the ultimate basis for continuing political leadership.[36] Having helped to promote economic development through the mechanism of capitalist expansion, it is all the more important to its own interests that the USA maintain its commitment to the principles of free trade which have underpinned both its hegemony and economic development throughout the world. Development is not, as the dependency perspective would have it, a zero-sum game in which one pole of the system can only prosper at the expense of the other. If based on free trade, it can provide both the means and the end to continuing American influence in the world.

American relations with the Third World therefore reinforce the argument that the emerging capitalist world order presents the USA with enormous opportunities for continuing leadership. But they also suggest a further lesson for American policy: the association with authoritarian, not to say murderous, regimes abroad that has characterized its period of hegemony has undermined America's legitimacy as a world leader in the eyes of Third World countries, and has helped in the process to discredit the capitalist system it represents. The extension of capitalism on which American interests depend will require consensus rather than exploitation and imposition through force if it is to be extended successfully to the Third World, and this in turn will require the re-establishment of American legitimacy. This can only be done if the USA gives greater substance to its democratic rhetoric in choosing allies abroad. In the 1990s, therefore, American foreign policy for the Third World should be directed towards eliminating the connection between defending capitalism and political repression. The demonstrable superiority of capitalism in generating wealth and the concomitant decline of the communist threat present a propitious set of circumstances in which America can extend its influence; but this will only be achieved if support of repression is eschewed in favour of a liberal policy which has faith in the efficacy of capitalism and democracy in winning the hearts and minds of Third World countries.

Notes

1. B. Moore, *The Social Origins of Dictatorship and Democracy: Lord and peasant in the modern world*, Harmondsworth: Penguin, 1966.
2. R.H. Chilcote and D.L. Johnson (eds.), *Theories of Underdevelopment: Modes of production or dependency*, Beverly Hills, Calif.: Sage, 1983.
3. The distinction between them was in fact developed in the well-known debate on the transition from feudalism to capitalism. See P.M. Sweezy *et al.*, *The Transition from Feudalism to Capitalism* (ed. R. Hilton), London: New Left Books, 1976.
4. H. Pirenne, *A History of Europe from the Invasions to the 16th Century*, London: Allen & Unwin, 1939; H. Pirenne, *Medieval Cities: Their origins and the revival of trade*, Princeton, NJ: Princeton University Press, 1952; A.F. Havighurst (ed.), *The Pirenne Thesis: Analysis, criticism and revision*, Lexington, Mass.: Heath, 1976, 3rd edn.
5. I. Wallerstein, *The Capitalist World-Economy*, Cambridge: Cambridge University Press, 1979.
6. *ibid.*
7. A.G. Frank, *Capitalism and Underdevelopment in Latin America*, New York: Monthly Review Press, 1967.
8. W.W. Rostow, *The Stages of Economic Growth: A non-communist manifesto*. Cambridge: Cambridge University Press, 1971, 2nd edn.
9. H. Magdoff, *The Age of Imperialism*, New York: Monthly Review Press, 1969.
10. J. Karabel, 'The failure of American socialism reconsidered', *Socialist Register*, 1979, pp. 204–27.
11. P. Baran and P. Sweezy, *Monopoly Capital*. Harmondsworth: Penguin, 1968.
12. K. Marx, 'The Eighteenth Brumaire of Louis Napoleon', in *Selected Works*, London: Lawrence & Wishart, 1968, pp. 97–180.
13. H. Marcuse, *One-Dimensional Man: Studies in the ideology of advanced industrial society*, London: Routledge, 1964.
14. R. Brenner, 'The origins of capitalist development: a critique of neo-Smithian Marxism', *New Left Review*, 104, July–Aug. 1977, pp. 25–93.
15. On the labour theory of value, see J. Elster, *Making Sense of Marx*,

Cambridge: Cambridge University Press, 1985, pp. 127–41.
16. K. Marx, 'The manifesto of the Communist Party', in *Selected Works., op. cit.*, pp. 35–63.
17. P. Anderson, 'The origins of the present crisis', *New Left Review*, 23, Jan.–Feb. 1964, pp. 26–53; P. Anderson, 'The figures of descent', *New Left Review*, 161, Jan.–Feb. 1987, pp. 20–77.
18. Bill Warren, *Imperialism: Pioneer of capitalism*, London: New Left Books, 1980.
19. P. Evans, *Dependent Development: The alliance of multinational, state and local capital in Brazil*, Princeton, NJ: Princeton University Press, 1979.
20. F.H. Cardoso and E. Faletto, *Dependency and Development in Latin America*, Berkeley, Calif.: University of California Press, 1979.
21. R. Dahl, *Pluralist Democracy in the United States*, New York: Rand McNally, 1967.
22. P. O'Brien (ed.), *Allende's Chile*, New York: Praeger, 1976.
23. H. Singer and J.A. Ansari, *Rich and Poor Countries: Consequences of international disorder*, London: Unwin Hyman, 1989, 4th edn, chapter 6.
24. J. Petras, *The US and Chile: Imperialism and the overthrow of the Allende government*, New York: Monthly Review Press, 1975.
25. P. Sigmund, 'Chile: what was the US role?', *Foreign Policy*, 18, fall 1974, pp. 142–66.
26. M. Honeywell (ed.), *The Poverty Brokers: The IMF and Latin America*, London: Latin American Bureau, 1983.
27. W.P. Bundy, 'Dictatorship and American foreign policy', *Foreign Affairs*, 54, 1, Oct. 1975, pp. 51–60; J. Kirkpatrick, 'Dictatorships and double standards', *Commentary*, 68, 5, Nov. 1979, pp. 34–45.
28. N. Chomsky, *Turning the Tide: US intervention in Central America and the struggle for peace*, London: Pluto, 1985.
29. A. Lowenthal, 'Jimmy Carter and Latin America', in K. Oye *et al.* (eds.), *Eagle Entangled: US foreign policy in a complex world*, New York: Longman, 1979.
30. W.E. James, S. Naya and G.M. Meier, *Asian Development: Economic success and policy lessons*, Madison, Wisc.: University of Wisconsin Press, 1989.
31. D. Halberstam, *The Reckoning*, New York: Morrow, 1986.
32. N. Chomsky and E. Herman, *The Political Economy of Human Rights. Vol. 1 The Washington Connection and Third World Fascism*, Boston, Mass.: South End Press, 1979.
33. C. Thorne, 'American political culture and the Asian frontier', *Proceedings of the British Academy*, 72, 1988.
34. M. Porter, *The Competitive Advantage of Nations*, London: Macmillan, 1989.
35. P.G. Cerny, 'Political entropy and American decline', *Millennium*, 18, 1, 1989, pp. 47–63.
36. For a contrary view which stresses the incompatibility of interests between countries of the North and South, see S. Krasner, *Structural Inequality*, Berkeley, Calif.: University of California Press, 1985. For perspectives more compatible with that taken here, see R. Packenham, *Liberal America and the Third World: Political development ideas in foreign aid and social science*, Princeton, NJ: Princeton University Press, 1973; R.I. Rothstein, *The Third World and US Foreign Policy: Cooperation and conflict in the 80s*, Boulder, Colo.: Westview, 1981.

CHAPTER SIX

THE 1960s: THE ACME OF AMERICAN POWER

In this chapter we will begin to trace the trajectory of American power in the world since 1960, and of US policy responses to it. In doing so we will need to choose between competing pictures that have been drawn: some have seen this period as one which began with the hubris of an imperial power followed by a prolonged period of retribution; others have viewed it as a time of long, steady decline; a third view accepts that it has been characterized by weakness, but confines this to the earlier part of the period and sees the 1980s as a decade of American resurgence. We can now put some historical flesh on the analytical bones of the ideas we have considered in earlier chapters, as a means of determining which of these views best captures America's role in the modern world.

The background to the 1960s is by now familiar. The USA enjoyed an historically unprecedented superiority as a world power after 1945 as a result of the devastation the war had wreaked on all other powers. This led to its adoption of a global role in which it took upon itself a virtually unlimited brief in world affairs. The justification for this was an absolute commitment to contain the spread of communism anywhere and everywhere. The rhetoric accompanying this undertaking divided the world into forces of light and darkness between which there was little room for compromise. The cold war mentality associated with the containment doctrine was so unqualified that it is hardly surprising that confrontations soon developed which involved more than rhetoric. The Berlin blockade was one example, but the greater involvement occurred in Asia where, after the 'loss' of China to communism, the USA was determined that the same fate should not befall Korea, and in line with its stated commitments was prepared to resort to arms to prevent this outcome.[1]

Under the Eisenhower administration somewhat greater restraint was shown, at least in rhetorical terms, although the policies of brinkmanship pursued by the Secretary of State, John Foster Dulles, maintained a constant level of tension in East–West relations.[2] This was heightened by the decision of the administration to rely on nuclear weapons for defence in this context rather than trying to match the Warsaw Pact in all aspects of conventional arms.[3] The USA also continued to take an active role in the affairs of countries where it saw political changes as inimical to its interests, the interventions in Guatemala[4] and Iran,[5] though not well known at the time, being among those that have now become well documented. Towards the end of the Eisenhower years, however, a sense of torpor appeared to prevail, and dissatisfaction was enhanced by the shock of the Soviet launch of the Sputnik satellite. This threw into question America's previously assumed technical superiority over the USSR, and raised fears that the USA was already in decline and losing the arms race with communism. An economic recession in the late 1950s contributed to the malaise, which developed into a generalized concern about decline and drift that seemed to be symbolized by the ageing occupant of the White House. It was these sentiments that Kennedy was able to exploit in his race for the presidency in 1960, and his victory owed much to the feeling that he would be able to revitalize the country.

Kennedy's election represented a revitalization of American society. A new, younger generation had come to power and under the slogan of the 'New Frontier' were looking to impose their stamp on America.[6] This aggressive, energetic attitude was reflected in the approach of the new administration to foreign affairs. The rhetoric of Kennedy's inauguration speech was confident and vigorous, and his famous pledge to 'pay any price, bear any burden' to defend freedom around the world appeared to resurrect an open-ended policy of containment. The toughness of the approach to communism was also apparent in the commitment 'never to negotiate from fear', though it was balanced by the accompanying 'but never fear to negotiate'. And this balance encapsulates the question that the Kennedy administration poses for America's role in the world: did this dynamism, when applied to foreign affairs, result in reckless warmongering, or was the uncompromising rhetoric a cloak designed to strengthen the negotiating hand of the administration, but also a cover for what would in practice turn out to be a measured, pragmatic and even-handed approach to the exercise of America's enormous power?[7]

The first, dramatic, episode in which the new administration became involved seemed to suggest that the former outcome was the most likely. The sponsorship of an invasion of Cuba by rebel forces in what turned out to be the fiasco of the Bay of Pigs gave the impression that Kennedy fully intended to match his strong rhetoric with action.[8] On closer inspection, however, a somewhat different interpretation seems more justified. In this case Kennedy was as much a victim of predetermined forces as an instigator of aggression. The rebel forces had been armed and trained by the USA under the Eisenhower administration, and commitments to support the invasion were already in place when Kennedy came to office. It would have been possible for him to renege on them, but very difficult to accomplish honourably without tarnishing the government's word and without making himself appear pusillanimous. As it was, he tried to limit involvement in the face of what appeared to be a strategy by the rebels to draw the USA into a full-scale invasion of Cuba. There is evidence to suggest that they were well aware that the Bay of Pigs invasion was unlikely to be successful. Their calculation was that, when the invasion force faced defeat, the USA would have no option but to escalate the conflict and deploy its own forces in order to save face and demonstrate that it would not abandon groups to which it had made commitments. They may also have calculated that the administration would be only too pleased to have such a rationalization for accomplishing their shared goal of toppling Castro.

In fact, when it became apparent that the invasion force faced a rout, Kennedy pointedly refused to commit US forces and allowed the mission to fail. This suggests that he was well aware of the dangers of escalation and would not commit US power on ground that he had not prepared himself. If he could not extricate the USA before the invasion, he made sure that he would not allow himself to be led into the more dangerous waters of full-scale conflict with Cuba. This suggests restraint and an awareness of the limits of US power, together with a desire to exercise it judiciously. It also indicates a willingness to pay a political price for these convictions, since he was indeed vilified as a weak leader, strong on rhetoric but feeble in action, and he did secure the enduring enmity of the exiled Cuban population. It may have been that the real failure of leadership was to allow the situation to develop as far as it did, but having done so the charge of recklessness cannot be sustained, over this episode at least.

The much greater challenge of the Cuban missile crisis arose the following year.[9] Once again Kennedy appeared to adopt a confrontational approach, putting his and America's prestige on the line. And, of course, in this instance the fact that the confrontation was with the USSR enhanced the gravity of the situation immeasurably because it introduced the possibility of nuclear escalation. To many, at the time and since, this fact seemed to make the risks involved in Kennedy's ultimatum to the Soviet Union to remove nuclear weapons from Cuba insanely disproportionate both to the threat and to the possible benefits of victory. In practice, however, the issue was handled with considerable diplomatic skill. Kennedy was always careful to give the USSR a way out of the confrontation without too much loss of face.[10] The practical conduct of the affair was more pragmatic and balanced than the public rhetoric suggested, and the end result was generally perceived to be a victory which enhanced American prestige and that of Kennedy personally.

Whether it proved to be of long-term benefit is a moot point. It indicated to the Soviet Union what the limits of adventurism were, but it also made its leaders determined never to place their country in a position where it had to back down from such a confrontation because of inadequate military capacity. It was the humiliation of the Cuban missile crisis which gave rise to the massive Soviet arms build-up over the succeeding decades, the aim of which was to achieve military parity with the USA. Certainly, once the Soviet Union felt more confident in its military capacity, particularly its naval strength, its involvement in world affairs and, to American eyes, its unwarranted interventions resumed. Direct confrontation with the USA was avoided and the struggle conducted by proxy, but that was due to the caution of both sides rather than to any long-term chastening of Soviet behaviour that could be traced back to the Cuban missile crisis. It may well be therefore that Kennedy's victory was a Pyrrhic one.

Perhaps the more important charge, however, is that victory or defeat mattered less than the fact that risking nuclear war in order to prove the toughness of his administration was an irresponsible gamble by Kennedy which could never have warranted the potential gains involved. It is on such a point of principle that any charge of recklessness over the missile crisis has to hang. The problem with such a charge is that it would have to apply to all positive action by the USA in resisting the perceived threat from the USSR, since the whole of Western defence strategy rested on the willingness ultimately to use nuclear weapons. The Cuban episode may have made this willingness more tangible, but the threat it implied was no different in kind from that which operated constantly in the European theatre. It follows that if Kennedy was reckless over Cuba, then the whole basis of US foreign policy, and that of the West as a whole, has been reckless, as indeed has that of the USSR since it has rested on the same premiss. Whether this line of argument is accepted, or the alternative that it is precisely this willingness that has prevented direct conflict in the East–West confrontation, it seems unreasonable to separate out the Cuban missile crisis as either an instance of recklessness or a victory for toughness. In fact it was quite consistent with, and an expression of, the whole of the underlying Western strategy.

On balance, then, it appears that the invigorating rhetoric of the

Kennedy administration was not translated into a new adventurism in American conduct in the world. The success over Cuba certainly strengthened the American hand in dealings with the USSR, but this did not encourage Kennedy to seek out other victories through confrontation. On the contrary, this strength was placed in the service of moderation as a contribution to the Nuclear Test Ban Treaty of 1963, since it permited Kennedy to reach a compromise with the USSR without the danger of his being subject to domestic political attack as soft on communism.[11] His even-handedness in practice showed that he was able to use his rhetoric rather than taking it literally, and indeed his well-known American University speech of 1963 showed that he felt strong enough by then to articulate in public a much more balanced approach to dealing with communism than he had done at the outset of his administration.[12]

Policy towards Latin America confirmed this impression that the goal of the administration was to use both carrot and stick in an effort to find a middle way between confrontation with and capitulation to the communist threat. The Alliance for Progress[13] did not forswear the imperialist assumption of US attitudes to Latin America, but it was a kind of intelligent reformism. It remained clear that, if forced to choose between left and right regimes, the USA would continue to favour the latter.[14] But the point is that the policy was an attempt to manipulate the development of Latin America in a direction which would foster liberal democratic but market-oriented regimes, and so prevent the choice having to be made.

The pre-eminence that the USA enjoyed in world affairs did not produce in the Kennedy administration a willingness to rest on its laurels. On the contrary, the administration continued to be driven by the imperatives of capital to exercise its power and to expand its sphere of influence wherever possible. But if there was no running out of steam, neither was there any headlong rush into adventurism. Positive policies were pursued, but in a balanced way which suggested that the imperatives governing them were not so extreme as to preclude the application of intelligence to their implementation. In short, the Kennedy administration sought to win the hearts and minds of the rest of the world rather than applying brute force as the instrument of an expansionary policy. However, the hearts and minds policy as conceived by the Kennedy administration perhaps implied an even greater degree of hubris than a less subtle policy would have done. It was because the 'best and brightest'[15] of the Kennedy years felt such confidence, both in their own ability and in the superiority of the American way over all others, that they entertained little doubt that they would be able to convince foreigners of this superiority. American influence would therefore be extended, but through the power of example and persuasion rather than by cruder techniques. In the battle with communism across the globe, they felt that the communists could only win by brute force. If both sides had the opportunity to put their case fairly to the uncommitted, there could be only one response: to choose freedom as represented by the USA over tyranny as represented by communism. Various techniques of persuasion, inducement and manipulation were the preferred instruments of policy, and force was to be used only in so far as it was necessary to gain a hearing.

Certainly the administration, and Kennedy in particular, had the capacity to create a more popular image for the USA in the world than had previously been the case. While not universally loved at home or abroad, Kennedy had the image of a youthful, dynamic leader untarnished by cynicism or failure and representing a country in the same mould, and this image has lingered in the memory from that period. It was in this sense that those few short years seemed so blessed for America, and provide the grounds for viewing them as the acme of American power in the world. The combination of power and popularity, energy and idealism which came together then has not been surpassed since, and represents a golden moment.

But the moment soon passed. The seeds of the destruction of that image had already been sown in South-East Asia. It is fascinating but fruitless to speculate on whether the Kennedy administration would have allowed the USA to be dragged into the Vietnam conflict to the extent that eventually happened.[16] The pragmatism Kennedy had shown and his unwillingness to allow the USA to fight others' battles for them might have prevented it.[17] But the confidence of the administration in its abilities and its message could have taken developments in either direction. On the one hand, if indigenous peoples were not prepared to fight communism themselves, it might have been seen that force was a substitute for a hearts and minds strategy and therefore doomed to failure. On the other hand, and perhaps more likely, the unwillingness to believe that any people could freely choose communism, which was how the nationalist appeal of North Vietnam and the Viet Cong was perceived by the USA, might have persuaded them that force was necessary to secure a fair hearing for the case for freedom, and they would then have been drawn into the conflict. Certainly after the coup which overthrew Diem, and in which Kennedy was implicated, the withdrawal option no longer really existed, at least in the short term.[18] Ultimately, to have avoided involvement would probably have required the Kennedy administration to add prescience to intelligence in the list of its qualities, and this even they were unlikely to have found possible.

There is no doubt that the Johnson administration lacked the prescience to avoid a tragedy in Vietnam, or that it was a turning point in America's role in the world, and we need some explanation of how this could have occurred.[19] If we seek the explanation in the basic imperative governing US policy, that of capitalist expansionism, its relevance to this conflict is not readily apparent. Certainly there were never sufficient economic interests in Vietnam to justify the costs of involvement; and indeed the war ultimately had a very harmful effect on the domestic economy and the US role in the world economy by inducing inflation and undermining confidence. If the link between the economic and political dimensions is to be made, it is necessary to stand back from the immediate causes of the conflict and to consider it in the broader context of America's role in the post–war world.[20]

As we have seen, the initial American policy after the war was one of containment, interpreted as the adoption of the role of world policeman, willing to intervene in any conflict in order to prevent communism expanding its influence. The absence of limits characteristic of this attitude meant that the USA itself adopted an approach as expansionist as that of which it accused communism. Such an absolutist approach to world affairs, and the uncompromising ideology that accompanied and justified it, could have arisen only out of supreme confidence born of the overwhelming relative power that the USA enjoyed. One consequence was the systematic downgrading of the potential costs of any overseas engagement. The possibility of defeat did not seriously enter calculations because the faith in both US resources and the attractions of what America stood for were total.[21]

A further consequence of this mentality was an obsession with linkage. Since the world was seen as divided in a competition between the USA and the communist world, all conflicts were linked as part of this grand struggle. The zero–sum perspective this produced, whereby any loss for the West was an equal gain for communism, led naturally to the domino theory.[22] This suggested that the loss of any single country to communism would lead inevitably to the loss of others because it would tilt the balance of power in the grand struggle towards the communists. This in turn led to a refusal to take nationalism seriously. The only conflict the USA was prepared to recognize was that between freedom and communism, and all conflicts had to be fitted into that mould. The idea of a nationalist conflict whose significance lay outside the grand struggle was not acceptable. The fact that, at least in the early stages of the war, US policy-makers treated the USSR and the People's Republic of China as part of the same monolith when in fact there were fundamental divisions between them demonstrates how blinkered by its own ideology the USA had become.

The blinkers were even more restricting in respect of the relations between China and Vietnam, since they had been enemies for centuries. Hence North Vietnam was seen as a tool of Moscow and Peking, the vehicle for their plan for world domination, rather than an autonomous country seeking its own independence. The anti-communist prism thus imposed on the struggle blinded the USA to its realities and caused grave miscalculations as to the nature of the enemy they were fighting, miscalculations which reinforced the tendency to underestimate the possible cost of involvement. Even more importantly, America's perception of the struggle left it with little room for manoeuvre in its response. In so far as Vietnam was defined as vital to the interests of the West because of its linkage to the grand struggle, the USA, having committed itself to this grand struggle, had no choice but to intervene. The perspective it adopted on world affairs therefore predetermined the general outlines of the policy it would follow, and it is the way in which America was impaled on the consequences of its own overweening ideology that justifies the description of its fate as hubristic.[23]

Involvement in Vietnam, then, was not the product of some direct economic interest on the part of the USA. Rather it was a test of the hegemonic post-war edifice that the USA had built upon its global economic interests. The sphere of influence it had developed was composed of a range of countries linked, as it were, by the chain of American protection. But because of the linkage no defeat could be treated as trivial: if it were permitted, all the other allies would lose confidence in American guarantees of protection and its hegemonic status would be undermined. However, it was in the nature of the monolithic enemy they thought they were facing to attack this chain at its weakest link, since this is where the possibilities for overthrowing a regime and installing communism were greatest. As a consequence, the USA ceded the initiative to the enemy in respect of choosing the ground on which confrontation would take place, and was left in the position where it would always have to fight on the ground least favourable to itself in order to prove its capacity to keep the chain intact. And once it was committed the imperative to fight to the bitter end was determined by the fact that it could not be seen to be defeated, not because of the loss of the territory nominally the object of the confrontation, and rarely because of any direct economic interest, but because of the loss of prestige the USA itself would suffer, without which its sphere of influence and the global economic interests it protected would quickly unravel.

The defence of the post-war order therefore left the USA with very little room for manoeuvre in its response to the communist challenge. The fact that this challenge materialized in Vietnam was almost secondary, since what was perceived to be at stake by US policy-makers went well beyond the fate of Vietnam itself. Equally, it was no accident that Vietnam should be so unpropitious an arena for the defence of this imperial edifice. In this sense, failure was virtually pre-ordained by the perspective that the USA brought to the war, and was the more tragic for that.[24] If it is now apparent why America had to defend its sphere of influence in this way, it is important to understand the nature of the edifice of alliances that it was defending. To the extent that it was economic interest, specifically free access for capital, which underlay the system of alliances the USA had developed, then although the maintenance of the edifice was a political/military enterprise, the purpose behind it was economic. The symbiotic link between economics and politics is established along the lines analysed in earlier chapters, where it was suggested that, if economics provides the initial dynamic underlying American behaviour, this is not inconsistent with the fact that the defence of its interests is necessarily and irreducibly a political and at times military enterprise.

The defence of the imperial superstructure in Vietnam thus had a dual character: it was necessary not only for its own sake as the symbol of American power in the world, but also in order to maintain an essential core of economic interest. The conception of this superstructure as one in which the metropolis is tied inextricably to all its clients by a chain of absolute commitment meant that an attack on any part of the edifice was vital, made as it was by an enemy which attacks a weak link as a preliminary to its ultimate goal of overthrowing the core. The response therefore had to be appropriately uncompromising. This inexorable logic which drew the USA into the Vietnam conflict meant that it was not a manufactured intervention. The rhetorical argument that if the USA did not fight communism on the beaches of South-East Asia it would eventually have to do so on the beaches of San Francisco had a kernel of truth inside the hyperbole. The interests at stake were both political and economic, and they were real. They were made all the more so by America's perception of its role in the world, and in this sense the Johnson administration was not deceived by its own rhetoric. American involvement in the Vietnam conflict, if not inevitable, at least had a powerful imperative driving it, and cannot easily be dismissed as either a mistake or a misperception by the USA of its interests.

If this explains why the USA was drawn into the conflict, it remains to explain why it did not withdraw sooner when the miscalculation of the costs involved and the fact that victory was impossible had become apparent. One explanation derives from the bureaucratic character of the US state.[25] Policy was invariably a compromise between the wishes of different factions within the bureaucracy, each strong enough to prevent the other's view from being adopted, but neither able to impose its own coherent strategy on the conduct of the war. The differences in philosophy turned on the interpretation of the containment policy. One group interpreted the term more literally and saw US action as essentially defensive, resisting communist encroachment but in effect seeking to maintain the status quo. The other took the policy to its logical conclusion and argued that the best way to contain the spread of communism was not simply to resist it on the periphery but to go to the heart of the beast and remove the problem at its source. The former outlook manifested itself in a commitment to a political solution based on winning over the hearts and minds of the Vietnamese population to the American cause, and was rooted in a more liberal, East Coast European-oriented arm of the US establishment. It was this group which had largely been responsible for formulating the US world-view in the post-war years and had evolved in an essentially moderate direction.[26] The second perspective was irritated by self-imposed constraints on US military activity, and argued for more extensive bombing, including Hanoi and even Peking if necessary. Its attitude was that if the USA was going to enter the war it should employ all the means at its disposal and not try to fight with one hand tied behind its back. This was the product of a newly emerging Sunbelt Pacific-oriented element of the establishment, whose growing strength reflected the increased importance of that dimension of US domestic life and the more conservative and aggressive frontier mentality associated with it.[27]

This division between a rollback and a containment approach had been a feature of US policy from the beginning of its adoption of a world view which turned on fighting communism.[28] So powerful were the advocates on each side, however, that in the context of Vietnam they reduced the President to the status of arbitrator rather than leader. By the manipulation of information and promises of ultimate success – the light at the end of the tunnel – Johnson was invariably persuaded that continued intervention would ultimately prove worthwhile. In the meantime in deciding how to prosecute the war he took the middle ground, rarely giving those who favoured escalation all they asked for, but equally rarely favouring those who wished to pursue a political solution. The US commitment thus grew by increments and any coherent overall strategy was lost in the welter of bureaucratic infighting.

This gave the conflict the character of a quagmire, which once entered became increasingly difficult to escape. And once Johnson had committed US prestige to winning the war, the issue became prestige and not the ostensible substance of the fate of Vietnam. Consequently, the more the USA was drawn into the quagmire, the more of its prestige was at stake and the less able it was to extricate itself. Although the USA was led into the conflict by the narrowness of its own vision of the world, and led further by this and by its own hubris into a gross miscalculation of the consequences of involvement, there remained none the less a core of rationality behind these weaknesses. Empires have to be defended, in America's case no less so for its empire being an informal one. It is the element of inevitability this rational core brings in which, when combined with the flaws in the perspective of the USA as protagonist, gives the whole episode, and Johnson's fate in particular, the aspect of a Greek tragedy.

American involvement may have brought about the downfall of one President, Johnson, but although his successor, Nixon, was elected on a platform of withdrawal from the conflict, this does not mean that the process of extrication was straightforward or that it implied abandonment of the American world-view and the interests which generated that involvement in the first place. Indeed, it does not even mean that the withdrawal, as conceived by Nixon and Kissinger, implied acceptance of an American defeat in Vietnam,[29] which is one of the reasons they were prepared to take a long time to secure the best possible terms for it. There were two principal constraints on the Nixon/Kissinger strategy for withdrawal. The first was their continuing adherence to the concept of linkage. Far from abandoning it they were more insistent than ever that, in the face of the challenge of Vietnam, America's standing in the world and its ability to protect its interests depended on not being seen to lose this conflict. Kissinger argued forcefully that a major power could not afford to appear selective in meeting its commitments to defend its allies.[30] The whole system of alliances which secured US interests was tied together, and a failure in one part would inevitably undermine US credibility everywhere and quickly lead to an unravelling of the system. In other words, Nixon and Kissinger accepted the rationale which had played such a large part in dragging the USA into the conflict in the first place.

This perspective would in itself have favoured an indefinite continuation of US involvement rather than withdrawal, but it had to be balanced against the other constraint which affected their policy. This was the domestic political constraint that the American public had voted for Nixon's promised withdrawal and was not prepared to accept continuing involvement. Disillusion with the war grew to unmanageable proportions after the Tet offensive in 1968, which was perceived as demonstrating the impossibility of an American victory,[31] and failure to deliver withdrawal would undoubtedly have had fatal political consequences for the Nixon administration. On the face of it, this would seem to place the two constraints in such direct opposition to each other that there could be no possibility of reconciling them, and Nixon would be forced to choose which to follow. However, it is essential to recognize the precise nature of public opposition to the continuation of the war. The US public was not against the stated aims of the war: the idea that the USA had a responsibility to resist the expansion of communism still commanded wide assent. Although some came to see the USA as the aggressor and to believe that the US action was morally indefensible, the majority continued to believe in the justness of the cause. What they were unwilling to countenance was the cost of pursuing it, specifically the cost in American lives.

There were other considerations: the cost to the domestic economy was becoming increasingly apparent by the late 1960s, and many were also concerned at the cost to American society of the domestic turmoil the divisions over the war were creating. The shootings at Kent State University, for example, demonstrated how turmoil that started over the war could spread and undermine the fabric of society. But the principal concern was that the USA should not continue to lose the lives of its soldiers in a war that it had become obvious could not be won in a conventional sense. These sentiments were heightened by the belief that, while the cause was just, the USA was bearing too much of the burden and the South Vietnamese too little in what was, after all, their own defence. The decline of the anti-war movement after conscription was ended is indicative of what was really exercising the protestors, and even the demonstrations against the extension of the war into Cambodia were more a revolt at the prospect of indefinite continuation of the war than against the war itself.[32] In short, the US public willed the ends of American involvement in Vietnam, but would not will the means.

It was the particular character of the disenchantment with the war that gave Nixon and Kissinger the opportunity to reconcile the two constraints under which they were operating. The strategy they devised for doing so was summed up in the phrase 'Peace with Honour'. It recognized that withdrawal was inevitable, but equally that the American public's attitude gave them scope to achieve it with a minimum loss of face. What it came down to was that Nixon knew he had the four years of his first term of office to reduce American casualties significantly. In the space thus allowed, the strategy was implemented brilliantly in a diplomatic sense. Its first aspect was the so-called Vietnamization of the war. This was in tune with American public sentiment because it shifted the burden of the war rather than changed the underlying policy. The American role increasingly became to supply *matériel* and relatively 'safe' military back-up in the form of bombing, while the Vietnamese provided the front-line troops and therefore suffered the casualties. This policy of shifting the burden of defence away from US troops and towards high-technology back-up of allies in the struggle against communism was generalized from this case in the 'Nixon Doctrine'.[33] Nixon realized that the USA could never again allow itself to be dragged into front-line struggles in foreign wars, and that the limits of American involvement would have to be carefully delineated after the experience of Vietnam.

In order for these restrictions on US involvement, as articulated in the Nixon Doctrine, not to give the impression that they were merely a recognition and acceptance of weakness and decline, the types of US involvement that were permitted had to be seen to be effective. In the case of Vietnam this applied particularly to the bombing campaign. It was essential to the peace with honour strategy that the North Vietnamese should not feel that the American commitment to withdrawal meant that they could afford to wait the Americans out without cost. In carrying out the bombing, therefore, the Nixon administration was brutally tough, and much more effective than the previous administration. The USA incurred no serious cost from the bombing campaign in terms of loss of life, and it was therefore not subject to the same domestic constraint that had undermined direct engagement of land-based forces. Consequently it could, and Nixon made clear that it would, continue indefinitely. This in itself was a significant lever in bringing the North Vietnamese to the bargaining table. The other factor that had to be dealt with, however, carried significance far beyond the Vietnam conflict itself. This was the relationship of North Vietnam to its backers in China and the USSR.

One reason American action had always been limited in prosecuting the war was the assumption that the communist powers would intervene if the USA overstepped certain, unspecified lines. The fear that such escalation could easily produce a direct and catastrophic superpower confrontation had been the major restraint on US freedom of action. It was the Nixon/Kissinger policy of *détente* which effectively neutralized this threat. By giving the communist powers an interest in continuing co-operation with the USA, it provided a counterweight to their solidarity with North Vietnam. The wedge that *détente* drove between the Soviet Union and North Vietnam thereby critically increased American freedom of manoeuvre in the conduct of the war, and strengthened its hand in the concurrent negotiations with North Vietnam. In addition, the policy of opening relations with China in order to play it off against the Soviet Union increased even further the effective neutralization of North Vietnam's backers and left it the more isolated.[34] The *détente* policy was designed for much broader purposes than its effect on the Vietnam war, but its impact in this theatre was critical to the implementation of the peace with honour strategy. By permitting the USA to act more aggressively without the fear of superpower reprisal, it provided greater leverage in extracting the concessions from North Vietnam that were a necessary condition of an 'honourable' peace settlement.

While the elements of the strategy may have become evident in retrospect, executing them required diplomatic and political skill of the highest order. Nixon and Kissinger walked a tightrope in balancing international commitments against domestic sentiment. If the circumstances meant that the most their strategy could hope for was to cope with the limits on American power, indeed its decline, then it must be said that in terms of *realpolitik* they made the best of these circumstances. Why then were they ultimately unsuccessful? The ignominy of the final US withdrawal and the completeness of the victory of North Vietnam can hardly be disputed. But that in itself does not contradict the argument that the Nixon/Kissinger strategy was a success in its own terms. The problem was that it was not seen through to completion. The reason for this was, of course, the Watergate scandal, which not only removed Nixon from office but also distracted his attention from foreign policy and undermined his authority for some time before. Without Watergate there is every likelihood that Nixon and Kissinger would have maintained sufficient control of the situation to prevent a complete victory by North Vietnam. After the effective withdrawal of American troops and with the communist powers neutralized, they would have been under very few constraints. There is every indication that they would then have been prepared to use military power in the form of a bombing campaign in order to gain sufficient time to extricate the USA on their own terms.[35]

The fact that Ford and Kissinger were not able to see through this strategy when the time came was a consequence of congressional disaffection and the restrictions it placed on their freedom to act. This disaffection was only in part a result of the conduct of the war; it was in fact much more the product of the weakening of the presidency brought about by Watergate.[36] But the problems of Watergate themselves were not unrelated to the peace with honour strategy. Its execution required secrecy, manipulation and even deception. In order for all its various pieces to be kept in motion it required a single guiding intelligence. This did not fit comfortably with the pluralistic nature of the American bureaucracy, or indeed the division of powers between the branches of government. Consequently, Nixon and Kissinger sidestepped these constraints by ignoring or deceiving these other elements of their own government. Such a concentration of power was almost bound to spill over into the domestic sphere. They gathered all power to themselves in order, as they saw it, to save the USA from international ignominy. They became, to themselves, the embodiment of the state. It followed that anyone opposing them, even from a position of relative ignorance of their purposes, was an enemy of the state and of the vital work they were carrying out on behalf of their country. Nixon's cavalier disregard for the niceties of constitutional restraint on his power amounted virtually to a contempt for the democratic process as something to be manipulated in order to give him the freedom to carry out his designs. It was the same mentality, then, which manifested itself in both the conduct of foreign policy and the excesses of Watergate. Brilliant though the foreign affairs strategy of the Nixon administration was, both in conception and execution, it was also fundamentally amoral and undemocratic. It thus revealed very starkly the tension between effectiveness in foreign policy and a pluralist democratic process. The fact that the Watergate crisis ultimately resolved this tension in favour of the democratic process does not make the implications any less sobering.

After the American withdrawal from Vietnam was completed, the post-mortem divided predictably along conservative and liberal lines. The conservative reaction was to stress that, once the commitment to intervene had been made, the USA should have done whatever was necessary to win the war. The mistake was to have restrained the US armed forces so as to prevent the employment of the military power that would have secured victory. This has the merit of a certain consistency, in so far as it stresses that it is insufficient to will ends without willing the means to achieve them. It is flawed in two other respects, however. Firstly, it sidesteps the question of whether the USA should ever have become involved. It therefore leaves the whole US world view, which is what prompted involvement in the first place, unchallenged. This amounts to a tacit endorsement of it, one which suggests that conservatives would be likely to be drawn into the same unwinnable conflicts again. The only alteration contemplated in the conservative analysis would be the tactical one of not restraining US military forces once the commitment had been made. But it is this undiluted belief in the efficacy of American military force to guarantee the success of involvement that is the second flaw. It bespeaks a crude and naive appreciation of the complexities of such conflicts, combined with a simplistic faith in US supremacy, which would almost certainly lead to further disasters.

The predominant liberal reaction to the defeat in Vietnam was that the USA should make its commitments to military intervention much more carefully than it had done in that case. It should do so only when it is supporting forces with strong indigenous backing, and should not intervene on behalf of lost causes at the risk of squandering its own prestige. While to some extent an expression of common sense, such a view does benefit greatly from hindsight and is thus of greater use in analysing past mistakes than in guiding future actions. It also suffers from a degree of wishful thinking, since the credibility of a hegemonic power does indeed depend on its capacity to defend all the outposts of its sphere of influence. Choosing only those battlegrounds where victory is certain is simply not compatible with hegemonic status, since by definition the hegemon must be able to win all its battles. If taken to the extreme, the liberal reaction would therefore amount to a tacit acceptance of the fact that the USA cannot maintain this hegemonic position and is reduced to the status of an ordinary country which can and must choose which battles to fight.

But perhaps more important than what divides the conservative and liberal reactions to the Vietnam débâcle is the agreement which persists beneath the surface differences. Both accept in their different ways that the goals of US policy are unchanged. The liberal view is more cautious about how extensive American sway can be and advocates a diplomacy which recognizes this, placing less faith in the force of arms than the conservative view. But that the American role in the world is to contain the spread of communism as far as possible is unquestioned in both perspectives. The differences revolve merely around the extent to which this can be done and the best tactics to pursue. The other point of agreement, equally significant for future US conduct, is that the USA should commit its own manpower to overseas conflicts only as the very last resort. Much greater stress should be placed on the support of indigenous forces, with the US commitment generally confined to the provision of material and technical support rather than its own personnel. The domestic political consequence of risking the lives of large numbers of soldiers was proven by Vietnam to be too great, and it was only by avoiding this constraint that maximum freedom to pursue the policy of containment could be ensured.

It was this shared perspective on the fundamentals of America's role in the world that permitted the reconstruction of the imperial ideology when a decent interval had passed after the humiliating conclusion to the US involvement in Vietnam. The media coverage of the plight of the boat people and of the post-war condition of Vietnam and Cambodia has been shown to have been tailored to the idea that the USA was right all along in fighting a regime that could produce such a repressive society.[37] In this context the Carter presidency is best seen as a hiatus. His commitment to a moral foreign policy based on respect for human rights was a natural but short-lived reaction to the excesses of the

Nixon administration. It did not reflect the strong image of a superpower to which most Americans still wished to cling. After the period of introspection produced by the defeat in Vietnam, the country resumed its normal confident, expansionist attitude to world affairs under the Reagan administration. The difference between it and pre-Carter administrations was that it had learned not to overreach itself, but to deploy US forces more judiciously, either committing them in areas where victory was cheap and danger slight, as in Grenada, or withdrawing them rapidly when they were in a no-win position and before US prestige became entwined with their fate, as in the Lebanon. It was therefore able to avoid catastrophe, but by changing tactics not goals.

The conclusion concerning this period when American power was at its height is that America's role is one which may be characterized by hubris or, to use Senator Fulbright's phrase, by the arrogance of power.[38] If the involvement in Vietnam which brought retribution and toppled the USA from its seeming invulnerability as a world power was not inevitable, then it was certainly not accidental. America's supreme role in the world required that its power be tested at some point, and it had to try to meet the challenge or forfeit its position. There was undoubtedly a core of rationality in the domino argument, and real interests were at stake for the USA in the conflict, even if this was as much the result of the US perspective on its role in the world as the consequence of an objective challenge. The core of the interests that the USA was defending remained economic; specifically, the key was the free access of capital to as large a fraction of the world economy as possible. It was communism which denied this access, particularly when combined with nationalism as in Vietnam, and this was why it had to be resisted. While the Soviet Union itself, as we argued in Chapter 3, may have posed a vital challenge to the integrity of the USA and thus thrown into relief the fundamentally political nature of American interests in international affairs, the same does not hold for the conflict in Vietnam. Literally vital interests were not at stake as they were in relations with the USSR; what was at issue was control of the sphere of American influence within which capital was permitted to move freely, an issue to which the domino theory was relevant, but in which the link to a communist world takeover was more a rationalization than a reason.

It follows that a degree of intransigence was necessary in American attitudes to liberation struggles, and to the wave of communist expansion of which they were perceived to be a part, for as long as communism persisted in denying access to private capital. However, the critical importance of the economic imperative does not alter the fact that economic interests had to be defended by political means. The fighting in Vietnam may have appeared to be very distant from the defence of core US interests, and many liberals rejected it for this reason. But in fact there was a clear chain of interest linking the two that was quite real and not simply constructed out of the fevered imagination and absolutist mentality of US cold warriors. With hindsight it would have been possible to avoid some of the mistakes made by the USA in its involvement, but it is difficult to see how involvement could have been avoided altogether. Certainly in the latter half of that involvement, under the guidance of Nixon and Kissinger, the USA pursued the political and diplomatic protection of its sphere of influence with exceptional vision and skill. It is fortunate that the fact that this was done on an amoral basis and with little respect for the niceties of the American constitution did not do more lasting damage to American democracy.

There is little doubt, though, that in protecting its domestic democratic institutions the USA forfeited, at least temporarily, some of its effectiveness in foreign affairs. Hindsight suggests that it would perhaps have been possible to reconcile morality and expediency a little more if the initial impulse to overreach itself had been curbed at the outset. But to expect this is to expect the USA to have been a different kind of country occupying a different place in world affairs. Vietnam was a tragedy waiting to happen; it remains to be seen whether the chastening effect of the lessons learned from it have increased the US capacity to cope with the other, less dramatic but no less important challenges to its leading world role. It is in this sense that Vietnam provides the essential backdrop to the responses successive administrations from Nixon through Carter to Reagan adopted to these broader challenges.

Notes

1. R. Foot, *The Wrong War: American policy, and the dimensions of the Korean conflict*, Ithaca, NY: Cornell University Press, 1985.
2. M.A. Guhin, *John Foster Dulles: A statesman and his times*, New York: Columbia University Press, 1972; R.A. Divine, *Eisenhower and the Cold War*, New York: Oxford University Press, 1981.
3. J. L. Gaddis, *Strategies of Containment*, New York: Oxford University Press, 1982; L. Freedman, *The Evolution of Nuclear Strategy*, London: Macmillan, 1981.
4. S. Schlesinger and S. Kinzer, *Bitter Fruit: The untold story of the American coup in Guatemala*, London: Sinclair Browne, 1982.
5. B. Rubin, *Paved With Good Intentions: The American experience and Iran*, New York: Oxford University Press, 1980, chapter 3.

6. A.M. Schlesinger, Jr, *A Thousand Days: John F. Kennedy in the White House*, Boston, Mass.: Houghton Mifflin, 1965; T. Soresen, *Kennedy*, New York: Harper, 1965.

7. R.J. Walton, *Cold War and Counter-Revolution: The foreign policy of John F. Kennedy*, Harmondsworth: Penguin, 1973.

8. *ibid.*

9. R.A. Divine (ed.), *The Cuban Missle Crisis*, Chicago, Ill.: Quadrangle, 1971; R.L. Garthoff, *Reflections on the Cuban Missile Crisis*, Washington, DC: Brookings, 1989, revised edn.

10. A. and R. Wohlstetter, 'Controlling the risks in Cuba', Adelphi Papers (April 1965), London: Institute for Strategic Studies, 1965.

11. S. Brown, *The Faces of Power*, New York: Columbia University Press, 1983.

12. J.F. Kennedy, 'Commencement address at the American University, Washington, June 10, 1963', in *Public Papers of the Presidents of the United States: John F. Kennedy, 1963*, pp. 459–64.

13. F.G. Gil, 'The Kennedy–Johnson years', in J.D. Martz (ed.), *United States Policy in Latin America: A quarter century of crisis and challenge, 1961–86*, Lincoln, Nebr.: University of Nebraska Press, 1988; A.M. Schlesinger, Jr, 'The Alliance for Progress: a retrospective', in R.G. Hellman and J.H. Rosenbaum (eds.), *Latin America: The search for a new international role*, New York: Wiley, 1975; J. Levinson and J. de Onis, *The Alliance That Lost Its Way: A critical report on the Alliance for Progress*, Chicago, Ill.: Quadrangle, 1970.

14. A.M. Schlesinger, *op. cit.*

15. D. Halberstam, *The Best and the Brightest*, London: Barrie, 1972.

16. Arthur M. Schlesinger, Jr, argues not: see his *Robert F. Kennedy and His Times*, Boston, Mass.: Houghton Mifflin, 1979.

17. See Kennedy's interview with Walter Cronkite, *Public Papers of the Presidents of the United States: John F. Kennedy, 1963*, pp. 650–53.

18. Senator M. Gravell (ed.), *The Pentagon Papers: The Defense Department's history of United States decisionmaking on Vietnam*, Boston, Mass.: Beacon, 1971.

19. J.P. Kimball, *To Reason Why: The debate about the causes of US involvement in the Vietnam war*, New York: McGraw-Hill, 1990.

20. F. Schurmann, *The Logic of World Power*, New York: Random House, 1974.

21. N. Chomsky, *American Power and the New Mandarins*, London: Chatto, 1969.

22. The theory was originally formulated by Eisenhower: see S. Brown, *The Faces of Power: Constancy and change in United States foreign policy from Truman to Reagan.* New York: Columbia University Press, 1983, p. 80.

23. L.H. Gelb and R.K. Betts, *The Irony of Vietnam: The system worked*, Washington, DC: Brookings, 1979.

24. G. Kolko, *Vietnam: Anatomy of a war 1940–75*, London: Allen & Unwin, 1986.

25. Schurmann, *op. cit.*

26. W. Isaacson and E. Thomas, *The Wise Men: Six friends and the world they made*, London: Faber, 1986.

27. K. Sale, *Power Shift: The rise of the Southern Rim and its challenge to the Eastern establishment*, New York: Random House, 1975.

28. D. Yergin, *Shattered Peace: The origins of the cold war and the national security state*, New York: Houghton Mifflin, 1979.
29. Seymour Hersh, in *Kissinger: The price of power – Henry Kissinger in the Nixon White House*, London: Faber, 1983, argues that despite publicly promising withdrawal, Nixon never had any intention of allowing the USA to suffer a defeat in Vietnam, and that his whole withdrawal strategy was premissed on the idea that it would only occur when the purposes of American involvement had been secured.
30. H. Kissinger, *The White House Years*, Boston, Mass.: Little Brown, 1979.
31. Assessments differ greatly as to whether this was an accurate perception. Many argue that the North Vietnamese won an ideological victory in the Tet offensive even though militarily they suffered a defeat. See G. Lewy, *America in Vietnam*, New York: Oxford University Press, 1978; Kolko, *op. cit.*
32. W. Shawcross, *Sideshow: Kissinger, Nixon and the destruction of Cambodia*, London: Hogarth, 1986, new edn.
33. R. Litwak, *Detente and the Nixon Doctrine: American foreign policy and the pursuit of stability 1969–76*, Cambridge: Cambridge University Press, 1984; V. Briodine and M. Selden (eds.), *Open Secret: The Kissinger–Nixon doctrine in Asia*, New York: Harper, 1972.
34. A.D. Barnett, *China Policy: Old problems and new challenges*, Washington, DC: Brookings, 1977.
35. R.M. Nixon, *The Memoirs of Richard Nixon*, London: Sidgwick, 1978; Kissinger, *op. cit.*
36. R. Woodward and C. Bernstein, *All the President's Men*, London: Quartet, 1974.
37. N. Chomsky and E. Herman, *The Political Economy of Human Rights. Vol. 2 After the Cataclysm: Postwar Indochina and the reconstruction of imperial ideology*, Boston, Mass.: South End Press, 1979.
38. W. Fulbright, *The Arrogance of Power*, New York: Random House, 1966.

CHAPTER SEVEN

·

NIXON AND CARTER: RESPONSES TO DECLINE

The brilliance of the Nixon/Kissinger strategy for withdrawal from Vietnam with the minimum loss of face should not obscure the fact that it was a strategy designed to cope with a manifest decline in American power in the world. As an exercise in damage limitation it was quite in contrast with the confident and aggressive US handling of the reconstruction of the post-war world only a short time before. The US experience in Vietnam was part of a wider process of American decline that became manifest in other areas in the 1970s. It was apparent, for example, on a variety of economic indicators: the US share of world trade was in decline, its rate of growth was below that of Japan and much of Western Europe, living standards were stagnant and again in relative decline, and America's pre-eminent position in overseas investment was also diminishing rapidly.[1] Our concern, however, is not to elaborate on the quantitative details of decline, but rather to consider the strategies that were developed for coping with America's reduced role in the world in the 1970s. The different strategies devised by the Nixon and Carter administrations (the Ford administration was not sufficiently distinctive to be relevant in this context) reveal some basic divisions in American foreign policy, and an evaluation of their successes and failures is therefore of more general significance than their short-term impact.

The response of the Nixon administration to decline was made manifest in dramatic fashion with the so-called Nixon shocks of August 1971.[2] The measures taken included not only restrictions on imports from Japan in recognition of the USA's deteriorating competitive position, but, more importantly, the effective ending of the convertibility of the US dollar for gold. We have already discussed the advantages to both the USA and the rest of the market world economy of the privileged position of the US dollar as a reserve currency. The loss of that position was therefore a considerable blow. It meant that the USA would no longer enjoy freedom from the same disciplines as other

131

countries through its ability to finance trade deficits simply by printing more money. This position had depended to a large extent on confidence in the strength of the USA, and once this was dented, principally as a consequence of Vietnam but also because of recognition of general US economic decline, it raised the prospect of a run on the dollar as overseas holders of the currency sought more secure havens for their capital and trading requirements. This left the US government with no choice but to end convertibility. However, the response of the Nixon administration was not merely one of acceptance of relative economic decline; it also declared an intention to fight back. There was to be no acquiescence to defeat.[3]

In the first place, the end of convertibility did not necessarily signal the end of a world financial role for the USA. It retained a significant, not to say a controlling interest in the international financial institutions which had been set up as part of the new global order after the war.[4] The IMF in particular gave the USA a powerful instrument for influencing the economic policies of other countries, an influence that was invariably exercised in a fashion which favoured the disciplines of market forces and enhanced the role of private enterprise.[5] Capital outflow from the USA continued to be massive,[6] and as a creditor nation and what remained by far the biggest single economy in the world, the USA still retained considerable power in the world economy. And the Nixon administration was not afraid to capitalize on the continuing American strengths once the burden of reserve currency status had been lifted. One illustration of this was its employment of the tactic of devaluation that the end of convertibility had made possible.

The USA was in a particularly favourable position to use devaluation as a means of increasing its economic competitiveness. The relatively small scale of its international payments compared to the size of its domestic economy meant that devaluation did not have a substantial inflationary domestic effect. For most other advanced economies any devaluation, which made imports more expensive in terms of the home currency, imported inflation into the domestic economy. This counteracted the benefits of increased competitiveness because it usually required restrictions to be put on home demand in order to eliminate inflationary pressures. This in turn slowed economic growth, reduced competitiveness and so prompted a further devaluation. For most countries, then, devaluation was an option of last resort.[7] It follows from this differential effect of devaluation that it was rational for America, in seeking to restore its relative economic position, to initiate a process of competitive devaluation between the advanced economies, since unlike the USA they could only be harmed by it. And it was for this reason that the Nixon administration pursued devaluation of the dollar not just as a means of realigning its external payments position, but in an aggressive competitive thrust to improve its position relative to its allies.[8]

A second element of this strategy was to pursue a policy of vigorous domestic growth. This was preferred to the alternative of responding to decline by tightening financial and monetary conditions in order to eliminate inefficient producers and so provide a basis for an economic revival after restructuring.[9] Whether growth or retrenchment was the best way to manage the economy was fiercely disputed on purely domestic grounds. But in respect of the international consequences, the reasoning of the administration was parallel to that of devaluation: growth would benefit the USA relative to its international partners because it would be effected partly at their expense. A domestic economic growth strategy for the USA was likely to result in high government deficits and suck in more imports, thereby worsening the trading position on manufactured goods. This in turn would lead to the raising of interest rates in order to finance the twin deficits. Higher interest rates would attract an inflow of capital from around the world, and in order to stem what would be an outflow from their economies, other countries would have to raise their interest rates. But this would make capital more expensive, which would reduce the level of investment in their economies, which in turn would lead to lower economic growth.

By initiating this process, and by virtue of the relative size of its economy, the USA was therefore able to invert the usual economic logic whereby high interest rates reduce growth. To attract the financing for its deficits the USA still needed to enjoy the confidence of owners of capital in other countries. But the stability of its economic and political system meant that investors felt it was a safe haven. Consequently, there was little difficulty in attracting the required capital. Size and stability were the US advantages in this competition with other capitalist economies, and the Nixon administration was not slow to capitalize on them even though, and perhaps because, the strategy worked at the expense of its partners.[10]

It should be stressed that these policies could easily have contradictory effects. After all, the encouragement of an inflow of capital would, other things being equal, lead to a rise in the value of the dollar and so counteract any devaluation tactic. What did provide the uniting element guiding US attempts to reconcile these contradictions was the increasingly mercantilist perspective of the Nixon administration.[11] It was determined to try to reverse economic decline by putting US national interest ahead of any overriding commitment to the well-being of the world economy. In the earlier hegemonic period, the interests of the USA and of the world economy were, almost by definition, virtually synonymous. Once this unity had been broken the USA was quick to choose its priorities. The clearest manifestation of this mercantilist approach was the willingness of the administration to control trade in the national interest.[12]

The USA had been the leading advocate of free trade as the means of reconstructing the post-war world economy, and it is difficult to imagine how the period of sustained growth after the war could have been achieved without it. But while the principle of comparative advantage provided the theoretical rationale for free trade by demonstrating how all countries, rich and poor alike, would benefit from it, there is also little doubt that rich countries like the USA benefited the most. This follows simply from the fact that free trade is a means of making all play by the same rules. On the basis of equal competition, it is clear that the strong will benefit more than the weak. As the strongest economy it was therefore quite rational for the USA to advocate free trade since it had nothing to fear from the competition. However, once it had ceased to dominate world economic affairs and had become uncompetitive in various areas, it began to have an interest in protecting some of its industries from overseas competition in order to ensure their survival and maintain domestic employment. In short, the USA joined the ranks of those countries which wanted as far as possible to have the best of both worlds, protection at home and free trade overseas.

This was a combination that Japan had largely achieved, and it was primarily against imports from Japan that the USA was prepared to employ restrictions.[13] In effect, it was signalling to the Japanese that their tactics were no longer acceptable, precisely because they had been too successful in the past, and at the expense of Japan's allies, including the USA. Formerly the USA had been willing to indulge these tactics, partly because it was strong enough economically not to be threatened by them, and partly because it had an interest in building up Japan as a strong society which could act as a bulwark against the spread of communism in the Far East. American unwillingness to continue this indulgence signalled the rise of tension that has continued to the present day. Although it has become more acute, the problem has not been resolved.

Part of the difficulty has been that the superior quality of Japanese consumer goods has meant that US consumers have continued to buy them despite restrictions; Japanese consumers, on the other hand, appear relatively impervious to the attractions of American goods, irrespective of the existence or otherwise of formal tariffs or restrictions. Each side has manoeuvred for position in this contest since the early 1970s, but it was from then that the USA felt the need to compete on equal terms and showed its willingness to do so at its partners' expense. It was no longer dominant and secure enough to be able to take responsibility for the health of the whole system, even at the expense of its own narrow advantage. The USA under Nixon did not start to pursue a dramatically nationalistic policy; rather it became an ordinary country seeking, from a position of weakness, to gain the best advantage it could. The point is that having to act like an ordinary country was in itself a radical departure for the USA.[14]

American relations with the Third World were also affected by this realignment of economic policy under Nixon. The Brandt report symbolized a widespread commitment to a new international economic order in which the developed economies would assist the impoverished parts of the world economy.[15] The argument for this was partly a sense of obligation, and partly self-interest. The new international economic order was envisaged to be a form of international Keynesianism which would redistribute wealth to poorer countries. These would have a high marginal propensity to consume, and the consequence would be a net increase in effective demand in the world economy. The effect would therefore be beneficial not only for Third World countries, but also, ultimately, for the advanced economies too because they would have enlarged markets in which to sell their output.[16] There was no question, however, that it was the element of sacrifice rather than self-interest that was stressed in this perspective, at least in the initial stages. And it was this which the administration rejected.

In line with the *realpolitik* approach of Nixon and Kissinger, it was calculated that Third World countries had little power to extract concessions, and that there was thus no need to compromise with them. Instead a continuation of an aggressive and indeed exploitative relationship in which Third World countries were viewed as sources of cheap labour and materials rather than markets was seen to fit better with the US national interest. Of course, as we saw in Chapter 5, there is a strong argument that in the long run it is the undiluted export of market capitalism which is most likely to promote both economic development in the Third World and US interests, however harsh the consequences in the short term. But it was on the basis of a different calculation of national interest that the US policy was pursued.

One area in which Third World countries did demonstrate power that had to be taken seriously was oil production. The development of OPEC as a cartel which was able to bring about a dramatic rise in the price of oil on world markets was a genuine shock to all advanced economies.[17] Once again, in earlier periods the USA would have been relatively immune from such a development since it had been self-sufficient in oil. By the early 1970s, however, this had ceased to be true, and although European and Japanese economies were more dependent on oil imports from OPEC countries, the US too was adversely affected. But in this instance the USA was able to turn this problem, if not to its advantage, then at least to a position which minimized the damage and left it better off relative to the other advanced economies. In the first place, the multinational oil companies, which were predominantly US based, were able to maintain a profitable position in the oil production process. More importantly, the vast profits which were made, especially by Middle East countries, needed to be reinvested in the world economy because their domestic economies could not absorb them through either consumption or investment. This task was carried out by international banks, an area in which at that time the USA was again pre-eminent. In fact the recycling they undertook strengthened their international position relative to their competitors. The area in which much of the recycling took place was in loans to Third World countries. This was a policy whose long-term consequences were close to catastrophic in the 1980s when world-wide interest rates rose. These left the Third World countries which were the recipients of the loans unable to maintain interest payments without unacceptable consequences for their standard of living. This in turn put the existence of many of the world's leading banks which had made the loans into jeopardy, and indeed threatened the collapse of the whole international banking system.[18]

In the short run, however, the effect was beneficial to the USA. The underlying reason why the OPEC challenge ultimately did little harm was that the OPEC countries depended on a healthy world capitalism.[19] Without it they would not have markets or investment opportunities. They had gathered considerable power to themselves and were able to play First World countries off against each other because of the latter's differential dependence on oil.[20] But the fundamental facts of interdependence meant that they could use oil only to effect some redistribution of wealth within the system, and not to threaten the stability of the system itself. To do so would have been to kill the goose which laid the golden egg. The net consequence was therefore a minimal shift in the balance of power, and one which the USA was able and willing to turn to its advantage against allies who were more dependent on OPEC oil and less able to recycle the increased profits from its production. In effect, therefore, the net transfer of wealth in respect of the advanced economies was from Europe and Japan to the USA via the OPEC countries.[21]

In sum, the economic response of the Nixon administration to the relative decline of the USA was an aggressive and relatively nationalistic one. It attempted to reassert the US position, if necessary at the expense of the mutual prosperity of the rest of the capitalist economies. However, it is important to recognize that, although as its hegemony waned US tactics became more competitive, any nationalistic tendencies were restrained by the interdependence of the world economy. Growing interdependence meant that if America went too far in beggaring its allies it too would suffer because its own economic health was increasingly dependent on overseas markets and investment opportunities. A new balance had to be struck, therefore, between competition and co-operation, one which recognized both that the USA was no longer so dominant that it did not have to choose between its interests and those of the world system, and also that the world economy was becoming increasingly interdependent. The balance drawn by the Nixon administration amounted to a new but tempered nationalism on the economic front.

But, as we have argued throughout, America's international economic role cannot be seen in a vacuum. It is always intimately tied up with its political role, and so we must consider the nature of that connection in this period. It might appear that the connection is a contradictory one, since *détente* is based on co-operation whereas the economic strategy was based on competition. The apparent contradiction is intensified in so far as the USA was pursuing an aggressive policy in respect of its allies and a co-operative one with its stated enemy. In fact the contradiction is more apparent than real because, as we argued in Chapter 3, the conception of *détente* as a policy of co-operation is a misreading of its nature.

The underlying premiss of *détente* was that the West was in crisis.[22] To some extent this was viewed as a broad historical trend and carried echoes of a Spenglerian perspective. Perhaps equally important, it was a reaction to the 1960s, a decade in which the moral challenges to the domestic social order were viewed by many as evidence of the spread of moral decadence in the USA. The problems raised by the adversarial mentality that developed in the 1960s were compounded by what was taken to be a sense of liberal guilt as to the world role of the West. The role of America in particular was seen as tainted by imperialist exploitation and a lack of respect for other cultures, especially those of the Third World. Clearly, the Vietnam war was the origin of much of this sentiment, but it became generalized into a feeling of self-loathing at the American role in the world. The net effect of these trends was to produce a loss of confidence, purpose and drive in the West, and particularly in the USA. The rise of America to world power status had been accompanied by a strong belief in the superiority of its own ideology as compared to communism. The 1960s, and specifically the Vietnam war, had undermined this self-belief and had replaced energy with torpor, and confidence with angst. The cancer which was undermining American resolution may have originated on the liberal wing of US society, but it had spread into the mainstream and even into those reaches of government responsible for conducting American foreign policy. Such a spiritual crisis was bound to cripple America in the fiercely competitive struggle with a communist world that retained an ideological commitment which gave it the strength, energy and discipline needed to impose itself on the world.[23]

In view of both its short- and longer-term roots, there was a tendency to see the decline of the West in quasi-spiritual and relatively deterministic terms, as a reflection of grand historical forces which could only be mitigated rather than reversed. *Détente* was a policy designed as the best way for the USA to cope with its inevitable decline. Its preoccupation was the superpower axis and the perennial struggle between the world's two leading ideologies, as represented by the USSR and the USA. Pessimism as to American prospects in this struggle were the essential backdrop to the strategy it embodied. This strategy was to adopt the logic of bargaining in place of the logic of confrontation.[24] Since the USA could no longer afford the latter as it lacked the will, or indeed the material strength, to win such confrontations, the object became to employ finesse to compensate for loss of strength. This was to be done by using, for example, continuing US advantages in the area of high technology as an influence on Soviet behaviour. By offering to extend the benefits of this technology to the USSR, and therefore holding out the prospect of assisting in Soviet economic development, it was expected that the Soviet Union would develop an interest in co-operating with the USA. In this way, policy was a consequence of a hard-headed calculation of the relative strengths of the protagonists. America's principal advantage was the productivity of its economic system, backwardness in which respect was the Soviet's Achilles' heel. The basis existed for a trade-off: US economic assistance for Soviet political restraint. And as economic co-operation intensified, it was calculated that the Soviet Union would become more rather than less dependent on American economic co-operation. If handled correctly, the use of the economic inducement would result in a long-term curbing of Soviet expansionism as the USSR became increasingly dependent on Western economic co-operation for its own domestic stability.

The second aspect of this strategy was to open friendly relations with China as a means of restraining Soviet power.[25] It had been a shibboleth of foreign policy that communism was a monolithic phenomenon which was centrally directed, and this precluded serious divisions between communist powers. This view was maintained despite all the evidence to the contrary with regard to the relations between China and the

USSR. In keeping with its more hard-headed approach, the strategy of *détente* recognized that national divisions were compatible with communism and could be exploited to reduce the power of the communist challenge as a whole, and of the Soviet threat in particular. One of the weaknesses of the Soviet position in the world was that it had to defend itself on two fronts, east and west. It was the cost of meeting both that had helped to distort its economic development by channelling excessive resources into the military sector. In opening up relations with China, the Nixon administration effectively increased the pressure on the Soviet Union from both directions, and thereby made it even more dependent on Western economic co-operation.[26]

In one sense, opening the door to China was a recognition of American weakness. For the first time in the post-war world it was forced to think in terms of balance of power strategies, manoeuvring alliances in order to maximize its position, where previously its hegemonic status had made such compromises superfluous. The principal obstacle to such pragmatism was the ideological barrier to making alliances with a power which had been the object of a demonology in the USA. This aspect of *détente* compromised the simple view of anti-communism even more than developing economic ties with the arch enemy in the Soviet Union. Although Nixon had made his political career out of precisely this form of uncomplicated anti-communism, it was characteristic of his administration's behaviour not to allow such ideological preconceptions to stand in the way of a strategy designed to further American interests from a position of relative weakness. It is a well-known irony that Nixon's earlier hard-line ideological career had provided an ideal background for just this form of pragmatism because it insulated him from the charge of being soft on communism, a charge it is possible to imagine him prosecuting with vigour had a more liberal administration attempted the same policy. But ultimately Nixon was given the space to overturn the old shibboleths because it was accepted that this was being done to further American interests and not to undermine them. In this instance too, therefore, nationalism was the key to US actions, even though the form it took differed markedly from America's policy in relations with its allies. The differences of form should not obscure the underlying unity of purpose.

In addition to a new degree of pragmatism, the policy of *détente* required a higher level of diplomatic skill than had perhaps been asked of the USA before. The question is not one of the calibre of individual diplomats, in which there is no reason to suppose the USA deficient compared to other countries, but of the more complex task presented to them by *détente*. It demanded the capacity to balance a number of considerations, not least placating domestic opinion in the face of this massive realignment, where previously superior American power had made the lines of policy relatively straightforward. And there can be little doubt that the policy was brilliantly executed, although more in secrecy by the inner clique surrounding Nixon and Kissinger and via the National Security Council than through the more open, conventional diplomatic channels.

In replacing direct confrontation with communism by more subtle and effective tactics, *détente* even resurrected the possibility of overturning its own premiss and reversing the decline of the West. The enhanced control over Soviet behaviour that *détente* permitted made it something more than a reaction to American weakness. By removing the ideological and moral straitjacket into which hegemony had tied the USA, it opened up the prospect of much more effective deployment of America's still considerable capacities. The attempt to eliminate moralism and its accompanying vacillations and to focus clearly and consistently on US self-interest as the governing principle of policy carried American diplomacy to higher levels of effectiveness, at least in the short run.[27] It is important to recognize, however, that it did not imply the elimination of ideology from policy, let alone any ideological softening in the attitude to communism. In this sense the greater surface pragmatism and its apparent ideological contradictions were only a mask for a renewed and more ruthless use of foreign policy to fight the same grand fight against communism that had been its guiding star since the war. In short, the policy of *détente* sacrificed form to content.

Although ostensibly a crusade against communism, the underlying purpose of US policy was at least as much a defence of its own sphere of influence in the world, and in this context *détente* certainly indicated no softening of the American line. The preoccupation with the USSR as the only other power capable of mounting a substantial threat to the American empire remained at the forefront of policy. The world continued to be seen in zero-sum terms where radical shifts of regime in any country were viewed as a gain for one superpower and an equal loss for the other. Local conflicts were seen through the prism of superpower relations with all countries placed in one camp or another and those in the US camp linked by the chain of US protection. Hence the imperative was to stand by the allies, not just for their sake but because the integrity of the whole sphere of American influence depended on the integrity of each of its parts.

One innovation that *détente* did bring to these unchanging goals was the idea encapsulated in the Nixon Doctrine that the USA would be much more wary in committing its own troops in defence of its allies. The responsibilities of friendship were taken to work both ways: US protection would no longer be interpreted as a willingness to defend allies by fighting their battles for them. Instead the US role would be confined to providing the level of material support they needed to fight these battles themselves. Since *détente* effectively precluded the possibility of direct confrontation between the superpowers, it became all the more likely that the continuing struggle would break out into open conflict on the periphery. Having absorbed the lesson of Vietnam, Nixon realized that such 'peripheral' struggles were vital but also that the USA could not fight them directly. This was accepted in part because it could not win them, but more importantly because to do so would reintroduce the possibility of dragging the Soviet Union into a conflict. This would defeat the object of *détente*, since it would result only in the movement of the site of direct superpower confrontation.

The American calculation was that it was better equipped to fight these struggles on the periphery than the Soviet Union because of its superior material resources, but only if the superpowers themselves did not become directly involved. In order to enhance the prospects of victory in these struggles, the USA attempted to create a series of regional powers which would be able to act as its agents in trouble spots and as a buffer between it and direct involvement. In the Middle East, for example, policy towards Israel and Iran was dictated by this strategy. It was innovative particularly in respect of Iran, which was given *carte blanche* by Nixon in terms of weapons procurement with the object of building its military capacity up to the point where it could police the region on America's behalf.[28] This policy put a premium on standing by such powers when both external and domestic challenges arose, and demonstrated quite clearly that the policy of *détente* was compatible with strong resolution to defend the US sphere of influence, and was indeed intended to be a more sophisticated method of doing so.

In so far as the strategy of *détente* did appear to be based on weakness, most of this impression stemmed from the constraints imposed upon it by the need for the USA to withdraw from Vietnam. While Vietnam was an important catalyst in educating the USA in the limits of its power, *détente* was intended to re-establish American power as far as possible by conducting policy on a more realistic but also more sophisticated, subtle and complex basis. One fatal flaw of the design, however, was its overtly amoral character. It was felt that the unduly moral basis upon which US foreign policy had previously been conducted gave it an unstable character which was inimical to the prosecution of long-term unchanging national interests, and that the unrealistic, not to say romantic, outlook it prompted led the USA ineluctably into conflicts which it could not win. By committing US prestige to the defence of moral values, it was bound to put that prestige at risk in areas where vital interests were not involved. Since the defence of those interests should be the sole criterion of foreign policy, previous policy had been ineffective. Moral indignation at communism also prevented the USA from dealing with communist powers in a way which maximized its use of its own resources, relationships with China being the obvious case.[29]

The weakness that stemmed from this amorality was not revealed in the area of foreign affairs as such. It became apparent rather in its implications for the process of conducting foreign policy. It meant that the policy process became essentially undemocratic, and this was not compatible with the American political system. The secrecy and manipulation of both the US bureaucracy and the Congress which characterized the implementation of *détente* were not accidental. They were an essential component of the strategy that only those in full awareness of the grand design should be permitted to carry it through. While perhaps a suitable outlook for a nineteenth-century autocracy manoeuvring within a complex balance of power, this was not appropriate to a modern democratic state. It was not possible to sustain a secretive, devious and manipulative foreign policy process within an open, democratic political system of checks and balances. It was virtually inevitable, therefore, that the administration would be brought eventually into fundamental conflict with the wider requirements of the US constitution. As it happened, this occurred over Watergate. Perhaps if it had not, the conflict would have been resolved at the expense of the Constitution or at least its effective subversion. We shall never know, but we do know that in this light Watergate was an episode which revealed the limits of the mentality which governed the *détente* strategy.

The argument for *détente* in this respect was that the focus on interest rather than ideology was a much more effective basis for the defence of national interest, and that open democratic processes were not an effective way of conducting complex strategies which required a strong element of central direction. This was especially true when dealing with adversaries not themselves encumbered by the checks and balances of democratic politics.[30] It is therefore a vital criticism of *détente* to suggest that besides being amoral it was not even effective. The basis for this criticism is the preoccupation with the grand contest between the superpowers that was part of *détente*. As we have indicated, this preoccupation led to all regional conflicts being viewed through the superpower prism and to a zero-sum mentality. In the first place, this encouraged a neglect of relations with many allies who were taken for granted and treated as objects of competition. We have seen that the thrust of intra-capitalist economic relations under Nixon was one of a more aggressive nationalism, thought by Nixon and Kissinger to be consistent with the nationalism of *détente*. The relative lack of concern of Nixon and Kissinger with economic relations, and their relative neglect of allies, particularly in Europe, blinded them to the fact that their policies in this area were actually undermining the effectiveness of the USA and the West. It was awareness of this connection rather than some ideological preoccupation *per se* which underpinned the stress on Western ideological unity and the gap between it and communism. In this sense, ideology and effectiveness were not only compatible but interdependent, and the stress solely on national interest self-defeating.

The other flaw in the *détente* strategy followed on from the superpower preoccupation and its accompanying zero-sum mentality. This perspective meant that the administration was unable to judge the true nature of local conflicts. All such conflicts were seen primarily in terms of their implications for the contest between the superpowers. But that context elevated every local conflict into a major test of American strength and resolution. This gave the USA no option but to support its allies irrespective of the justice of their cause or the likelihood of their being able to defeat a domestic challenge. By tying US prestige to particular, often autocratic, governments in peripheral countries solely on the grounds of their anti-communist credentials, the USA was condemning itself to having always to support unpopular, unjust and unviable regimes. The ironic conclusion must be that, although the genesis of *détente* lay partly in a determination to avoid the mistakes that the USA had made in supporting incompetent and unpopular allies in Vietnam, the blinkered vision it imposed on foreign policy condemned it to repeat those mistakes. The challenge to the Shah of Iran came to be the most notorious example, and demonstrated just how inadequate this dimension of the *détente* strategy was.

Judged on its own criterion of effectivness, then, the *détente* stategy was to prove deeply inadequate. Its flaws were an amorality which made it incompatible with domestic democratic processes, an obsession with the USSR which led to the neglect of allies and undermined its stated aim of fighting communism, a blinkered attitude to the rest of the world which would inevitably drag the USA into conflicts it could not win, and a stress on interest at the expense of ideology which failed to recognize the importance of the latter in the defence of the former. The brilliance of the Vietnam withdrawal and of the manipulation of the Soviet Union and China have to be set against these substantial deficiencies. In fact the development of domestic politics after Watergate meant that a reasoned balance sheet in judgement of *détente* was not drawn up by the electorate. *Détente* became discredited by association with a disgraced administration. As a strategy for coping with US decline it had many strengths; but there were alternatives, and the revulsion against the Nixon era which led to the election of Jimmy Carter meant that an alternative strategy would be given the opportunity to test its effectiveness.

The most notable initial feature of the Carter presidency was the prominence given to morality as the basis for American foreign policy. The emphasis on human rights was clearly a deliberate attempt to overturn the *realpolitik* approach taken by Kissinger and Nixon.[31] The policy was widely accused of naivety and being a product of Carter's lack of experience in foreign affairs by those who viewed international relations as an arena where interests took precedence over principles. In fact the Carter policy rejected the distinction between the two rather than simply being unaware of it. It was based on the premiss that it was possible to reconcile interests and ideals in the conduct of foreign policy. Indeed, in the case of the United States it could even be argued that it was necessary to do so. This was because the American role in the world rested to an unusual degree not simply on its material wealth or its military capability, but on the moral vision of freedom, justice and respect for individual liberty that it embodied. In a world where most of humanity were denied this liberty, the influence of the USA lay in capturing their aspirations, and this could only be done if it showed the same repect for human rights abroad as it claimed to do at home.[32]

Carter's approach argued that it was misleading to suppose that, because such factors were intangible compared to weapons stocks, they were any less important in affecting the conduct of nations. If the object of US policy was to defend its sphere of influence from communism, then it had to be taken seriously that this was an ideological competition for the hearts and minds of the uncommitted, and in this struggle the US conception of freedom and liberty was infinitely more appealing than the communist version. It was therefore in the US interest to live up to its ideals so that its appeal was not tarnished. To confine policy to the realm of *realpolitik* was thus to throw away America's most precious asset in the struggle with communism. Far from being realistic, the construction of an opposition between interests and ideals, and placing an emphasis on the the former, was to miss the essence of what the USA represented and therefore of how best it could pursue its interests.

Another respect in which the approach of the Carter administration differed from Nixon's was in relations with other advanced capitalist powers.[33] Again the goal was the same, maximum effectiveness in the struggle against communism, but where the Nixon/Kissinger approach had interpreted this to imply a focus on direct relations with the communist powers at the expense of the capitalist allies, the Carter administration reversed the priorities. Its preoccupation was with the intra-capitalist axis rather than the superpower one, on the grounds that the divisions among the allies consequent upon the Nixon policies weakened both the West generally and the US specifically in the competition with communism. It was also much more aware of the dangers to world capitalism itself of the competitive nationalism of the Nixon era, and placed itself firmly in the internationalist camp which harnessed US interests to the emergence of a world capitalist system. The influence of the Trilateral Commission was substantial in this respect, and most of the senior foreign policy officials in the administration were members of it.[34] By bringing together politicians, businessmen and academics from Europe, Japan and the USA, the Commission helped to forge an international consensus which curbed the competitive tendencies of the leading capitalist countries. The object was to increase strength through co-operation in recognition of the interdependence of the world economic system, which meant that countries would prosper either together or not at all.[35] This implied a diminution of US pre-eminence, as had the Nixon strategy, but responded to it in a less confrontational fashion.

The initiation in 1977 of regular economic summits between the leaders of the leading capitalist powers in order to try to co-ordinate the cycles of economic policy were evidence of this new approach.[36] In opting for an internationalist rather than a mercantilist position as a strategy for coping with decline, the Carter administration was recognizing the necessity of supranational political arrangements to match the internationalization of the economic system. This aligned it with the free-trade ethos of multinational corporations and against protectionist approaches to maintaining America's role in the world. The underlying logic of the position was that protectionism was self-defeating, since it could only enhance American uncompetitiveness in the longer run. The move towards a global economic system was irreversible, and if the USA tried to exclude itself because it could no longer dominate the process, it would be the loser.[37] The point was that it was not a loss of power to other nation-states which had to be resisted; the real challenge was to find a role for the USA in the new, co-operative arrangements between nations that would have to emerge. Political power would still be the necessary support mechanism for international capitalism; far better for the USA to embrace the logic of internationalism and play a leading and constructive role in the new arrangements than to try to hold on to the past hegemony and its outdated nationalistic perspective. This would not only secure its own prosperity, it would also fit the West better for the competition with communism and, through its combination of economic dynamism and individual liberty, maximize the attraction of the Western camp to the uncommitted countries of the world.[38]

This liberal alternative to the strategy of the Nixon years also sought to reconcile ideals and interests by avoiding the pitfalls of committing the USA to propping up unstable, exploitative regimes in the name of anti-communism. It argued that the USA tarnished its own democratic credentials by this policy, and thus wasted its greatest asset in world affairs: its moral appeal to unfree peoples. By judging each regime in terms of its own criteria of respect for human rights and access for capital, it could avoid the mechanistic linkage that resulted from the zero-sum approach to Soviet influence throughout the world. This would extricate the USA from the vicious circle of committing its prestige to the defence of the indefensible, and so make it easier to avoid being dragged into conflicts of the type exemplified by Vietnam. In a curious way, this implied much greater faith in the US system than the Nixon approach had done. It rested on the belief that the wealth and freedom of the USA made it a much more attractive model than communism, and the USA could win the struggle with communism by relying on these strengths. Compromising its principles by supporting unpopular, oppressive regimes was therefore both unnecessary and counterproductive.

This approach was significant also because it amounted to a refutation of the theory that it was the imperatives of capitalist accumulation which forced the USA to operate a reactionary foreign policy. It showed that there was scope for an enlightened foreign policy without contradicting those imperatives. On the contrary, being on the side of the good guys was good for business. Increasing the moral stature of the USA in the world by confining support to regimes which respected human rights and enjoyed popular support was the best way to export the American system, including access for its capital. An illustration of this policy in action ocurred in Africa with the independence struggles of what became Zimbabwe.[39] By not allowing the apparent Marxist sympathies of ZANU to blind it to the reality that ZANU was far more a popular nationalist movement fighting a just anti-colonial cause than a puppet of Moscow, the Carter administration, and specifically Andrew Young, the Ambassador to the United Nations, was able to help facilitate its victory. As a consequence it gained influence with the new government which, for all its socialist and nationalist rhetoric, proved amenable to discussing access for American capital because it recognized that this promised much more assistance on the path of development than the dead hand of totalitarian communism. Thus, having faith in its own assets, wealth and freedom, as appealing to both the idealist aspirations and economic self-interest of Zimbabwe,

US policy was able to support a just cause and further its own economic interests, while at the same time preventing the spread of Soviet influence in southern Africa.

The Carter administration was faced with a much greater test of its policy by developments in Iran, however, and as it turned out this exposed some of its flaws, to fatal effect for the political health of the administration.[40] When the Shah of Iran, whom Nixon had given the role of defending US interests in the region, came under domestic attack, the Carter administration attempted to pursue a middle path. Previous policy would have dictated unconditional support on the grounds that allies once chosen had to be defended from internal and external attack if the US sphere of influence were to remain intact. Conscious, however, of the Shah's domestic unpopularity and the poor record of his regime on human rights, Carter declined to provide such unconditional support, in the form of either additional arms or tacit approval for suppression of the revolt. In effect he permitted the Shah to fall, where Kissinger and Nixon would have defended him to the death. This policy was pursued largely on the grounds already outlined, that in the longer run the USA would become stronger for dissociating itself from oppressive client regimes. But part of the calculation underlying it was also that the new regime which would emerge from the Iranian revolution would have a middle–class, technocratic orientation; it would continue to be sympathetic to the USA, but would perform much better on human rights. Again, the expectation was that US ideals and interests would be better reconciled without the Shah, and this was given precedence over unconditional loyalty to the friends of a previous administration.

The miscalculation as to the likely nature of the post-Shah regime proved disastrous. The Carter administration overestimated its ability to manipulate the situation so as to produce a friendly governmment in Iran, lost control and ended up faced with an intensely hostile, radical Islamic government inspired by Ayatollah Khomeini. This led to criticism within the USA that the new policy had gambled and failed, producing instability and reducing US influence in an area vital to world peace and US interests, charges which were difficult to refute. The situation was greatly exacerbated, of course, by the taking of US hostages. This is something that could have happened whatever the US policy and would have been extremely difficult to resolve. In that sense the hostage trauma was an unfair test of Carter's approach, since it did not result from it. But in the context it seemed only to confirm the criticism that his policy was one of weakness rather than enlightenment. If anything, the Carter administration payed the price for the weaknesses of the previous administration, which had sanctioned the repression by the Shah and so made the USA reviled in the eyes of the new regime in Tehran. The real problem was trying to change policies in midstream. It was the Nixon administration's policy which had created the tension and hatred in Iran that ultimately led to the hostage crisis, but it was the Carter administration which paid the price. In retrospect it is possible to see that it was the previous Nixon policy which in fact condemned the new Carter approach to failure, but the irony was that it did so in such a way that the blame fell on the latter.

Fairness is not a prime attribute of politics, however, and Carter's domestic opponents were not slow to generalize from the failure of policy in Iran to a critique of the administration's whole approach as weak, misguided and exacerbating US decline.[41] Carter's handling of the domestic economy had left him vulnerable to political attack, but his exposure to criticism was intensified by the failure of the hostage rescue attempt, again something which, while it might have revealed other kinds of weakness, was not in fact a legitimate test of a liberal approach to foreign relations. The Soviet invasion of Afghanistan was also seized upon as evidence of American weakness since, it was argued, the USSR only felt able to do it because the USA was no longer strong enough to impose penalties on it. The invasion also reconfirmed in the eyes of many the image of the Soviet Union as bent on world conquest. The actual explanation of the invasion was much more parochial, but that did not prevent political capital being made of it in the USA.[42] Carter's response to these developments, especially Afghanistan, was to try to reverse his policies and revert to something much more like the hard anti-communist line of previous administrations. This was in fact the worst course as it only added an impression of inconsistency and indecisiveness to that of weakness. The Carter administration was plagued by divisions between liberals and hard-liners in foreign policy,[43] and Carter's inability to choose between them was a failing which rebounded on the liberal approach because it meant that it was never pursued consistently and with perseverance.

Although the Carter administration achieved some other successes in foreign policy, such as the Camp David accords between Israel and Egypt,[44] there can be little doubt that by the end of its term the liberal alternative was widely perceived as a failure. The question is whether this was because it was poorly executed by the Carter administration, whether it was a victim of circumstances, or whether its failure was a result of inherent flaws in the approach. The answer is that it was a combination of all three. In some respects the policy was not even carried through, as with the case of Chile, where even the appalling human rights record of the Pinochet regime did not lead to a complete withdrawal of US support.[45] Too many US interests were at stake, and so Carter, while trying to influence the Chilean government to improve human rights, was effectively constrained by the principle of interest. And this reveals the rather naive, perhaps even hypocritical dimension that was the inherent flaw of this policy. In attempting to reconcile ideals and interests it was bound in some cases to be squaring a circle. In the final analysis interests would always take precedence, and the nature of American interests as a hegemonic capitalist power would be bound to require it to resist calls for a new international economic order which envisaged a massive transfer of wealth from the First to the Third World,[46] and on occasion to support inegalitarian and thus potentially oppressive regimes, rather as the Nixon administration had done. This is not to deny that bad luck, vacillating leadership, shortage of time and domestic vulnerability did not also contribute to the discrediting of the liberal approach, and make it appear a form of self-inflicted, guilt-driven weakness which was leading the USA to give up something for nothing in its role in the world.

Equally, there can be little doubt that the liberal critique of earlier policies had considerable validity. The USA had pursued policies which were unnecessarily reactionary because of a fundamental insecurity among advocates of *realpolitik*. Distrustful of the functional superiority of the American system in world affairs, they masked their lack of faith in a cloak of machismo through which the USA would prove its toughness by neglecting moral scruples in favour of confrontation with the communist menace wherever it showed its face. If pursued properly, a liberal policy could defeat communism by winning over the uncommitted; but in a way that would put the USA on the side of regimes which enjoyed genuine popular support and did not have to resort to terror to prop up themselves and their American backers. Countries could be won over to the American side by moral and economic example. Economic plunder and political repression would therefore become superfluous and indeed counterproductive.

The fact that there was scope for a more enlightened approach that could capitalize on, rather than squander, American moral standing in the world was not enough to save the Carter administration. Just as the flaws, accidents and circumstances associated with the Nixon approach had swung the pendulum in a liberal direction, so its own inadequacies provided the momentum for a swing back to a more aggressive policy which was determined to restore the American position in the world by whatever means necessary. The frustration and anger of those Americans who were not willing to tolerate what they saw as an acquiescence in American decline were brilliantly articulated by Ronald Reagan in the 1980 election campaign, and the election result meant that he would have the opportunity to try to reverse the trend and produce a resurgent America. In the next chapter we will consider how well his administration measured up to that task in the 1980s.

Notes

1. S. Gill and D. Law, *The Global Political Economy*, Hemel Hempstead: Harvester Wheatsheaf, 1988; J. Agnew, *The United States and the World Economy*, Cambridge: Cambridge University Press, 1987; A. Szymanski, *The Logic of Imperialism*, New York: Praeger, 1981, chapter 15.
2. D. Calleo, *The Imperious Economy*, Cambridge, Mass.: Harvard University Press, 1982; R. Parboni, *The Dollar and Its Rivals*, London: New Left Books, 1981.
3. S. Gill, *American Hegemony and the Trilateral Commission*, Cambridge: Cambridge University Press, 1990, chapter 4.
4. W. Scammell, *The International Economy Since 1945*, London: Macmillan, 1989, 2nd edn; B. Tew, *The Evolution of the International Monetary System 1945–77*, London: Hutchinson, 1977; R. Solomon, *The International Monetary System 1945–81*, New York: Harper, 1982, revised edn.
5. B. Nowzad, *The International Monetary Fund and Its Critics*, Princeton, NJ: International Finance Section, Princeton University, 1982; F.A. Southard, *The Evolution of the International Monetary Fund*, International Finance Section, Department of Economics, Princeton University, 1979.
6. Calleo, *op. cit.*, p. 243.
7. The history of the UK economy in the late 1980s shows that such problems were not confined to the 1970s.
8. Parboni, *op. cit.*
9. At around the same time the Heath government in the UK followed a similar growth strategy. It was unsuccessful, and the alternative option of retrenchment was the one pursued by the Thatcher government in its early years.
10. Calleo, *op. cit.*, chapter 6.
11. H.O. Schmitt, 'Mercantilism: a modern argument', *The Manchester School*, 47, 2, June 1979, pp. 93–111.
12. Gill, *op. cit.*
13. H.M. Holland, *Managing Diplomacy: The United States and Japan*, Stanford, Calif.: Hoover Institute, Stanford University, 1984; A. Iriye and W. Cohen (eds.), *The United States and Japan in the Postwar World*, Lexington, KY: University of Kentucky Press, 1989.
14. R. Rosencrance (ed.), *America as an Ordinary Country: US foreign policy and the future*, Ithaca, NY: Cornell University Press, 1976.
15. Independent Commission on International Development Issues, W. Brandt, Chairman, *North–South: A programme for survival – a report*, London: Pan, 1980.
16. C.A. Jones, *The North–South Dialogue: A brief history*, London: Pinter, 1983; J.N. Bhagwati (ed.), *The New International Economic Order: The North–South debate*, Cambridge, Mass.: MIT Press, 1977.
17. P. Terzian, *OPEC: The inside story*, London: Zed, 1985.

18. H. Lever and C. Huhne, *Debt and Danger: The world financial crisis*, Harmondsworth, Penguin, 1985.
19. Gill and Law, *op. cit.*, chapter 13.
20. It was this which made the organization of a counter-cartel so difficult, though the USA did attempt something of the kind with the formation of the International Energy Agency. See Gill and Law, *op. cit.*, chapter 13.
21. The Trilateral Commission, in line with its more co-operative approach, advocated that this recycling be extended to include the developing countries of the 'Fourth World'. See R.N. Gardner, S. Okita and B.J. Udink, 'OPEC, the trilateral world and the developing countries: new arrangements for cooperation 1976–80', Triangle Papers, no. 7, New York: Trilateral Commission, 1975.
22. G.W. Nutter, *Kissinger's Grand Design*, Washington, DC: American Enterprise Institute, 1975; P.W. Dickson, *Kissinger and the Meaning of History*, Cambridge: Cambridge University Press, 1978.
23. T. Szulc, *The Illusion of Peace: Foreign policy in the Nixon years*, New York: Viking, 1978.
24. S. Brown, *The Faces of Power: Constancy and change in United States foreign policy from Truman to Reagan*, New York: Columbia University Press, 1983, chapter 22.
25. J.K. Fairbank, *The United States and China*, Cambridge, Mass.: Harvard University Press, 1979, 4th edn.
26. C. Bell. *The Diplomacy of Detente: The Kissinger era*, London: Robertson, 1977.
27. H. Kissinger, *American Foreign Policy*, New York: Norton, 1977, 3rd edn.
28. B. Rubin, *Paved with Good Intentions: The American experience and Iran*, New York: Oxford University Press, 1980; F. Halliday, *Iran: Dictatorship and development*, Harmondsworth: Penguin, 1979.
29. J.L. Gaddis, *Strategies of Containment: A critical appraisal of postwar American national security policy*. New York: Oxford University Press, 1982, chapters 9 and 10.
30. G.D. Cleva, *Henry Kissinger and the American Approach to Foreign Policy*, Lewisburg, PA: Bucknell University Press, 1989.
31. N. Chomsky, *Human Rights and American Foreign Policy*, London: Spokesman, 1978; E.B. Haas, 'Human rights: to act or not to act', in K. Oye *et al.* (eds.), *Eagle Entangled: US foreign policy in a complex world*, New York: Longman, 1979.
32. S. Brown, *The Faces of Power: Constancy and change in United Stages foreign policy from Truman to Reagan*, New York: Columbia University Press, 1983, chapter 28.
33. R. Keohane, 'US foreign economic policy towards other advanced capitalist states', in Oye *et al.*, *op. cit.*
34. Gill, *op. cit.*; H. Sklar (ed.), *Trilaterialism: Elite planning for world management*, Boston, Mass.: South End Press, 1980.
35. R.C. Cooper, 'Economic interdependence and foreign policy in the 70s', *World Politics*, 24, Jan. 1972, pp. 159–81.
36. W.H. Buiter and R.C. Marston (eds.), *International Economic Policy Coordination*, Cambridge: Cambridge University Press, 1985; M. Artis and S. Ostry, 'International economic policy coordination', Chatam House Papers, no. 30, London: Royal Institute of International Affairs/Routledge, 1986.

37. Gill, *op. cit.*
38. R.K. Olson, *US Foreign Policy and the New International Economic Order: Negotiating global problems 1974–81*, Greenwich, CT: Westview, 1981.
39. D. Rothchild, 'US policy styles in Africa', in Oye *et al.*, *op. cit.*
40. Rubin, *op. cit.*; Halliday, *op. cit.*
41. F. Halliday, *The Making of the Second Cold War*, London: New Left Books, 1983.
42. N.P. and R.S. Newell, *The Struggle for Afghanistan*, Ithaca, NY: Cornell University Press, 1981.
43. The principal division was between the Secretary of State, Cyrus Vance, and the National Security Adviser, Zbigniev Brzezinski. See their memoirs: C. Vance, *Hard Choices: Critical years in America's foreign policy*, New York: Simon & Schuster, 1983; Z. Brzezinski, *Power and Principle: Memoirs of a National Security Adviser 1977–81*, London: Weidenfeld & Nicolson, 1983.
44. S.L. Spiegel, 'The United States and the Arab–Israeli dispute', in Oye *et al.*, *op. cit.*
45. R.A. Pastor, 'The Carter administration and Latin America: a test of principle', in J.D. Martz (ed.), *United States Policy in Latin America: A quarter century of crisis and challenge, 1961–86*, Lincoln, Nebr.: University of Nebraska Press, 1988; A. Lowenthal, 'Jimmy Carter and Latin America', in Oye *et al.*, *op. cit.*
46. Gill and Law, *op. cit.*, chapter 14.

CHAPTER EIGHT

REAGAN AND THE RESURGENCE OF AMERICA IN THE 1980s

America's decline through the 1970s, while undisputable, should not be exaggerated. In economic terms the decline was relative rather than absolute, and its military and cultural domination had remained largely intact. The strategies pursued by the Nixon and Carter administrations did have some effect in combating the process of decline. The Nixon strategy was brutal in its economic nationalism, but sophisticated and far-reaching in its diplomatic aspect. Its depth of understanding of the nature of America's role in the world could not mask its amoral character, however, and the discredit brought upon the Nixon administration by Watergate gave Carter the opportunity to pursue an alternative strategy which attempted to capitalize on America's moral authority. This too was cut short, partly by the misfortune in Iran and partly by weak and vacillating implementation. While each strategy demonstrated certain strengths, in both cases these were undermined by weaknesses which gave domestic political opponents the opportunity for effective criticism, and so led to a reversal of the direction of foreign policy. Just as Carter had been a reaction to Nixon, so Reagan was a reaction to Carter and he came into office determined to adopt a much more aggressive stance towards reversing American decline.

The perspective of the Reagan administration on the 1970s was unequivocal. It was seen as a period of unrelieved decline, both domestically and internationally, both spiritually and economically. The source of the problem, however, was the weak leadership the country had received, particularly from Carter, and not any inherent deficiency. America retained the capacity to be the dominant nation in the world, but it would require a reversion to traditional values, inspired by strong leadership, to halt what had been an unnecessary process of drift and decline.[1]

Although these feelings, which spread across a wide spectrum of society, coalesced with the election of Reagan, they had been a significant factor in American political life for some years previously.[2] Reagan himself had come to prominence as a national political figure with a speech at the 1964 Republican Party convention. The Party candidate, Barry Goldwater, was heavily defeated by Lyndon Johnson in the presidential election that year, but the impact of Reagan's speech demonstrated that he had articulated some sentiments that were deeply held among those who were concerned at what they perceived to be the liberal drift of American society, and who felt that their point of view was not receiving sufficient response from the existing parties. This current of resentment adopted a variety of guises before becoming the orthodoxy of the Reagan years: it was, of course, instrumental in electing Reagan himself as Governor of California, but it was also courted at the same time in the national arena by George Wallace, and eventually was appropriated by Richard Nixon into the 'silent majority' which found its voice in his election. Indeed, it is possible to argue that if the disgrace of Watergate and the consequent Carter interregnum had not happened, the New Right,[3] as it came to be called, would have become dominant without the need for the Reagan crusade.

As it was, the setbacks of the 1970s only increased the resentment fuelling this current of opinion and led to its transformation into a much more organized and effective political force. The lobby groups which organized themselves around the emerging New Right banner were spectacularly efficient fund-raisers and political operators, and, in their neo-conservative aspect, political thinkers and advocates who were all the more effective for being disaffected liberals who had seen the light and converted.[4] But the driving force of the movement remained a fervour, often expressed in fundamentalist religious terms, among working- and lower-middle-class Americans that their country's destiny had been hijacked and led astray by an unholy alliance of welfare cheats and guilt-ridden Washington liberals, of atheists and federal bureaucrats, a perspective in which racial antagonism was never far below the surface.[5]

This fervour was channelled into political effectiveness by the New Right political organizers, initially through single issues such as campaigns on tax revolts, school prayers, anti-abortion and anti-bussing, and through targeting of individual liberal politicians who symbolized where the country had gone wrong. Gradually the movement generalized its appeal around a traditional concept of the family and was able to make powerful allies with elements of capital, again principally located in the Sunbelt,[6] and established lobbies such as the National Rifle Association, who found its philosophy congenial to their own aims and who were able to help provide the financial lubricant so necessary to success in the American political system. Eventually the movement was rounded off with the creation of Reagan into its messianic figure, who could lead it from the wilderness into the Oval Office and begin implementing its agenda to turn America around. The result was a political tidal wave which, whatever the statistics of Reagan's margin of victory, was widely accepted as heralding a sea change in America's politics and its role in the world.

In the economic sphere the new administration's diagnosis of failure was that the USA had lost touch with the roots of its historical economic dynamism – the power of the free market to generate wealth.[7] Decline had been due to an excessive growth of the state, which had encumbered the market both by regulation and by redistributing resources from productive free enterprise to parasitical welfare expenditure. The taxation required to finance this redistribution had undermined incentives, thus cutting output and instituting a vicious economic circle. And the public spending associated with redistribution had also been the root cause of the inflation which plagued the economy in the 1970s, a problem greatly accentuated by the excessive power of trade unions in extracting wage increases not warranted by productivity levels. The corporatist post-war accommodation between labour and capital had come adrift because it had lost sight of the fundamental truth that profit was the engine of economic growth, and that creation of an environment in which profits could be made was the primary task in any successful capitalist economy. Instead the preoccupation had come to be with the distribution of wealth rather than its creation. This was to put the cart before the horse, and the result was the stagflation which characterized the economy in the 1970s.

There was also a moral dimension to this economic decline.[8] The growth of welfare had created what became known as a culture of dependency in which too many people who were capable of taking responsibility for providing for their own and their family's needs had instead come to rely on the state to look after them from cradle to grave. It was in fact the 1960s from which this cancer had derived. This was seen as a time in which family values and the work ethic had been undermined by a hedonistic, indulgent philosophy which seemed premissed on the idea that the world owed everyone a living and that sacrifice and self-denial were old-fashioned and outdated. Moral decrepitude had been manifested as well in a decline of religious observance, the link between which and personal responsibility, hard work, self-sacrifice and economic accomplishment had always been at the core of the strength of American society.

The solution to this complex of disintegration was to restore the free market to its proper place as the keystone of the economy, and to redress the drift towards the working class and away from capital that had characterized the post-war political economy.[9] The first priority in this respect was to reduce state expenditure, especially on welfare-related programmes, both for its financial and for its moral effect. As important was to reduce inflation by controlling the money supply. The preoccupation with Keynesian demand management which had dominated post-war macroeconomic policy, had turned attention away from monetary policy, and this had to be reversed if inflation was to be conquered. The new emphasis was to be on the supply side of the economy where wealth was generated. Here taxes were to be reduced in order to increase incentives and the investment that would produce new wealth. It was also believed that reduced rates of taxation would not necessarily reduce government revenue, since they would so liberate incentives that output would increase and government would, in a reversal of the vicious circle of the 1970s, collect the same sum by taking a smaller percentage of a larger national product.[10] The question of distribution was to be relegated to second place while the balance between wealth creation and distribution was redressed. In general, however, the distribution problem too would be solved, not by state intervention but by the trickle-down effect of the new wealth, which would percolate through the economy as investment created jobs and wages for those willing to work as well as profits for investors. As a final corollary of this economic strategy, there was to be an accompanying campaign to reassert traditional spiritual values of personal responsibility, the family and religion as a means of guaranteeing the moral basis for a healthy economy.[11]

This comprehensive condemnation of America's domestic ills was matched in the international sphere, where the analysis ran parallel.[12] Here too America had lost touch with its roots. The old verities remained as true as ever: the great struggle in the modern world was between freedom and tyranny, and in that struggle the USA was the torchbearer of freedom while communism, specifically the Soviet Union, was the incarnation of tyranny. The clarity of this division, the consummate evil of the enemy and the manifest justness of its own cause, should have given the USA great confidence in playing its role on the world stage. But in recent years America had lost its self-belief. This was a result of a liberal guilt complex which cast doubt on America as the defender of freedom and instead agonized over whether it had come to be the leading imperial power, with all the connotations this term carried of exploitation and oppression. Flirtation with socialism at home had led many liberals to adopt a questioning attitude to American hegemony abroad, and this had paralysed conduct of foreign policy in which clear and certain guidelines were necessary for effective action.

The Vietnam war had been instrumental in prompting this soul searching, and the true purpose of the war, preventing the expansion of communism, had been lost sight of. But the 1960s had produced a wider moral crisis which went beyond the war issue and infected foreign policy as much as domestic. In the name of peace, love and freedom, the capacity to make clear distinctions between right and wrong had suffered. Without this the ability to take responsibility for protecting the good and fighting the evil was greatly impaired, and the result was paralysis and a foreign policy incapable even of defending America's palpable interests, let alone fighting the wider cause. The problem was therefore defined less as one of decline than as an inability or unwillingness to use the capacity America retained which was sufficient to maintain its position as the leading world power.

The further complication was that in the post-Vietnam era this guilt-ridden mentality had expressed itself in anti-military prejudice. It had passed the buck for a failure of political nerve in fighting the war on to the military, and had taken revenge on it once the demands of war mobilization were removed by reducing military expenditure at the first opportunity. These cuts had become generalized, and military spending continued to be reduced in order to make room for rapidly increasing spending on welfare. While this was happening, the Soviet Union, untroubled by such guilt, was embarked upon a massive arms build-up. The contrast was striking, and the consequence was a rapid decline of American military power. The failure of will thus produced both symbolic and objective weakness, and Soviet confidence and adventurism grew in proportion to it, as the invasion of Afghanistan had shown.

Once again the solution to the problem grew directly out of the diagnosis. The first requirement was to increase American military strength. If this required a large increase in expenditure and other items of spending had to be cut in compensation, then so be it. This was not an area in which compromise was any longer possible; too much damage had been done. Strong defence was the precondition for all other forms of desirable activity, and the reversal of its neglect therefore had to be the absolute priority. While the increased capacity this would produce was important in itself, its greatest significance lay in the signal it would send to the Soviet Union of renewed American self-confidence and strength of purpose.

The fact that the USA was prepared to make sacrifices in order to ensure a strong defence was a signal to domestic constituencies of new priorities too, reflecting the mandate the new administration had been given. This mandate and the willingness, indeed eagerness, of the administration to implement it gave added force to the purely military dimension of the struggle with communism. Ultimately, that had always been a battle of wills, and under Reagan America would show that it had regained the stomach for the fight. These signals were intended not only for the Soviet Union. New threats from terrorists of various stripes had emerged as a major problem, particularly from radical Islamic movements and especially in the area of hostage taking. Again Reagan's rhetoric indicated that such challenges would be met much more vigorously under his administration. The same applied to Third World nationalist governments which attempted to exploit American imperial guilt. If there were to be negotiations with any of these enemies, communist, Islamic, nationalist or terrorist, they would be undertaken only from a position of strength befitting America's power. The initial object was to reassert that strength and to leave no one in any doubt that America was number one in the world and would act to the limits of its power to defend its interests.[13]

The purposes of the new Reagan administration in 1981 could hardly have been more clear cut. How well were they realized? In the economic sphere there was an initial tightening of monetary policy combined with tax cuts, as prescribed. The stimulative effect of tax cuts would take time to work their way through the economy, however, while the depressive effects of tight money made their impact more quickly. The result was a short-run recession characterized by low growth and rapidly rising unemployment. From a long-term perspective this was not necessarily a bad thing, for the assumption was that its rigours involved a shaking-out of the less productive parts of the economy and a stimulus to more efficient practices. This type of recession would therefore eventually produce a leaner, fitter economy better able to compete in world markets. However, the political pressures associated with a depressed economy are acute and short term. It quickly became clear that, whatever its long-term benefits, this economic policy would cost the administration's supporters dearly in the 1982 elections as the polls showed public support plummeting. The response of the administration was to stimulate the economy in what looked remarkably like the type of Keynesian manoeuvre that had been previously condemned as a source of economic weakness. This stimulus was achieved, moreover, by means of a massive budget deficit that out of office Reagan would no doubt have been the first to condemn as profligate and evidence of a lack of political will and economic discipline.[14]

This volte-face was reconciled with the administration's ideology in two ways. First, the deficit was the result not just of increased government expenditure, but also of the substantial tax cuts it had enacted. These were designed to increase incentives and thereby to stimulate economic growth. This would eventually increase government tax revenues. So it was possible to see the deficit as a necessary device, but one which would be temporary and self-correcting, lasting only until the effect of the tax cuts had eliminated it. Second, the deficit was also the result of massive increases in military expenditure. As we have seen, these were the absolute priority of the administration and so could not be compromised. The fact that they were the source of the problem was important, however, because it meant that this deficit was not like earlier ones. It was not produced out of political weakness to buy off certain constituencies and sap the the moral fibre of the nation. On the contrary, it was a sacrifice necessary to rebuild that fibre. Indeed, it had the useful political consequence of actually increasing the pressure for cuts on welfare expenditure. If the deficit was to be limited at all and its military component was sacrosanct, then it was only the welfare component that was available to bear the brunt of the cuts. This was an excellent lever for the administration in its struggles with Congress over changing the values of American society. In effect, the administration had three goals: tax cuts, military strength and a balanced budget. They were incompatible in the short term, and so the last was sacrificed to the first two. The fact that this compromise quickly engendered rapid growth in the economy and produced a revival in the administration's political popularity no doubt also helped to make the ideological quandaries involved less troublesome.[15]

The danger inherent in this apparently painless solution to the Reagan administration's problems was that, like previous Keynesian stimulation, it would set off a cycle of inflation, something again the administration had come into office determined to eradicate. In order to see why this did not happen we have to consider some of the international implications of this economic policy. The substantial federal budget deficits it involved were financed by the sale of government bonds. As the quantity of these which needed to be sold rose, so did the interest rates at which they were offered. The reason this did not have the inflationary effect that might otherwise have been expected is that a large proportion of the bonds were purchased with foreign rather than domestic capital. The early 1980s was a period when the mobility of capital across national boundaries increased phenomenally and became one of the most striking aspects of the internationalization of capitalism.[16] It was also a time when the trade surplus run by the Japanese economy began to generate significant capital funds for overseas investment. As a consequence Japanese, and indeed European,[17] capital flowed into the USA to buy the bonds which financed the budget deficit. Foreign investors were attracted partly by the high interest rates and partly by the fact that the USA was still seen as the safest of havens for capital in a risky and uncertain world. This external financing produced an infusion of capital, which increased supply without squeezing domestic capital, and without therefore putting the same inflationary pressure on the economy.[18]

External financing had another major beneficial effect, that of producing a strong dollar.[19] The purchase of US government bonds by overseas financiers increased demand for the dollar, which rose in value as a result. As the need for external finance continued, investors came to expect a continuing rise in the dollar. These expectations increased their desire to invest in the USA in the hope of making speculative gains. Before long the investors were making a larger return from the increasing value of the dollar than from the interest rates which had attracted them in the first place. The combination of high interest rates and speculative gains then reinforced demand and so pushed the dollar even higher. Apart from the symbolic significance of a strong currency to a country bent on asserting its power, a further consequence was to make imports of consumer goods cheaper in dollar terms, and this too helped to reduce the domestic rate of inflation.

This amounts to a description of a politician's dream, economic growth without pain, and it is worth reviewing the sequence which brought it about. High military spending, which was necessary to American resurgence, gave rise to a large budget deficit. This spurred growth in the economy, but was financed largely by an infusion of capital from overseas. This in turn created a strong currency, cheapened the price of consumer goods and helped to prevent growth from generating high inflation. Economic resurgence indeed! But it is important to note that, whether it was the intention or not, this painless growth was achieved at the expense of other capitalist countries, in a manner similar to the Nixon years. High US interest rates inevitably pushed rates up in other countries, which had to attempt to stem the flow of capital out of their own economies. While in the USA the infusion of capital was financing growth, in other capitalist countries the consequent high interest rates were choking off investment and so reducing growth. Similarly, the high American dollar meant that the imports for other countries denoted in dollars became more expensive, and this increased their domestic rates of inflation.

In a sense, then, the USA solved its economic problems by exporting them, in respect of both growth and inflation, where its improvement was only possible at the expense of the economic well-being of its capitalist competitors. The fact that the USA was able to play by one set of rules while other countries were forced to play by another more conventional set was primarily the result of the greater size and stability of the US political economy. And in the early Reagan years the administration showed no compunction about using these factors, where it still enjoyed an advantage, in order to regenerate dynamism in its economy. In many respects the magnitude of the movements involved meant that the policy amounted to something even more aggressively nationalistic than Nixon's had been a decade earlier. The impetus may have been domestic and political, but the consequences for America's international economic position soon became apparent, and the continuation of these policies would not have been countenanced unless these effects were acceptable to the administration. If they were not the object of the policy as such, then they were at the very least acceptable consequences of it.

There were some significant differences compared with the Nixon strategy, however. The approach of the Reagan administration was less mercantilist; this was a consistent extension of its ideological commitment to the virtues of the free market at home.[20] But, as we have seen, ideology was not allowed to become a barrier to self-interest, and more substantial as a basis for the continuing commitment to the free movement of goods and capital than its theoretical virtues was the fact that without this freedom the USA would not have been able to attract the overseas capital on which its economic strategy had come to depend. Reconciliation of free trade with US national interest was possible because the Reagan administration had devised a strategy which produced rapid domestic economic growth by taking advantage of free international movement of capital. Restrictions on imports of goods therefore became superfluous and indeed counterproductive because they would have eventually led to restrictions on capital flows. American dependency on international capital to sustain its policy of growth was indicative of the increasing involvement of the USA, along with other leading industrial powers, in the world economy in the 1980s. The level of interdependence took a quantum leap in this decade, and the interests in perpetuating it had become so strong that it is doubtful if the Reagan administration could have retreated into an isolationist or nationalist economic policy with any hope of success even if its free-market philosophy had not already made it disinclined to do so.[21]

This marked a significant change of options in the decade since the Nixon administration, and in recognizing this the Reagan strategy showed resourcefulness by turning internationalization to its advantage rather than attempting to turn the clock back or to steal undue national advantage, both of which tactics could enjoy only short-term success at best. It remained an aggressive policy which sought to foster internationalization through the extension of the market system world-wide, rather than through any concept of international co-operation that was a euphemism for the transfer of wealth to less developed countries. Hence its unsympathetic response to Third

World demands at the Cancun conference in 1981, and its advocacy of an extension of the market as the solution to the ills of less developed economies.[22]

The point about such a policy, harsh as it seemed, was that it took as its premiss the fact that America remained the single most important economic unit in the world, and that notions of decline were exaggerated because they underestimated the degree of structural power the USA retained to influence the development of the world economy in the free-market direction. In this way, the policy furthered American national interests not simply by asserting the power it had always possessed but had been unwilling to use, but also by harnessing the higher level of integration into the world economy to its ends.[23] Rather than acquiescing in decline by seeking some spurious co-operation in a new international economic order that ran counter to the fundamentals of a capitalist economy, and that would undermine the basis on which American strength rested, it determined to use its power to help create the type of world economy from which America would benefit, but which would also generate, through market forces, greater wealth in other countries.[24]

In this it showed itself domestically superior to the Carter administration because by promoting rapid growth it reconciled the interests of domestic constituencies such as trade unions and small employers, whose concern was keeping employment in the USA, and those of US-based multinational corporations with a vested interest in free international trade. It was the potential conflict between these two interests which had been a constant threat to the political position of American Presidents ever since the USA had lost its effortless domination of the post-war world economy, which had obviated the need to choose between them. In demonstrating its willingness to shift direction and reverse its initial deflationary policies in the face of this threat, the Reagan administration appeared to gain a remarkable triumph which achieved the best of all possible worlds. As we have seen, much of the initial impetus for it was to protect the political popularity of the administration, and part of its remarkable success was to achieve this goal too as Reagan was rewarded with a handsome election victory in 1984.[25]

This strategy for reversing economic decline appeared almost too good to be true, and time was to demonstrate that it did indeed suffer from major flaws. The first of these was that it helped to create a massive balance of payments deficit for the US economy. International trade had grown relative to total GNP and was no longer insignificant in proportion to it.[26] And with the dollar no longer acting as the world's reserve currency, this meant that a deficit was not sustainable in the long term without severe consequences. The most obvious remedy was one that had been applied elsewhere, a general dampening of domestic consumer demand so as to restrict the flow of imports. But this would undermine the economic growth that allowed the strategy to reconcile so many conflicting goals. In addition, it did not follow that domestic producers would be able to take up the slack if imports were curbed. The strong dollar, by making imports cheap, had led domestic corporations to abandon vast areas of production for consumer demand because they were uncompetitive. Revival of such domestic industries would not be a simple matter, certainly not without a degree of economic intervention that was anathema to the administration. In producing a consumer boom, economic policy had in fact undercut much domestic industry, and once the ensuing balance of payments deficit had to be addressed, the consequences of earlier actions became apparent. The alternative method of financing the balance of payments deficit was an inflow of long-term capital to compensate for the trade deficit. But this implied the sale of domestic assets to foreign capital; not just government bonds, but also property and industrial assets. While acceptable in the short term perhaps, this sort of sale would eventually generate an outward flow of capital as profits were repatriated, and would thus only exacerbate the problem in the long run. This strategy therefore amounted to mortgaging the future to pay for current consumption.

In fact the inward flow of foreign capital was the principal method by which the economic boom of the 1980s was financed, and the consequence was to turn the USA from the largest creditor nation in the world economy at the start of the decade into the largest debtor by its end. The scale of the transformation in this respect was quite phenomenal and will produce a substantial drain on future income for the USA. For America to be in this position of major debtor gives its economy characteristics associated with those of Third World countries and is difficult to reconcile with a hegemonic role. The consequences of debtor status for America's freedom of manoeuvre on the international political and economic stage are significant and are a form of retribution for the excessively expansionist policies of the early 1980s. This weakness was compounded by a reversal in the fortunes of the US dollar, also a consequence of earlier policy. As the strength of the dollar came to depend increasingly on the speculative aspect of the inward flow of capital to the USA, so it became inevitable that eventually the speculative bubble would burst and the currency would move into a classic reversal as investors lost confidence in its future value and began to remove short-term funds. This in turn made the deficit more difficult to finance, increased the price of imports and so added to inflation. In general, the effect produced was exactly the opposite of the benign spiral that had characterized the early part of the decade.

The administration's international economic strategy in its second term recognized these flaws, and the movement of James Baker III to the Treasury signalled that eliminating them would be given high priority.[27] Baker was the principal instigator of a shift of emphasis in international economic policy. Where his predecessor, Donald Regan, had pressed for an unrestricted market approach to the world economy, Baker launched a series of initiatives aimed at increasing international economic co-operation. These were intended to tackle the consequences of the massive international debt problems that had arisen as a result of high interest rates in the early 1980s, and which were threatening the stability of the international banking system. He also sought to manage a slow-down or soft-landing of the domestic economy and a gradual decline in the value of the dollar to avoid the precipitous falls that an unfettered market might have produced. This recognition of the virtues of co-operation, though belated, was significant because it revealed the limits to which the more nationalist policies of the first term could be taken in an age of growing interdependence. The Reagan economic strategy to reverse American decline, while brilliantly successful initially, bought its success at the cost of exacerbating that decline in the longer term. The remedies devised to extricate the administration from its political unpopularity at the beginning of the decade were of a short-term nature and only worsened the situation in respect of the underlying trends towards American economic decline. What they did was buy popularity by reinforcing consumption at the expense of investment, and cover the deficiencies this produced by the import of foreign capital. This was the opposite of what was required to produce the long-term productivity gains that were the only path to true economic resurgence. Despite the effort to reverse these trends in the second term of the administration, they created fiscal, trade and currency weaknesses in the latter part of the decade which will make it all the harder for the economy to recover its international competitiveness.

One necessary component of the shift in economic emphasis in the second term was a reduction in the massive growth of defence expenditure undertaken in the first term. But the issues involved obviously transcended economic management, and this raises intriguing questions about their relation to the changes of the Reagan years in the international political arena, which if anything were even more dramatic than the roller-coaster of American economic fortunes. We need to consider the political trajectory of the Reagan years in order to discover whether the avowed goal of restoring America's position as the leading world power was more successfully approached in this arena than it had been in the economic field. The initial stance of the Reagan administration was an aggressive reassertion of the American mission in the world to combat tyranny in general and communism, inspired by the Soviet Union, in particular.[28] This stance was couched in more extreme rhetoric than had been heard for more than a generation, and was encapsulated in the Reagan Doctrine which suggested that, rather than be content to defend its own sphere of influence, the USA would seek to take the offensive and eliminate communism from countries where it already held sway. The ideological offensive peaked with Reagan's famous characterization of the Soviet Union as an 'empire of evil'. But the rhetoric was backed up by a massive rearmament programme which left no doubt as to the seriousness of purpose of the administration and its willingness to intensify the struggle with communism to the point of direct confrontation. Since, as we have seen, the short-term domestic economic consequences of rearmament were benign, at the outset the relationship between economics and politics was harmonious and mutually reinforcing.

During the course of the administration this tough stance was also backed up by a number of examples of aggressive action. Perhaps the most obvious examples are the bombing of Libya and the invasion of Grenada,[29] both of which were clear attempts to demonstrate that the USA was no longer hamstrung by its own inhibitions from using its military capacity. But equally, both episodes were principally symbolic in character, in so far as they contained little risk of escalation to more serious levels of conflict. This raises the possibility that the Reagan administration chose its battlegrounds very carefully, mindful of the Vietnam experience, and only committed itself where the risks of serious reverse were minimal and the chances of victory were high.[30] Certainly both these incursions, unlike Vietnam, paid a considerable domestic political dividend, although they were viewed with concern by US allies overseas. The American public managed to convince itself that they were symbolic of renewed American vigour to a degree that their limited and rather tawdry character would not appear to warrant.

The question arises, then, of whether the rhetoric was designed for its symbolic value whereas actions were in fact calculated with great prudence and avoided wherever defeat, and thus domestic unpopularity, was a possibility. American policy in Central America would appear to bear this hypothesis out.[31] At the beginning of the administration this area was a major preoccupation. It was felt that it had come to represent American weakness, illustrated, for example, by the treaty agreeing the reversion of the Panama Canal at the end of the century. And this weakness had given rise to rebellions, successful in Nicaragua, almost so in El Salvador, which would embody the march of communism into America's own 'backyard'. This could hardly be tolerated by a country wishing to sustain regional power status, let alone one aspiring to world leadership.[32] Such a direct challenge had to be answered, and certainly the public statements of the administration raised the prospect of direct military intervention as a very real one. And yet it did not happen. The threat was combated by substantial aid, to the government of El Salvador and to the Contra rebels of Nicaragua, and even by threatening military manoeuvres by US military forces in the region. But in retrospect it is clear that the strategy was one of grinding down the opposition forces rather than risking US lives in direct confrontation.[33]

This strategy was particularly apparent in Nicaragua, where support of the rebels and maintenance of a constant high level of tension did gradually succeed in impoverishing the country and causing sufficient disillusion among the Nicaraguan population with their Sandinista leaders to persuade them to opt for an alternative regime sympathetic to the USA.[34] It may have been that what tipped the balance away from direct intervention was not just the administration's awareness of the lessons of Vietnam as encapsulated in the Nixon Doctrine, but lack of public support in the USA for intervention and congressional restraint consequent upon it and upon the Iran–Contra affair.[35] Whether it was these restraints or the administration's own prudence, or indeed the effective diplomacy of other Central and Latin American countries in the Contadora group,[36] the balance of policy which resulted proved remarkably successful in achieving a sympathetic regime in Nicaragua without having to abandon respect for democratic procedure or resort to crude imperialist intervention.

Prudence and a pragmatism belied by the administration's rhetoric were evident in other areas too. If policy in the Middle East could hardly be described as a resounding success, then in that respect it was no different from that of other US administrations or other countries. It would not be reasonable to criticize the Reagan administration for failing to achieve objectives that have proven beyond all who have been involved. Of more significance was its reaction to the serious reverse it did meet in Lebanon when a suicide attack killed hundreds of American soldiers.[37] Rather than escalate its involvement or seek retribution against those responsible, it withdrew. The episode was a humiliating one, but attention was soon moved on, whether by intention or coincidence, to the invasion of Grenada, which was authorized within a week of the bombing in Lebanon. By cutting its losses in this way, the Reagan administration minimized the damage to American prestige and avoided the trap of being dragged into a quagmire, as had happened in Vietnam.

Similarly, awareness of the limits of American power was shown in the handling of its own hostage crises in the Middle East. It was as hamstrung as Carter had been by this form of terrorism; the difference was that the Reagan administration was sufficiently skilful to prevent the issue ever becoming a test of its virility because its credentials had been established in other areas, both rhetorically and practically. Toughness elsewhere thus created space for a relatively measured and passive approach that was the only response possible without incurring damage to America's own prestige. Again in the Philippines[38] protestations of support for the Marcos regime and a continuing commitment to defending all links in the chain surrounding the American sphere of influence did not blinker the administration into defending the indefensible, as had happened in earlier administrations. In the end the Reagan administration showed some skill in proving capable of reconciling itself to the Acquino regime while continuing to protect vital US interests in the major military bases located in the Philippines.

It was relations with the Soviet Union that were of overriding importance for the Reagan administration, as for previous ones, and the success in other areas of its mixture of extreme rhetoric and pragmatic action would amount to little if it were not replicated in this crucial relationship. It too was subject to an extraordinary transformation during the course of the Reagan years. Initially the American stance was one of confrontation, rhetorical at the outset but soon manifest in more material terms.[39] As we saw in Chapter 4, the deployment of Cruise missiles arose primarily out of concerns within the Western alliance about the nature of the tie between America and Europe. But its ramifications for relations with the USSR were equally important. As seen from the Soviet perspective, it was an attempt to escalate the threat to them and to raise tension. In particular, because it raised the possibility of a successful nuclear first strike, it caused grave concern as to whether the USA was intending to fight a 'limited' nuclear war in Europe. Cruise missiles made this a possibility which, although devastating to both sides, would leave the USA in a stronger position relative to both Europe and the Soviet Union. Mutual assured destruction had made aggression unthinkable, but the development and advocacy of intermediate nuclear weapons had the potential to destablize the order that had been achieved in Europe. Added to this, the hostile rhetoric with which the Reagan administration confronted the Soviet Union raised fears in both Europe and the USSR as to exactly what American intentions were.[40]

These concerns were greatly intensified by the announcement of the Strategic Defense Initiative or 'Star Wars'.[41] Although Reagan claimed that this was a defensive initiative designed to make nuclear war impossible by providing a protective shell over the USA which would intercept any nuclear attack, it was not seen that way by the Soviet Union. It was assumed that complete protection from attack was unachievable; but it was possible that the USA could develop the capacity to intercept sufficient missiles to be able to limit the damage done by a Soviet nuclear attack. If this happened, the USA would have the capacity to survive a nuclear attack while inflicting total destruction on the USSR. In this sense, 'Star Wars' would make it possible for the USA to 'win' a nuclear war. Despite American protestations that the system was intended solely for defensive use, the fact that it also carried this offensive potential could not help but aggravate Soviet suspicions. Military strategy, after all, is conducted in terms of capacities rather than intentions, however honourable these may be at the time of expression. Particularly in view of Reagan's aggressive rhetoric about the need to roll back the influence of communism in the world, the idea that the USA would develop this capacity but never use it was one to which the Soviets were understandably reluctant to trust their fate.[42]

These fears of aggressive American intent, and the belief in Europe and the Soviet Union that the USA was seeking to reverse its decline to the extent of seeking world domination by military means, reached their peak in the mid-1980s. The level of tension thus engendered made all the more remarkable the transformation that occurred in the second part of the decade. It was replaced by a level of *détente* undreamt of even in the Nixon years, and the headlong rush of events has yet to produce a stable pattern in the relationship. This is in part because the USA has yet to determine an unequivocal response to the momentous changes in the nature of the threat it faces. Even more important are the tensions that the transformation of the Soviet Union have brought to the surface in that society, tensions so severe that the eventual outcome of the struggles they engender is by no means clear. What is clear, however, is that the transformation that is taking place is a profound one, and the question is whether the policies of the Reagan administration can be seen as being the major cause of what may prove to be the emergence of a more secure and peaceful world.[43]

The claim which has been made by the supporters of the Reagan strategy is that the early confrontation was a necessary prelude to the succeeding era of peace and *détente*.[44] The argument is that the Soviets respect only strength, and American rearmament was necessary to convince them that the West had not declined into weakness, but remained willing to make the sacrifices required to ensure that the Soviets could not defeat them. The role of rhetoric in articulating Western values and strength of purpose was vital, and it was one at which Reagan was particularly adept. But equally important was the escalation of the arms race. This had a purpose beyond its ostensible one of strengthening Western defence, vital though that was. It may have been an economic sacrifice for the USA, though given the short-term boom it generated in the US economy even this much is doubtful. The point, however, is that the principal objective of Soviet policy for years had been to achieve parity with the USA on the world stage, and this goal left it with no option but to match the US build-up. However, this required the Soviet Union to increase even further the proportion of its much smaller economic resources that it had to devote to military production. It is this which proved too much for the Soviet economy. The contrast between the impoverishment it had brought to its people and Western affluence became unsustainable and threatened the stability of Soviet society. And this finally convinced Soviet leaders that radical change was necessary.

In effect the consequence of the American rearmament strategy was to beggar the Soviet Union into submission by making the cost of the competition more than the Soviets could sustain. The transformation of the Soviet Union is therefore a general vindication not only of the superiority of the Western political and economic system, but also of the strategy of negotiation from strength pursued by the Reagan administration. Fears of American aggressive intent have been proven to be groundless, and the superior vision of those who decided to try to achieve peace through strength confirmed.

The truth of such claims is undoubtedly exaggerated. It is indeed presumptuous and ethnocentric to imagine that anything the West alone could have done would have sparked such a radical transformation of Soviet society. To see this simply as a triumph for the West is to miss the historical scope and complex origins of what has been happening in the USSR and Eastern Europe. More importantly, it fails to grasp that the pressures which have brought about this transformation, though massive, are internal to the communist system. Western influence, whether in promoting or retarding these changes, has been essentially marginal. The core of truth in the claim, however, does indeed lie more in the economic impact of the arms race than in American postures of toughness which in themselves are likely to produce only a response in kind given the long-standing Soviet goal of being treated as equals by the USA on the world stage. The fundamental problem of the Soviet system has been its failure to deliver an acceptable standard of living to its people. The source of the problem lies in the inadequacies of its economic structure, but the military burden it has taken upon itself has been a contributing factor to its economic weakness. In so far as Soviet military expenditure is a response to Western levels, and this is only one factor determining it, then the US rearmament of the 1980s might be seen as the straw which broke the camel's back. It is in this sense that American intransigence did make some contribution to hastening the changes in the USSR, though no more than a marginal one.

More important than precise distribution of credit or blame for the changes in the USSR is the effect they will have on world affairs. There can be little doubt that the Soviet Union has initiated a process of transformation which will leave unchanged very few of the assumptions on which the post-war world order was based. Whatever pattern of security arrangements emerges in Europe and elsewhere, they are going to require fundamental adjustments in American thinking. The decline of communism and the *rapprochement* with the West have put an end to a post-war era characterized above all by bipolarity between the superpowers. The effect on the USA of a multipolar world will be complex. On the one hand, its pre-eminence will be diminished without the discipline which the communist threat permitted it to exercise in its area of hegemony. On the other, as the sole remaining superpower it will not be reduced to the level of just one player among many in the shifting alliances that will produce a balance of power in a multipolar world. Its singular position will give it the opportunity to orchestrate the new world order and perhaps even to conduct its harmonies; all the more so, since such harmony, if it is to be achieved, will rest on an economic system which will become global but of which the USA remains the leading exemplar. This is not to suggest that recent developments in the communist world should be interpreted as giving the USA licence to languish in the comforts of victory over the old enemy. The cold war may be over and capitalism may have triumphed, and it would be easy to see this as the ultimate vindication of the American role in the modern world. A moment of indulgence in self-congratulation may be in order, but anything more will blind the USA to the new challenges that the emerging world order will pose, challenges which will be no less daunting for lacking the clear and familiar outlines of the communist threat.

It is in this context that the mixed achievement of the Reagan administration must be judged. It was above all an administration of paradox,[45] one in which its deeds belied its rhetoric, its bark proved worse than its bite. Assuming office with the highest of ideological profiles, it proved thoroughly pragmatic in international affairs, to the disappointment of many true believers on the New Right who helped to put it into power. But this is perhaps too generous, since the concept of paradox may be thought to be a euphemism for an administration of two halves which was forced to reverse itself on most major issues. In its first term it pushed for international economic liberalization on a market basis, whereas in its second it stressed international political co-operation to restrain the market; in the first term there was economic growth and a strong dollar, in the second economic stagnation and currency decline; in the first term there was military build-up and marked hostility to the Soviet Union, in the second there were cutbacks in spending and armament levels and an undreamt-of degree of co-operation with the USSR.

This picture is drawn too sharply for the reality, but the real issue is whether there were any threads of constancy which might account for this apparent pattern of reversal. Partisans would suggest that the theme of negotiation from strength provides the unifying link which underpinned the balance that the administration sought to strike between the competing pressures upon it. Pressures for economic internationalization competed with national economic interest, pressures for peace competed with readiness for war, above all pressures for the reassertion of American strength were in conflict with the limits of American power. This may be true up to a point, but the real legacy of the Reagan administration remained contradictory. On the one hand, it left an economic legacy of enduring weakness exacerbated by its short-term 'solutions', the consequences of which were only partly ameliorated in the second term.[46] Awareness of this weakness was one of the factors which made Reagan respond so positively to the overtures of Gorbachev and the peace dividend they promised. But this provides an ironic connection with the positive aspect of the Reagan legacy, the reassertion of America's will and leadership in the world, the willingness to stand for something and to use its power to try to bring it about. The final paradox is that, although the Reagan administration weakened America in the international economic arena, in the process it restored America's self-belief and faith in its own exceptionalism.[47] It therefore provided the platform from which the USA can take advantage of the opportunities that the decline of communism and the internationalization of capitalism will bring in the 1990s.

Notes

1. N. Podhoretz, 'The new American majority', *Commentary*, 71, 1, Jan. 1981, pp. 19–28.

2. M. Davis, *Prisoners of the American Dream*, London: Verso, 1986, chapter 4; M.W. Miles, *The Odyssey of the American Right*, New York: Oxford University Press, 1980.
3. G. Peele, *Revival and Reaction: The right in contemporary America*, Oxford: Clarendon, 1984; A. Crawford, *Thunder on the Right*, New York: Pantheon, 1980.
4. P. Steinfels, *The Neo-Conservatives*, New York: Simon & Schuster, 1980.
5. M. Novak, *The Rise of the Unmeltable Ethnics: Politics and culture in the 70s*, London: Macmillan, 1973; H.O. Patterson, *Ethnic Chauvinism: The reactionary impulse*, New York: Stein & Day, 1977.
6. K. Sale, *Power Shift: The rise of the Southern Rim and its challenge to the Eastern establishment*, New York: Random House, 1975.
7. M. Friedman, *Capitalism and Freedom*, Chicago, Ill.: University of Chicago Press, 1962; M. and R. Friedman, *Free to Choose*, New York, Harcourt, 1980.
8. G. Gilder, *Wealth and Poverty*, New York: Basic Books, 1981.
9. S. Rousseas, *The Political Economy of Reaganomics: A critique*, Armonk, NY: Sharpe, 1982.
10. This idea was dignified by the theory of the Laffer curve, named after the economist who attempted to quantify these variables and who acted as an adviser to the administration.
11. F. Lekachman, *Greed Is Not Enough: Reaganomics*, New York: Pantheon, 1982.
12. N. Podhoretz, 'The future danger', *Commentary*, 71, 4, Apr. 1981, pp. 29–47.
13. S. Brown, *The Faces of Power: Constancy and change in United States foreign policy from Truman to Reagan*, New York: Columbia University Press, 1983, chapter 33.
14. D. Stockman, *The Triumph of Politics*, London: Bodley Head, 1986.
15. F.F. Piven and R.A. Cloward, *The New Class War: Reagan's attack on the welfare state and its consequences*, New York: Pantheon, 1982; T. Edsall, *The New Politics of Inequality*, New York: Norton, 1984.
16. L. Tsoukalis (ed.), *The Political Economy of International Money*, London: Sage, 1985.
17. The UK was one of the biggest European contributors to this inflow of funds after the Thatcher government, as one of its earliest acts, eliminated all controls on the flow of capital in and out of the UK.
18. K. King, 'US monetary policy and the European responses in the 1980s', Chatam House Papers no. 16, London: Royal Institute of International Affairs/Routledge, 1982.
19. R. Parboni, 'The dollar weapon from Nixon to Reagan', *New Left Review*, 158, July–Aug. 1986, pp. 5–18.
20. H. Nau, *International Reaganomics: A domesticist approach to world economy*, Washington: DC: Georgetown Center for Strategic and International Studies, 1981.
21. M. Stewart, *The Age of Interdependence: Economic policy in a shrinking world*, Cambridge, Mass.: MIT Press, 1983.
22. Secreteria de Relationes Exteriores, *Cancun 1981: Framework, debate and conclusions of the meeting on international cooperation and development*, Mexico City, 1982.

23. S. Gill, *American Hegemony and the Trilateral Commission*, Cambridge: Cambridge University Press, 1990, p. 106.
24. Of course, many resisted the idea that the market was the solution to Third World problems and saw the Reagan strategy as simply a cloak for reasserting its imperialist and exploitative domination of the Third World. See E. Augelli and C. Murphy, *America's Quest for Supremacy and the Third World*, London: Pinter, 1988.
25. M. Davis, *Prisoners of the American Dream*, London: Verso, 1986, part 2.
26. International Monetary Fund, *Balance of Payments Statistics, Yearbook*, Washington DC, yearbook, 32, 1981 onwards.
27. Gill, *op. cit.*, p. 108.
28. F. Halliday, *The Making of the Second Cold War*, London: New Left Books, 1983.
29. R.A. Burrowes, *Revolution and Rescue in Grenada: An account of the US Caribbean invasion*, New York: Greenwood, 1988.
30. C. Bell, *The Reagan Paradox: American foreign policy in the 1980s*, Aldershot: Elgar, 1989.
31. M.D. Hayes, 'Not what I say, but what I do: Latin American policy in the Reagan administration', in J.D. Martz (ed.), *United States Policy in Latin America*, Lincoln, Nebr.: University of Nebraska Press, 1988.
32. J. Kirkpatrick, 'US security and Latin America', *Commentary*, 71, 1, Jan. 1981, pp. 29–40.
33. J. Pearce, *Under the Eagle: US intervention in Central America and the Caribbean*, London: Latin American bureau, 1982; M. McClintock, *The American Connection: State terror and popular resistance in El Salvador*, London: Zed, 1985.
34. J. Valenta and E. Duran (eds.), *Conflict in Nicaragua: A multidimensional perspective*, London: Allen & Unwin, 1987; L. Cockburn, *Out of Control: The story of the Reagan administration's secret war in Nicaragua*, London: Bloomsbury, 1988.
35. J. Marshal *et al.*, *Iran–Contra: Secret wars and covert operations in the Reagan era*, Boston, Mass.: South End Press, 1987.
36. Valenta and Duran, *op. cit.*, chapter 9.
37. S.L. Spiegel, *The Other Arab–Israeli Conflict: Making America's Middle East policy from Truman to Reagan*, Chicago, Ill.: University of Chicago Press, 1985; B. Rubin, 'The Reagan administration and the Middle East', in K. Oye *et al.* (eds.), *Eagle Defiant: United States foreign policy in the 1980s*, Boston, Mass.: Little Brown, 1983.
38. R. Bonner, *Waltzing With a Dictator: The Marcoses and the making of American policy*, London: Macmillan, 1987.
39. N. Chomsky, *Towards a New Cold War*, London: Sinclair Browne, 1982; A. Dallin and G.W. Lapidus, 'Reagan and the Russians: United States policy toward the Soviet Union and Eastern Europe', in Oye *et al.*, *op. cit.*, N. Chomsky, J. Steele and J. Gittings, *Superpowers in Collision: The cold war now*, Harmondsworth: Penguin, 1982.
40. R. Scheer, *With Enough Shovels: Reagan, Bush and nuclear war*, London: Secker & Warburg, 1983.
41. M. Charlton, *The Star Wars History: From Detente to Defence – the American strategic debate*, London: BBC Publications, 1986.
42. Soviet suspicions were reinforced by American intransigence on the 'Star

Wars' issue in the strategic arms limitations negotiations. See S. Talbot, *Deadly Gambits: The Reagan administration and the stalemate in nuclear arms control*, New York: Knopf, 1984.

43. H. Haftendorn and J. Schissler (eds.), *The Reagan Administration: A reconstruction of American strength?*, Berlin: Walter de Gruyter, 1988.
44. M. Cox, 'Whatever happened to the "Second Cold War"? Soviet–American relations: 1980–88', *Review of International Studies*, 16, 2, Apr. 1990, pp. 155–172.
45. Bell, *op. cit.*
46. M. Friedman, *Day of Reckoning: The consequences of American economic policy under Reagan and after*, New York: Random House, 1988.
47. C. Coker, *Reflections on American Foreign Policy since 1945*, London: Pinter, 1989, chapter 1; R. Garson, 'The rise and rise of American exceptionalism', *Review of International Studies*, 16, 2, April 1990, pp. 173–9.

CHAPTER NINE

———— · ————

AMERICA IN THE 1990s: DANGERS AND OPPORTUNITIES

The start of the 1990s has been a period of massive upheaval in international affairs, and one in which the implications for America's role in the world are equally momentous. The outcome of the present transition is unclear and indeed unknowable. Many have suggested that it will result in a decline in American importance that is the fate of all great powers; and yet, paradoxically, American success in the Gulf war has given rise to suggestions of a new world order in which the United States will achieve a paramountcy dwarfing even its earlier post-war hegemony. It has been the argument of this book to reject both extremes: the 1990s undoubtedly present threats to America's role as a leading world power, but they also offer enormous opportunities for continued and indeed extended influence so long as the USA accepts the fact that this new order will be a multipolar one which permits leadership but not total domination by any nation.

The changes taking place in world affairs which have the greatest significance for America's role are the collapse of communism as a social system and the concomitant internationalization of capitalism, to the point where its globalization becomes a real and almost immediate prospect. Forces of this scale alter the parameters within which all nation-states operate, but these changes are fundamentally favourable to the USA and offer great scope for it to attain a pivotal role in a new world order. America is the only power with the combination of political, cultural, ideological, economic and military attributes necessary to this role. However, there are dangers attendant on this transformation too, and it is by no means certain that the USA will not decline. The purpose of this chapter is to assess what will be required for America to avoid the dangers that the 1990s present, and to maintain a leading role in the modern world even as that world is transformed to an extent inconceivable just a few years ago.

It is essential to this task to have an understanding of the theoretical basis of American behaviour in the world since the war, irrespective

175

of whether or not this is described as imperialist. Theories which address this issue tend to give primacy to either economics or politics as explanatory categories, with the result that they become unduly one-sided since both are clearly relevant. Economic factors are the best starting point for analysis, however, because they explain the fundamental dynamism of capitalist society. Marxist theories of imperialism fail in their ambitious goal of establishing the necessity of imperialism to capitalism on the grounds that, without imperialism to offset it, the tendency of the profit rate to fall would result in the collapse of capitalist society. What they do offer is a convincing explanation of the essentially expansionist nature of capitalism. The imperatives of competition and accumulation dictate that capitalism either expands or dies. Even if it does not logically imply imperialism, this basic feature inevitably affects the policy and behaviour of the leading capitalist power.

One consequence is that the state will act to provide an international environment in which capital accumulation can take place, and this imperative has certainly been applicable to the American case. But the irony is that this effect may not be the exploitative one conjured up if the term 'imperialism' is employed to describe it. Even in the Marxist framework, capitalism is progressive at a certain stage of history because it provides the material wealth which is the only basis upon which a superior form of society can be constructed. If considered at the global level, which is the most appropriate one today, capitalism retains that progressive character; it follows that the United States too, as the international standard bearer of capitalism in the modern world, has played a progressive role in this sense. While the element of competition that is at the heart of capitalism creates pressure for exploitation and can become destructive, self-defeating and irrational, it also, by virtue of the wealth it generates, creates the basis for common interests and thus for co-operation between states which wish to maximize their own prosperity. The principle of comparative advantage demonstrates why the free movement of goods, services and capital across national boundaries is essential to meeting this goal, and the implications of this for the behaviour of the USA are inimical to the monopolistic restrictions classically associated with imperialism.

The validity of some aspects of the Marxist theory of imperialism does not therefore entail acceptance of the condemnatory stance usually associated with it, or of the connotation that economic factors are the primary explanatory category. The drive for expansion on which it focuses must have a congenial environment in which to work itself out, and this is something it cannot provide for itself. Provision must be a political process, and this alone would make politics an irreducibly important explanatory element in any complete theory. In this respect, therefore, politics and economics are in a symbiotic relationship, though one where the economic imperative is so broad that it remains compatible with a wide range of policy options. As applied to the United States this perspective suggests that we will not understand American behaviour if we fail to recognize the vital part that provision of a congenial environment for the expansion of capital has played in it, but neither will we understand it if that is all we recognize.

This symbiosis is only one aspect of the role of politics in this context. Its importance is reinforced by the fact that it is in the political realm that the literally vital matters of security and indeed survival in a nuclear age are acted upon. It is the logic of behaviour by nation-states based on these considerations to which realist theory is addressed, and which demonstrates the importance of an irreducible concept of power in interstate relations that goes beyond any connection with economic systems. Indeed, there is scope for considerable tension between political and economic imperatives deriving from the differing concepts of interest they imply: if the imperative of capital is towards globalization, prosperity and co-operation in international affairs, then that of realist theory is towards the centrality of nationalism, insecurity and antagonism relieved only by a balance of power. In sum, the principles governing the behaviour of a major capitalist power such as the United States are the result of a complex interaction of economic and political factors which can be at once both symbiotic and antagonistic, and which defy any simple formulation. Such principles remain very abstract and establish only the parameters within which policy is constructed. A fuller understanding requires more specific consideration of how these principles have been made manifest in the American case.

Whether the USA is best described as an imperialist power is a trivial question in the sense that it is obviously not literally so, and any such characterization based on its power in world affairs is no more or less valid than the prejudices of those making it. Nor is it the case that the USA can be described as imperialist in the sense that its domestic stability is dependent on the fruits of its exploitation of the rest of the world. The magnitudes involved are insufficient to sustain such an argument, and indeed in the case of capital flows operate in the reverse of the required direction. This is not to suggest that American policy is unconstrained by economic imperatives. Their precise effect is difficult to isolate, however, because the drive for economic expansion and the requirement for political security have influenced policy in the same direction for much of the post-war era. Having arrived at a position of dominance immediately after the war, the American desire to consolidate and extend it was threatened principally by the challenge from communism, in particular from the USSR. But since communism at once challenged both freedom of access for capital and American notions of democracy and liberty, the defence of one became synonymous with protection of the other. The Manichaean construction of the communist threat evident in the practice of containment justified the adoption of an aggressive stance by the USA to protect its interests, despite protestations of purely defensive intent. While the political threat was real enough, especially after it took on a nuclear aspect, this unmediated construction of it undoubtedly owed much to the economic imperative for which it provided such an effective rationalization.

As a consequence of this interpretation, the USA became associated with unjust regimes and the support of exploitation, and this prompted the perception of its role in world affairs as imperialist. But the better overall characterization of the period of American dominance is as one of hegemony, the critical difference being the element of consensus associated with the latter term. This consensus was not an entirely natural phenomenon, having being constructed in part by American intervention in the domestic order of countries in its sphere of influence during the early post-war years; but neither could it have been sustained on a purely manufactured basis. The appeal of the American hegemonic order lay more in the attractions of the economic dynamism and prosperity which it promised than in the defence against a much exaggerated threat of communist world domination. It is the element of systemic reproduction, initially at the economic level but also drawing in political and cultural dimensions, which provides the basis of the case for the essentially benign nature of American hegemony. During this hegemonic era the world economy enjoyed an unprecedented period of growth, and this was not incompatible with the American national interest since, if other countries benefited from the combination of dynamism and stability that its hegemony supplied, the USA benefited most of all. This makes all the more acute the issue of whether both American and wider interests can be protected in the transition from its hegemonic phase to the coming era of multipolar, global capitalism.

It is the superpower relationship with the USSR which has dominated American policy since the war. The American analysis of the Soviet Union as intent on world domination lay at the origin of the cold war and gave the USA response of containment such an uncompromising character for much of this period. The combination of Soviet nuclear capacity in a system of nation-states characterized by insecurity and uncertainty, together with the denial of access to capital it represented, meant that this threat was real, notwithstanding the fact that it frequently suited America's interests to exaggerate it in order to rationalize its own expansionary intentions. As a result, the dominant motif of superpower relations has been one of confrontation, both directly and by proxy. None the less, the containment mentality has not prevented the USA from adopting a more pragmatic approach in practice than its ideological rhetoric would have suggested. American policy towards the Soviet Union has in fact been characterized by a series of swings between open hostility and *détente*, although even when *détente* was pursued with the greatest subtlety by Kissinger and Nixon in the 1970s, it remained a more sophisticated method of achieving the constant goal of containment rather than a repudiation of it. This makes all the more dramatic the latest swing of the pendulum in the 1980s, in which the overt confrontation of Reagan's 'evil empire' phase has been succeeded by a level of *détente* which calls into question the whole premiss of containment.

Although it is the nuclear dimension which gives the superpower relationship its fundamental character, and capacities in this respect have not fundamentally changed, the collapse of communism as it has been known in Eastern Europe and the Soviet Union has been primarily an economic phenomenon. It has occurred because the planned economies have been unable to satisfy the minimum demands of their populations, and the only and necessary alternative will be the evolution of some form of market system. Part of the reason for the economic ineffectiveness of the Eastern bloc has been the enormous military burden that the cold war placed on its resources, and this burden has applied to the USA as well, though with rather more mixed consequences. Of much more importance for the USA, however, are the implications of the former communist sphere being opened up to the penetration of private capital. This presents all the capitalist economies with considerable opportunities for wealth creation, but the USA continues to bear a special responsibility for an orderly transition to a more international capitalist economy, since this requires political leadership as well as economic dynamism. The danger for the USA is that it will negotiate the integration of the communist countries into the capitalist sphere successfully at a political level, but in doing so will only open the way for others to reap the economic harvest.

This is not to suggest that the USA should do other than continue to co-operate in the process of orderly transformation of the Soviet Union: to do otherwise would foster the all too evident possibility of a reactionary reversal based on military power that would not only recreate an oppressive internal regime, but would almost certainly reintroduce a level of tension in world affairs inimical to American and Western interests. While the political element of this relationship is vital, therefore, this does not diminish the importance of its economic aspect. On the contrary, if the opportunity created by the economic flaws of the communist system can be grasped, it can reshape world politics into a much more co-operative configuration and remove the spectre of potential nuclear holocaust which the old logic of confrontation generated. Taking this opportunity will require a particular mixture of co-operation and competition between the capitalist powers, a balance which the USA will have the critical role in developing.

The problem in this context is America's economic decline relative to these other powers. At the height of its hegemonic phase, economic supremacy and political domination created the space in which the USA could promote stability without suppressing competition. As the period of such unequivocal domination passes, it is possible that the element of competition for markets between national capitals could get out of hand. There is always the temptation for any country to act as a free rider, not only allowing the USA to bear the burdens of political and military leadership, but also protecting its national industries and domestic constituencies while taking advantage of free trade practised by others. If taken too far, this can institute a cycle of retaliation which begins with the spread of mercantilism, but which the history of the twentieth century demonstrates can easily intensify to the point of open conflict. The functional superiority of the models of capitalism in Germany and Japan, in particular, as compared to the United States in itself creates pressure for the USA to defend its interests by retreating into mercantilism, and this element has been by no means absent from US policies in recent years.

There are counter-pressures which favour co-operation, however. The mutual prosperity which free trade can bring has become more evident in the post-war years, just as the history of the pre-war years showed the self-defeating nature of economic nationalism. The growth in interdependence that has occurred under American hegemony makes the link between the interests of the world economic system and its component parts ever more real and apparent. Circumstances are propitious for this tendency to accelerate and become irreversibly dominant in international economic affairs in the 1990s. The quantum leap in the mobility of capital around the world has created an environment in which international implications become major constraints on the national economic policy decisions of all countries. Similarly, the growth of multinational corporations is creating an international capitalist class whose basic interest lies in the free movement of factors of production across as much of the globe as possible. This class is enhancing its coherence through such agencies as the Trilateral Commission, and is acting as a powerful influence on national governments which are themselves developing ever more elaborate formal mechanisms of policy co-ordination.

The decisive factor favouring co-operation between capitalist powers in the 1990s is the prospect, made real by the collapse of communism, of extending the market system into hitherto closed areas of the world economy. In an historical inversion of substantial significance, it is the attractions of collective prosperity based on an economic system shared with the former communist world that will come to replace the discipline exercised on the capitalist countries under American hegemony by the existence of a common enemy. This dialectic is made all the more compelling by the fact that it was the discipline of the external enemy which permitted the USA to foster international economic co-operation, thereby demonstrating the superior productivity of capitalism over communism, and so hastening the collapse of the enemy that had generated it in the first place. The decline of communism, while it deprives the USA of this tool for maintaining order in the capitalist world, also presents it with an opportunity to resurrect its leadership on the basis of managing the common interest in the orderly expansion of capitalism. Intra-capitalist relationships will displace the relation between the superpowers at the centre of world affairs, but they will continue to require political leadership to prevent their destructive aspects becoming paramount. The USA is the only power with the combination of qualities to be able to provide this leadership, which if it will lose something of its hegemonic aspect, will gain from being exercised across a broader canvas.

Since the globalization of capitalism is the key to this prospect for continuing American leadership, it must extend to relations with the Third World. These have represented the darker side of American hegemony, in which economic exploitation and political repression have been the more typical pattern than co-operation based on consensus. It is possible that globalization could become a euphemism for more of the same, even for enhanced exploitation based on an ultra-imperialist alliance of capitalist and former communist countries of the more developed world. Whether this will be the case depends on the nature of the relation between capitalism and the less developed countries. The dependency perspective, in which capitalist prosperity has been historically dependent on the surplus extracted from the Third World, suggests that further exploitation of the periphery by a reinforced metropolis is indeed the most likely prospect for the 1990s. If, on the other hand, the idea is accepted that capitalism must by its nature replicate itself as it expands, then this will have fundamentally benign implications for the Third World in an era of globalization. It is the latter perspective, which adopts the classical Marxist argument on the fundamental character of capitalism but inverts the implications usually derived from it, that is the more valid one.

This should not lead to any sanguine view that replication is likely to prove a painless process. The dislocations and social strain inherent in rapid development preclude this, and the exploitative element inherent in a system driven by inequality reinforces it. The extension of capitalism to the periphery has already given vent to authoritarian tendencies, and further rapid development makes it unlikely that they will be dislodged in the short term. The USA has been deeply implicated in the oppression associated with the expansion of capitalism. This has been as much the result of the exaggerated interpretaton of the communist threat, whereby any resistance to exploitation was seen as a manifestation of the communist drive for world-wide domination, as it has of the requirements of protecting capitalism in the Third World. Consequently, the demise of the communist threat is likely to make what was always unnecessary become evidently superfluous and indeed counterproductive to American influence over this aspect of globalization. If reduced concern about the spread of an alien philosophy is accompanied by greater faith in the power of capitalism itself to create a democratic consensus on, and a shared interest in, economic growth between the metropolis and the periphery, then the United States could regain the legitimacy that its support of oppressive regimes has forfeited in the eyes of many in the Third World.

Successful relations with the Third World will also require the USA to improve its economic competitiveness. The need to do so if it is to provide leadership for other advanced capitalist societies is perhaps obvious. But the success of the newly industrializing countries, which have opted to follow variations on the Japanese model of economic development rather than the type of free enterprise represented by the USA, shows that the danger of economic decline is more pervasive than would have been conceivable until recently. If a sufficient number of countries overtake the USA economically, then even if it regains its political legitimacy it will cease to be of relevance to less developed countries, which will look to more successful models to emulate. Beyond a certain point America's political, cultural, ideological and military advantages will be cancelled out by economic ineffectiveness, and its potential role as the pivot of a multipolar world system could be undermined as newly industrializing and advanced capitalist countries coalesce to form new centres of gravity which leave America marginal to the process of economic development that is the key to the new world order. This is perhaps the greatest danger facing the USA, and the irony is that its very success in prompting Third World development will make the task of avoiding economic irrelevance all the more challenging in the 1990s.

Much of the answer to whether the USA will show sufficient flexibility to avoid these dangers and grasp the opportunities of the 1990s is indicated by its conduct as a world power during its hegemonic phase. The picture is a mixed one. Despite the constant thread of containment, American policy has defied easy generalization as each administration has sought both to rectify and to avoid repeating the mistakes of its immediate predecessor. Kennedy inherited a legacy from the early post-war years of American supremacy that was possessed of only a dim awareness of the limitations of US power, and his inaugural rhetoric did nothing to suggest that such an awareness would be his guiding light. The practice, even in such events as the Cuban missile crisis, was rather more measured, but none the less left a fatal legacy of hubris to the Johnson administration which suffered retribution in Vietnam.

While never inevitable, American involvement in Vietnam was the natural consequence of a policy of unlimited containment which perceived conflict through the prism of a zero-sum game with the Soviet Union, which saw all conflict, however far removed, as linked to the battle against communism, and which could not tolerate even a minor reverse in that great conflict. The open-ended commitment to the defence of its sphere of influence left the USA vulnerable to attack at the weakest link in its chain of alliances, and unable to prevent its own prestige being drawn into a struggle on the least favourable terrain. Once its prestige and dependability as an ally were volunteered into the equation, real interests were indeed at stake, not of a direct economic sort since these were of little consequence in Vietnam, but the more fundamental interest of the very capacity of the USA to sustain its hegemony and the political and economic alliances around the world on which it depended. The quagmire that resulted from this ill-judged commitment dented American confidence both at home and abroad precisely because issues of real moment for American power had been put at stake, and the experience left the country chastened and painfully aware of the limits of its power.

By the same token, the importance of these issues made American leaders unwilling simply to abandon the conflict or to countenance straightforward defeat because of the implications for the exercise of US power everywhere else in the world. And yet by the late 1960s the continued or indeed escalated involvement that might have held some hope for victory had been made impossible by domestic political considerations. The task facing the Nixon administration was to resolve this contradiction. Its strategy of peace with honour came as close to achieving this as possible by extricating the USA from the quagmire while minimizing the loss to its prestige. It formed part of a wider strategy of *détente*: this was a creative response to America's reduced status which used previously untapped resources, such as a *rapprochement* with China and the creation of economic ties binding the USSR to the West, to further American interests. In the economic sphere, the Nixon administration sought to limit the damage from reduced American dominance by adopting a mercantilist strategy which confronted the growth of Japanese economic power in particular, and generally pursued US national interest even at the expense of America's international capitalist partners.

How successful the combination of *détente* and mercantilism would have been in the long run was never to be established because implementation of the Nixon administration's grand design to combat American decline was cut short by the effects of the Watergate scandal. It suffered from internal weaknesses as well. Economically, it fought against the underlying trend to internationalization in the capitalist world economy and would have proved divisive and destructive, gaining short-term advantage through the selfish exercise of American power at the expense of its longer term interest in precisely this process of internationalization and the sponsorship of co-operation it required from a country aspiring to leadership. Politically, *détente* was flawed by its obsession with superpower relations to the virtual exclusion of equally important intra-capitalist ones. Despite its dramatic change of tactics, it failed to alter the fundamentals of the containment perspective, and so suffered from the long-standing weaknesses associated with it. To these it added a further one: an amorality which, in the name of protecting the national interest, failed to recognize the vital role played by America's moral and ideological appeal in sustaining its hegemony.

The Carter administration entered office determined to reverse these priorities. On economic policy it was firmly committed to the Trilateralist line, and sought to foster the development of an international capitalism based on free movement of goods, services and capital, and improved co-ordination with other capitalist powers. Even more importantly, it sought to create an international environment built on universal respect for human rights as understood in America. This amounted to an ambitious attempt to extend American ideological hegemony, and thus to reconcile morality and interest. The concept of rights entailed in the Carter approach was quite compatible with the globalization of capitalism, since it conceived of the free market as the source of prosperity and thus as the bulwark of liberty. It demonstrated a faith in the capacity of capitalism to win over the uncommitted in the struggle against communism by the combination of prosperity and liberty it offered; policy could and should therefore dispense with the support of oppressive regimes as allies in the struggle against communism. For America to compromise its own highest ideals in the conduct of international affairs was therefore seen not only as wrong in itself, but also as counterproductive to the pursuit of the US national interest.

This enlightened approach too was cut short before its longer-term worth could be evaluated, partly as a result of its inherent limitations and partly due to circumstances beyond the administration's control. The most obvious instance of the latter was the revolution in Iran and the ensuing hostage crisis. The hostility to America which produced the crisis was the result of earlier American policies, but Carter's liberal approach, through a combination of bad luck and miscalculation, proved incapable of resolving it. It was thus left open to charges of weakness which were taken up vigorously by the increasingly powerful voice of the New Right. These were amplified after the Soviet invasion of Afghanistan, which was perceived on the right as a form of Soviet adventurism made possible by Carter's pusillanimous liberal approach to foreign affairs. He attempted to reverse much of his policy in the face of these attacks, but this only reinforced the impression of vacillation to which earlier instances of indecisiveness had given rise. However convincing the more sophisticated arguments behind this liberal approach may have been, in practice the policies which resulted gave the appearance of naivety and, more importantly, acquiescence in American decline, rather than the vigorous reaction to it that the American people clearly demanded once the trauma of Vietnam had receded. Their response was to elect in Ronald Reagan a leader who was determined to restore American pre-eminence in the 1980s by whatever means were necessary.

The anger that Reagan articulated stemmed from the belief that decline was unnecessary. It was felt that the United States had betrayed the principles that had made it not just a great power but an historically privileged one which could and should serve as a universal model. In his first term the regeneration of America was pursued aggressively: rhetorical confrontation with the forces of evil, located variously from Central America to the Soviet Union, was backed up by a massive increase in military capability and a nationalist economic policy which although it was couched in the rhetoric of the free market in practice achieved growth in the USA at the expense of other capitalist countries. But the economic policy in particular suffered from serious flaws, since its very success in generating growth created imbalances in the economy, which manifested themselves in an overvalued currency and twin deficits in government expenditure and the balance of payments. Growth on this basis was not sustainable, and the administration, notwithstanding its strongly ideological initial cast, showed a pragmatic streak in its second term in reversing the emphasis of economic policy. Most significantly, it avoided the temptations of economic nationalism and recognized the fact that interdependence had reached a stage where American economic well-being could not ultimately be purchased at the expense of the rest of the capitalist world. Accordingly, the administration sought greater international economic co-operation on matters such as debt refinancing, and demonstrated a willingness to compromise in respect of domestic expansion and currency values in the search for sustainable longer-term growth.

One sacrifice required to bring the economy into balance was a slow-down in the extraordinary increase in military expenditure that had taken place in Reagan's first term. Although its economic effects were profound, the rationale for this build-up had been to demonstrate American willingness to use its power, notably in the confrontation with the Soviet Union that remained the touchstone of policy. Its reversal would therefore have serious political implications. But these were dwarfed by the momentous change in American relations with the Soviet Union that took place in the second term. It was argued that the military build-up and indeed the initial aggressive posture were vindicated, since they had always been intended as a temporary measure necessary to allow the USA to enter negotatiations with both its capitalist allies and its communist opponents from a position of strength. Further, by increasing the burden of military expenditure on the Soviet economy in its attempt to keep up with the USA, the arms build-up exposed the weakness in the Soviet economic system, hastened the advent of *perestroika* and forced the Soviet Union to abandon its aims for world domination.

Whatever the contribution of the initial policy stance to subsequent developments, and it would seem that their origins were more deep-seated and beyond the scope of American control, the more significant point is that Reagan proved willing to respond to Soviet overtures and to demonstrate a pragmatism that belied his early rhetoric. The legacy of his administration has been as mixed as the policies pursued in it. The weaknesses of the American economy were exacerbated rather than resolved, and its relative decline was not halted during the 1980s. This remains the Achilles' heel of the USA's efforts to maintain its position in the world. On the other hand, political leadership was reasserted, and this placed the Bush administration in a good position to take advantage of the dramatic events in the communist world and of the extension of the market system to promote continuing American leadership in world affairs.

Relative economic decline has not been reversed under the Bush administration. It has continued to co-operate with the process of economic internationalization, although the dangers of conflict remain apparent in areas such as GATT talks on free trade and relations with Japan. But the relative feebleness of the American contribution to the reconstruction of Eastern Europe is in notable contrast to the dominant role that the USA played in the equivalent process in Western Europe at the time of the Marshall Plan, and is eloquent testimony to the dangers facing the USA. The underlying difficulty is domestic paralysis in reforming the structure of the US economy. Since the problem is insidious rather than dramatic, it appears to be beyond the capacity of the American political system to generate the necessary radical action, its pluralistic structure producing stalemate rather than the decisiveness that is required. Bush's dilemma is that, if the budget and trade deficits are not brought under control, the slow but inexorable decline of the American economy will continue; but if he does curb them, it will be at the expense of current consumption and therefore almost certainly at the expense of his own political popularity. The short-term pressures which result from the exigencies of the American political cycle do not inspire confidence that he will have the freedom of manoeuvre to take a sufficiently long-term view. The American public does not give the appearance of being ready to make the sacrifices involved, and Bush's political opponents, who control Congress, are unlikely to make the task of redressing the balance between consumption and investment any easier. The problem is compounded by a reluctance on the part of the administration to contemplate the strategic intervention in the free market that characterizes the more successful capitalist economies. The purpose of such intervention is to ensure the modernization of economic structure rather than to curb competition, and by eschewing it the Bush administration is adopting a literal interpretation of capitalist ideology which may cost America dear.

What, in summation, are the principal dangers threatening America's role in the world as it approaches the end of the century? For many who see the USA as a power in decline, the source of the problem lies not in the international sphere at all, but in the domestic weakness of American society. This is manifest in the massive and growing social inequality that is part of the legacy of the Reagan years. The growth of an underclass has been given point by the contrast with the conspicuous consumption of the rich, but the interconnectedness of these trends has become ever more apparent as patterns of broken families, lower educational attainment, rising crime rates, drug dependency and other symptoms of social pathology have spread through society. The USA appears to have forgotten the lessons of social democracy, and has sacrificed the long-term stability and consensus it brings for a short-term, get-rich-quick mentality that is dignified by the invocation of market forces, but which is producing a brutality, callousness and waste of human potential that is eating away at its vitality. The crass consumerism which has been one manifestation of this mentality in the 1980s is also symptomatic of an imbalance between consumption and investment that is not a sustainable basis for long-term economic growth. Already the excessive reliance on credit is reaping its rewards: the signs that the bubble has burst are evident in the demise of junk bonds and the collapse of the savings and loans industry. But the real bills in reduced standards of living have yet to be paid, and when they are the damage done to productive investment, already weakened by a bias towards military production, can only be exacerbated.

If the roots of decline are domestic, they will, on this view, have consequences which reverberate in the international arena. Rivalry with other capitalist powers will grow: the temptation to protect domestic inefficiency behind tariff walls will be considerable in a political system unwilling or unable to impose the sacrifices necessary to restore competitiveness. Other countries will inevitably respond to US mercantilism in kind, with the result that the free-trade order which has underpinned post-war prosperity will be fatally damaged. Conflict will not cease at this point; the mutual racism that has come to tinge American–Japanese relations gives an unpleasant foretaste of the way in which nations which have been competitors can become perceived as enemies. This could institute a vicious circle in which the USA, by attempting to use its political power to compensate for economic decline, succeeds only in exacerbating it. Should this continue, America will be drawn into ever more adventurist activities in a forlorn attempt to reassert its former pre-eminence. Far from restoring a healthy balance between economics and politics, this will give rise to fantasies of a new world order that is no more than a euphemism for a *pax americana* in which the USA throws its weight about as the world's military policeman. Such a path can end only in ruination, whatever short-term successes it might enjoy in the window of opportunity created by the decline of its rival superpower. The ruination would come because the USA would be trying to resolve its weaknesses at the expense of the rest of the world; in the process it would have lost touch with the trend towards globalization upon which its successful hegemony has been based, and in which its best hope for continued influence lies, thereby perverting its own dynamism into a reactionary stance based on fear of, rather than capitalization on, the historical tide.

Seen in this light, American strategy in the Gulf crisis contains the seed of great danger. If victory breeds a renewed American belief in its own invincibility, it will increase the temptation to rely on political and military might as a solution to all problems, including its own progressive economic decline. Concern that calculations of this nature lay behind the American reaction to the invasion of Kuwait is reinforced by the difficulty in otherwise explaining the intransigence of its response. The USA had, after all, been a recent supporter of Iraq, and other countries even more dependent on Gulf oil, such as Germany and Japan, did not feel that such a belligerent response to the invasion was necessary. This is not to deny that vital interests were at stake and that an Iraqi takeover of much of the oil reserves in the Gulf would have been intolerable to Western interests. It is to question whether a war could have been felt to be worth the risks entailed if that was all that was at issue. Protecting vital American and Western interests in the face of Iraqi expansionism could, it would appear, have been secured without such drastic action; that the USA was intransigent beyond what was needed suggests a hidden agenda that can only be explained in terms of a desire to take advantage of Soviet decline in order to assert its pre-eminence in a forceful fashion. The Gulf crisis would on this view be seen as an ideal diversion from domestic weakness and an opportunity for America to establish for itself a dominant, militaristic role in world affairs.

The danger is accentuated by the swift and (for America) relatively painless victory that was achieved. It arises not only from the possibility that this victory will prove a Pyrrhic one which, far from creating a new order in the Middle East, will induce only further instability by altering the balance of power in the region and creating even greater anti-Western resentment. More generally, the danger of victory lies in any illusion it may create in the USA as to its power to dominate the contemporary world. If the USA were, in effect, to rely on a form of imperial tribute to mask its internal weaknesses and maintain a leading world role, it would inevitably be driven into repressive and exploitative policies which would make the retribution and decline all the more extreme and ugly when it occurred; and occur it would, since little can be more certain than that the rest of the world would not tolerate such an anachronistic imperium. The danger, therefore, is that success in the Gulf will lead the USA not into accepting the reduced role in world affairs its relative decline demands, but instead into a desperate strategy of compensation and overreach which will ultimately prove more damaging to the world and to American influence in it.

That the potential for such a degeneration of America's role in the world exists cannot be denied; but on further examination the danger appears exaggerated and a more optimistic prognosis is in order. If we reconsider the problem of domestic weakness, the importance of social inequality for America's world role may be questioned. Inequality is hardly a new phenomenon, and the continuing deprivation of black Americans, for example, has had little discernible effect in undermining America's role in the post-war world. It may be a harsh truth, but the connection between the two spheres is not established by recent historical experience. More importantly, it is essential to recognize the kind of society the USA is: much of its dramatic inequality stems from its nature as an immigrant society. Many of the indices of poverty and apparent social pathology are distorted by the presence of large recent immigrant populations. This is not to justify their circumstances, but it is to remind ourselves that immigration has been historically more a source of dynamism and vitality in American society than any token of degeneration, and this despite the inequality which inevitably accompanies it. International comparisons can therefore be misleading, since the USA is a continental society that carries an internal Third World dimension, whereas Japan, for example, is much more homogeneous.

This point is equally valid in respect of economic comparisons. The diversity of the American economy, which includes low-wage, relatively primitive enclaves, for example around the Texas–Mexico border, can give a misleading impression of weakness if comparisons with more homogeneous advanced economies are made solely on the basis of average indicators. Inferiority on these does not necessarily imply that the USA is uncompetitive in the more advanced sectors. Indeed, this form of diversity has its strengths, notably in ensuring a continuing supply of cheap labour for both manufacturing and service sectors; the difficulties that the Japanese economy is running into are instructive in this context. None of this is to deny that the USA must find an appropriate niche in the world economy, and that at each level of its economy it must be competitive. But assessment of this positioning must take account of the variegated nature of the American economy, the continuing capacity of which to sustain both advanced and developing sectors can be viewed as a source of resilience and strength, rather than implying weakness in comparison with other countries which focus their energies more exclusively on the advanced sectors.

The broader implications of this reassessment of domestic weakness are to suggest that America has little need to try to compensate for it by a dangerous strategy seeking dominance through mercantilism and military power. A degree of strategic political intervention both to modify market forces domestically and to support national economic interests abroad would be desirable. The USA is no longer strong enough to stand above the fray while other countries intervene to support their national economic interests, and the ardour with which the interests of US firms in rebuilding the Gulf have been supported by the American government indicate that this lesson has been learned abroad at least. But this is quite a different matter from acting to undercut the fundamental principles of free trade as the preferred basis for the world economic order. US interests remain attached to the free movement of capital, goods and services because it is in their operation that America's best hope for world leadership lies. There is thus no necessary contradiction between American national interests and those of the developing international capitalist class. On the contrary there is scope for co-operation between the two, since private interests cannot operate effectively on a global scale without the political guarantees of stability that the US state is in the best position to deliver.

In respect of other capitalist powers too there is ample scope for co-operation based on a division of labour rather than mutually destructive antagonism, and for essentially the same reason that other nations need the stability that the United States is uniquely equipped to provide. The American deficit on international payments and its consequent debtor status is revealing in this respect. It has frequently been seen as an indicator of potential conflict because it has to be financed by the other capitalist powers and this creates a degree of dependency not compatible with world leadership. There are undoubtedly limits to this process, but the political stability of the USA has made it a safe haven for capital, and as other powers come to invest more and more in the US economy they develop less and less interest in damaging it. There is clearly a basis here for a constructive division of labour in which the American contribution to the common interest of securing the extension of capitalism through the globe is primarily political and where necessary military; if one consequence of this is an economic imbalance, then other, wealthier countries are likely to remain only too willing to finance it as a price to be paid for a secure world environment.

The point is that this would amount to a genuine division of labour based on mutual interest and not a prop for a decrepit giant and it would therefore be a sustainable basis for international affairs. But it would require acknowledgement of mutual dependency rather than any attempt by the USA to extract tribute for military dominance. This would of itself place limits on US ambitions and undercut the possibility of imperial hubris. It would also require the USA to acknowledge that, although it has a distinctive and leading contribution to make to the new world order, interdependence combined with America's own strengths and weaknesses mean it cannot be an all dominating one. Its critical contribution lies in the management of the globalization process and therefore a willingness to adapt and to seek collaboration rather than domination as the motif of policy. Only if this is understood will the USA secure its place as the first nation among equals in the 1990s.

From this perspective the American handling of the Gulf crisis bodes well. It demonstrates clearly that, notwithstanding its economic vulnerability, the USA remains the only country in the world capable of providing the leadership such a crisis demands. It is the fact that fundamental economic interests have been threatened by the prospect of Iraqi domination of the Gulf, not just for the USA but for world capitalism at large, that has determined the uncompromising American response, not any imperial ambition on its part. And it is a measure of the gravity of the threat that what had appeared to be the byword of US policy after Vietnam was forsaken: committing *matériel*, but not risking the lives of its troops to fight others' battles except in cases where the risk was minimal and the glory easily won, such as the Grenada and Panama invasions. Equally, the other lesson of Vietnam, never to send troops into battle with one hand tied behind their back, as it is commonly phrased, was echoed throughout the conflict. But what the Gulf war illustrates with great clarity is both how essential political and military capacity are to the defence of economic interests, and just how dependent international capitalism remains on America to defend these interests. This is all the more true in a period of transition between the old order and the new when the parameters of action are not clearly defined. It is the process of establishing what the limits of the acceptable will be in this new order that the Gulf war was at least in part about.

American leadership has been facilitated by Soviet decline, but even so the decisiveness of the American action in building a coalition under United Nations auspices and holding it together up to and beyond the advent of war is impressive testimony to its awareness of the requirements of, and capacity for, leadership in a post-hegemonic, multipolar world. The firm reaction of the USA to the threat not only to its interests but to the stability of the capitalist world suggests that it possesses the will to adopt the leadership role required of it. Equally important, however, is the fact that American leadership was carried out by consensus rather than by military adventurism. A coalition of remarkable breadth was painstakingly constructed and sustained throughout the conflict, and its solidarity not only enhanced the power of the military force brought to bear, but it also helped to convince Iraq that victory was not possible. Whether or not this consensus is maintained in rebuilding the Gulf, its success in prosecuting the war must help to convince American government that this consensual approach yields better and more sustainable results. It would be naive to suppose that in future crises such a widespread coalition could always be constructed, since the common interest will rarely be so apparent, but the lessons of the Gulf will remain valid if the USA continues to tailor the widest possible consensus in each crisis and creates a pattern of shifting coalitions to manage world affairs whose common feature is to retain the USA at their centre.

In conclusion, the 1990s will see a shift in the balance between politics and economics in international affairs. A world bifurcated into competing capitalist and communist camps, with all the attendant hostility and danger of nuclear annihilation, will recede. In this world the American role was hegemonic in relation to the capitalist sphere and principal antagonist in respect of the communist one, its pre-eminence assured. As the globalization of capitalism creates a world unified around the principles of market economies, the American role must either evolve or decline, since the threats to its position are substantial. Its dominance will be threatened by the absence of a single fault-line of hostility which made so many countries dependent on its nuclear protection. The liberating effect of the globalization of capitalism also threatens to create new economic powers with which the USA will be unable to compete. The breakdown of bipolarity could lead to the development of new allegiances which may coalesce into alliances, creating new power blocs that leave the USA marginalized.

A new politics will be required to ensure that the common interests in the capitalist system are translated into international co-operation, rather than allowing the competitive tensions inherent in capitalism to produce destructive levels of national conflict and exploitation as the dominant characteristic of this new order. It is the dynamic for expansion, to which the Marxist theory draws our attention, that presents the best hope of avoiding the realist nightmare of international anarchy in a post-hegemonic era. But the Marxist and realist theories of capitalism and nation-states respectively, taken together with the lessons of twentieth-century history, demonstrate the dangers involved and the difficulty of constructing a political framework within which the progressive aspects of capitalism can be allowed to work themselves out on a world-wide scale. If the underlying dynamic of globalization favours the development of a world economic system based on a judicious balance of competition and co-operation, of nationalism and internationalism, then internationalization of the capitalist economy must add a new dimension to world affairs; it cannot replace national aspirations and interests, but must act as a counterweight preventing them from degenerating into antagonism, and reflecting the collective interest without suppressing national identity or function. This will require a gyroscopic agency which can act as a stabilizer at the centre of a more pluralist international system based on shifting alliances. This is the role that the USA is best equipped to fulfil, and it is one which potentially offers greater influence than its previous one of hegemon in a more circumscribed capitalist world.

Management of complex interdependence will be necessary to establish the balance between consensus and conflict in this plural system. Its task will be to avoid the descent into the anarchy of national competition predicted by some realist theorists, a threat which will continue to exist just below the surface of even a single world economic system. But it will have to be achieved through the agency of existing nation-states, if only because the alternative of a legitimate and omnipotent world government is utopian. Further, it will need to be based more on neo-liberal principles of strategic intervention in markets than on any concept of welfare corporatism that dominated the post-war consensus, if it is to preserve the mobility of factors of production that is the essence of an efficient market system. The growing coherence of an informal transnational hegemonic bloc located in multinational corporations, academia and national and international political institutions will provide a significant resource in facilitating the management of global capitalism. But while it can influence nation-states, it can never replace their political contribution to the creation of a stable environment in which capital can expand and prosper. And although internationalization will produce new patterns of power among nation-states, successful management of the global economy involving the creative interplay of national and collective interests will continue to require political leadership. The United States is uniquely equipped to take the lead in the management of complex interdependence not just because of its own combination of attributes as a world power, but also because its own national interest corresponds to this goal.

The implication for American policy is therefore that the USA should clearly embrace globalization and help fashion it to the higher purpose of co-operation and prosperity, rather than retreating into an isolationist or mercantilist mentality which seeks only narrow sectional advantage and rejects any responsibility for the wider political framework of the global economy. It was during America's hegemonic phase that the groundwork for globalization was laid, since it was the universalism of systemic reproduction that provided the legitimacy underpinning America's hegemonic appeal. To reject the consequences of its own success and resist the transformation it has helped bring about would therefore betray these universal principles and would certainly do nothing to preserve American hegemony beyond its natural life. To restate the case rather less idealistically, American national interest in the post-war world has been identified with the expansion of capitalism, and its policies have been driven by the law of value and the logic of capital accumulation it entails. To desert that logic because it has outgrown American ability to control it would be folly, since US national interests remain tied to the expansion and development of the capitalist system on a global scale.

The adoption of a positive attitude to globalization as an opportunity to maintain American influence in the world should not distract from the adjustments this will require, since the 1990s do not offer the prospect of a simple continuation of American hegemony. The USA will maximize its power by accepting some diminution of it: it will need to show flexibility in relinquishing the domination over its allies that economic and military supremacy gave it in the post-war era in order to cultivate a role as first among equals within a more collaborative framework of international relations. This does not mean that it will have to confine itself to hegemony in the Americas, ceding equal status to Japan in Asia and Germany in Europe, as some have suggested. Globalization will not permit such neat divisions of influence, and the USA remains the only power capable of operating on a scale commensurate with the process. It will, however, have to accept the disciplines of free trade and avoid the temptations of protectionism to which its relative economic weakness will give rise. Since its domestic political system appears incapable of achieving the balance between consumption and investment necessary to international competitiveness, the external stimulus of open competition is the best hope of attaining it. Although, as we have seen, domestic weakness is easily exaggerated, it remains the case that unless more is done in this regard American pretensions to world leadership will be undermined.

If the USA is to retain its legitimacy and consensus as the basis for action across the wider span of the capitalist world, it will also have to avoid the identification with political oppression and exploitation which many of its policies have produced. The justification for these policies has been that they were a necessary evil in the fight against communism. The fixation on the communist menace warped American foreign policy by systematically playing down all other considerations and providing a justification for repression. This rationale was largely spurious and US interests could have been better protected had its foreign policy been more consistent with its claimed role as the embodiment of liberty and democracy. The point will become all the more pressing as the communist threat recedes and new principles of foreign policy have to be articulated. The fundamental principle which will best serve American interests is to take the lead in managing the extension of the capitalist system around the globe. The liberal approach to foreign policy, best exemplified by at least part of the Carter administration, may have been unrealistic in the circumstances of its time and inept in its execution, but its attempt to make morality and interest mutually reinforcing will take on new relevance in the 1990s.

If these adjustments are made, the transition from the era of hegemony will not signal a period of American decline. Rather than coming to an end, American hegemony will be transcended. Having given rise to a new era of global capitalism the fundamental conditions now exist for the United States to move on to a higher plane in which it will employ its unique combination of ideological legitimacy, cultural appeal, military strength, political will and economic power across a wider stage and become the primary shaping influence on a new world order. This will require it to demonstrate faith in its ability to capitalize on the opportunities presented by the new order, rather than allowing policy to be governed by fear of its dangers. The American century has not yet come to an end, and the extent to which it proves capable of taking the opportunities which the 1990s present will determine America's role in the post-modern world.

SELECT BIBLIOGRAPHY

Agee, P., *Inside the Company: CIA diary*, London: Penguin, 1975.

Agee, P. and L. Wolf (eds.), *Dirty Work: The CIA in Western Europe*, London: Lyle Stuart, 1978.

Agnew, J., *The United States and the World Economy*, Cambridge: Cambridge University Press, 1987.

Alperovitz, G., *Atomic Diplomacy: Hiroshima and Potsdam*, London: Secker & Warburg, 1966.

Anderson, P., 'The figures of descent', *New Left Review*, 161, Jan.–Feb. 1987, pp. 20–77.

Anderson, P., 'The origins of the present crisis', *New Left Review*, 23, Jan.–Feb. 1964, pp. 26–53.

Arendt, H., *The Origins of Totalitarianism*, London: Allen & Unwin, 1958.

Aron, R., *The Imperial Republic*, Englewood Cliffs, NJ: Prentice Hall, 1974.

Arrighi, G., *The Geometry of Imperialism: The limits of Hobson's paradigm*, London: New Left Books, 1978.

Artis, M. and S. Ostry, 'International economic policy coordination', Chatam House Papers, no. 30, London: Royal Institute of International Affairs/Routledge, 1986.

Augelli, E. and C. Murphy, *America's Quest for Supremacy and the Third World*, London, Pinter, 1988.

Baran, P. and P. Sweezy, *Monopoly Capital*, Harmondsworth: Penguin, 1968.

Barnet, A.D., *China Policy: Old problems and new challenges*, Washington, DC: Brookings, 1977.

Barnet, R. *Allies: America, Europe and Japan since the war*, London: Cape, 1983.

Barone, C.A., *Marxist Thought on Imperialism: Survey and critique*, London: Macmillan, 1985.

Barratt-Brown, M. *The Economics of Imperialism*, London: Penguin, 1974.

Begg, D., S. Fischer and R. Dornbush, *Economics*, London: McGraw-Hill, 1987, 2nd edn.

Bell, C., *The Diplomacy of Detente: The Kissinger era*, London: Robertson, 1977.

Bell, C., *The Reagan Paradox: American foreign policy in the 1980s*, Aldershot: Elgar, 1989.

Bell, D., *The End of Ideology: On the exhaustion of political ideas*, New York: Free Press, 1960.

Bell, D., *Marxian Socialism in the United States*, Princeton, NJ: Princeton University Press, 1967.

Bertram, C., 'The implications of theater nuclear weapons in Europe', *Foreign Affairs*, 60, 2, winter 1981–2, pp. 305–26.

Bhagwati, J.N. (ed.), *The New International Economic Order: The North–South debate*, Cambridge, Mass.: MIT Press, 1977.

Bialer, S. and M. Mandelbaum (eds.), *Gorbachev's Russia and American Foreign Policy*, Boulder, Colo.: Westview, 1988.

Bleaney, M., *Underconsumption Theories: A history and critical analysis*, London: Lawrence & Wishart, 1976.

Bobbitt, P., L. Freedman and G. Treverton (eds.), *US Nuclear Strategy: A reader*, London: Macmillan, 1989.

Bonner, R., *Waltzing with a Dictator: The Marcoses and the making of American policy*, London: Macmillan, 1987.

Brandt, W., *North–South: A programme for survival – report*, London: Pan, 1980.

Brenner, R., 'The origins of capitalist development: A critique of neo-Smithian Marxism', *New Left Review*, 104, July–Aug. 1977, pp. 25–93.

Brewer, A., *Marxist Theories of Imperialism: A critical survey*, London: Routledge, 1980.

Briodine, V. and M. Selden (eds.), *Open Secret: The Kissinger–Nixon Doctrine in Asia*, New York: Harper, 1972.

Brown, S., *The Faces of Power: Constancy and change in United States foreign policy from Truman to Reagan*, New York: Columbia University Press, 1983.

Brzezinski, Z., *Power and Principle: Memoirs of a national security adviser 1977–81*, London: Weidenfeld and Nicholson, 1983.

Brzezinski, Z., 'Post-communist nationalism', *Foreign Affairs*, 68, 5, winter 1989–90, pp. 1–25.

Buiter, W.H. and R.C. Marston (eds.), *International Economic Policy Coordination*, Cambridge: Cambridge University Press, 1985.

Bukharin, N., *Imperialism and the Accumulation of Capital* (ed. K. Tarbuck), London: Allen Lane, 1972.

Bukharin, N., *Imperialism and the World Economy*, London: Merlin, 1972.

Bundy, McG., G.F. Kennan, R.S. McNamara and G. Smith, 'Nuclear weapons and the Atlantic alliance', *Foreign Affairs*, 60, 4, winter 1982, pp. 753–68.

Bundy, W.P., 'Dictatorship and American foreign policy', *Foreign Affairs*, 54, 1, Oct. 1975, pp. 51–60.

Burrowes, R.A., *Revolution and Rescue in Grenada: An account of the US Caribbean invasion*, New York: Greenwood, 1988.

Calleo, D., *Beyond American Hegemony: The future of the Western alliance*, New York: Basic Books, 1987.

Calleo, D., *The Imperious Economy*, Cambridge, Mass.: Harvard University Press, 1982.

Calleo, D. and B. Rowland, *America and the World Political Economy*, Bloomington, Ind.: Indiana University Press, 1973.

Camps, M., '"First World" relationships: the role of the OECD', Atlantic Paper, no. 2, Paris: Atlantic Institute for International Affairs, 1975.

Cardoso, F.H. and E. Faletto, *Dependency and Development in Latin America*, Berkeley, Calif.: University of California Press, 1979.

Cerny, P.G., 'Political entropy and American decline', *Millennium*, 18, 1, 1989, pp. 47–63.

Charlton, M., *The Star Wars History: From detente to defence – the American strategic debate*, London: BBC Publications, 1986.

Chilcote, R.H. and D.L. Johnson (eds.), *Theories of Underdevelopment: Modes of production or dependency*, Beverly Hills, Calif.: Sage, 1983.

Chomsky, N. *American Power and the New Mandarins*, London: Chatto, 1969.

Chomsky, N., *Human Rights and American Foreign Policy*, London: Spokesman, 1978.

Chomsky, N., *Towards a New Cold War*, London: Sinclair Browne, 1982.

Chomsky, N., *Turning the Tide: US intervention in Central America and the struggle for peace*, London: Pluto, 1985.

Chomsky, N. and E. Hermann, *Manufacturing Consent*, New York: Pantheon, 1988.

Chomsky, N. and E. Herman, *The Political Economy of Human Rights. Vol. 1 The Washington Connection and Third World Fascism. Vol. 2 After the Cataclysm: Postwar Indochina and the reconstruction of imperial ideology*, Boston, Mass.: South End Press, 1979.

Chomsky, N., J. Steele and J. Gittings, *Superpowers in Collision: The cold war now*, Harmondsworth: Penguin, 1982.

Cleva, G.D., *Henry Kissinger and the American Approach to Foreign Policy*, Lewisburg, PA: Bucknell University Press, 1989.

Cockburn, L., *Out of Control: The story of the Reagan administration's secret war in Nicaragua*, London: Bloomsbury, 1988.

Coker, C., *Reflections on American Foreign Policy since 1945*, London: Pinter, 1989.

Cohen, G.A., *Karl Marx's Theory of History: A defence*, London: Oxford University Press, 1979.

Cohen, G.A., 'Marxism and functional explanation', in J. Roemer (ed.), *Analytical Marxism*, London: Cambridge University Press, 1986.

Cooper, R.C., 'Economic interdependence and foreign policy in the 70s', *World Politics*, 24, Jan. 1972, pp. 159–81.

Cox, M., 'Whatever happened to the "Second Cold War"? Soviet–American relations: 1980–88', *Review of International Studies*, 16, 2, Apr. 1990, pp. 155–72.

Cox, R.W., 'Gramsci, hegemony and international relations: an essay in method', *Millennium*, 12, 2, 1983, pp. 162–75.

Crawford, A., *Thunder on the Right*, New York: Pantheon, 1980.

Dahl, R., *Pluralist Democracy in the United States: Conflict and consent*, New York: Rand McNally, 1967.

Davis, M., *Prisoners of the American Dream*, London: Verso, 1986.

Deschamps, L., 'The SDI and European security interests', Atlantic Paper, no. 62, London: Croom Helm, 1987.

Dickson, P.W., *Kissinger and the Meaning of History*, Cambridge, Cambridge University Press, 1978.

Divine, R.A. (ed.), *The Cuban Missile Crisis*, Chicago, Ill.: Quadrangle, 1971.

Divine, R.A., *Eisenhower and the Cold War*, New York: Oxford University Press, 1981.

Dixon, C.J. et al., *Multinational Corporations in the Third World*, London: Croom Helm, 1986.

Dobson, A.P., *The Politics of the Anglo–American Special Relationship 1940–87*, Hemel Hempstead: Harvester Wheatsheaf, 1988.

Edsall, T., *The New Politics of Inequality*, New York: Norton, 1984.

Elster, J., 'Cohen on Marx's theory of history', *Political Studies*, 28, 1, Mar. 1980, pp. 121–8.

200 America in the modern world

Elster, J., *Making Sense of Marx*, Cambridge: Cambridge University Press, 1985.

Elster, J., 'Marxism, functionalism and game theory', *Theory and Society*, 2, July 1982, pp. 453–82.

Emmanuel, A., *Unequal Exchange: A study of the imperialism of trade*, London: New Left Books, 1972.

Etherington, N., *Theories of Imperalism: War, Conquest and Capital*, London: Croom Helm, 1984.

Evans, P., *Dependent Development: The alliance of multinational, state and local capital in Brazil*, Princeton, NJ: Princeton University Press, 1979.

Fairbank, J.K., *The United States and China*, Cambridge, Mass.: Harvard University Press, 1979, 4th edn.

Fann, K.T. and D.C. Hodges (eds.), *Readings in US Imperialism*, London: Porter Sargent, 1971.

Fieldhouse, D.K., *The Theory of Capitalist Imperialism*, London: Longman, 1967.

Foner, P.S., *The Spanish–Cuban–American War and the Birth of US Imperialism*, New York: Monthly Review Press, 1972, 2 vols.

Foot, R., *The Wrong War: American policy and the dimensions of the Korean conflict*, Ithaca, NY: Cornell University Press, 1985.

Frank, A.G., *Capitalism and Underdevelopment in Latin America*, New York: Monthly Review Press, 1967.

Freedman, L., *The Evolution of Nuclear Strategy*, London: Macmillan, 1981.

Freedman, L., *The Troubled Alliance: Atlantic relations in the 1980s*, London: Heinemann, 1983.

Friedman, B.M., *Day of Reckoning: The consequences of American economic policy under Reagan and after*, New York: Random House, 1988.

Friedman, M., *Capitalism and Freedom*, Chicago, Ill.: University of Chicago Press, 1962.

Friedman, M. and R. Friedman, *Free to Choose*, New York: Harcourt, 1980.

Fulbright, W., *The Arrogance of Power*, New York: Random House, 1966.

Gaddis, J.L., *The Long Peace: Inquiries into the history of the cold war*, New York: Oxford University Press, 1987.

Gaddis, J.L., *Russia, the Soviet Union and the United States: An interpretive history*, New York: McGraw-Hill, 1990.

Gaddis, J.L., *Strategies of Containment: A critical appraisal of postwar American national security policy*, New York: Oxford University Press, 1982.

Gardner, R.N., S. Okita and B.J. Udink, 'OPEC, the trilateral world and the developing countries: new arrangements for cooperation, 1976–80', Triangle Papers, no. 7, New York: Trilateral Commission, 1975.

Garson, R., 'The rise and rise of American exceptionalism', *Review of International Studies*, 16, 2, April 1990, pp. 173–9.

Garthoff, R.L., *Detente and Confrontation: American–Soviet Relations from Nixon to Reagan*, Washington: Brookings, 1985.

Garthoff, R.L., *Reflections on the Cuban Missile Crisis*, Washington: Brookings, 1989, revised edn.

Geiger, T., *The Future of the International System: The United States and the world political economy*, Boston, Mass.: Unwin Hyman, 1988.

Gelb, L and R.K. Betts, *The Irony of Vietnam: The system worked*, Washington, Brookings, 1979.

Gilder, G., *Wealth and Poverty*, New York: Basic Books, 1981.

Gill, S., *American Hegemony and the Trilateral Commission*, Cambridge: Cambridge University Press, 1990.

Gill, S., 'US hegemony: its limits and prospects in the Reagan era', *Millennium*, 15, 3, 1986, pp. 311–36.

Gill, S. and D. Law, *The Global Political Economy*, Hemel Hempstead, Harvester Wheatsheaf, 1988.

Gilpin, R., 'The multinational corporation and American foreign policy', in R. Rosencrance (ed.), *America as an Ordinary Country: US foreign policy and the future*, Ithaca, NY: Cornell University Press, 1976.

Gilpin, R., *The Political Economy of International Relations*, Princeton, NJ: Princeton University Press, 1987.

Gilpin, R., 'The richness of the tradition of political realism', *International Organisation*, 38, 1984, pp. 287–304.

Gilpin, R., *US Power and the Multinational Corporation*, New York: Basic Books, 1975.

Gilpin, R., *War and Change in World Politics*, Cambridge: Cambridge University Press, 1981.

Godson, J. (ed.), *Challenges to the Western Alliance*, London: Times Books, 1984.

Gordon, D., 'The global economy: new edifice or crumbling foundations?', *New Left Review*, 168, Mar.–Apr. 1988, pp. 24–64.

Graebner, N.A. (ed.), *The Cold War: Ideological conflict or power struggle?*, London: Heath, 1963.

Graebner, N.A. (ed.), *Manifest Destiny*, New York: Bobbs Merrill, 1968.

Graham, E.M. and P.M. Kruger, *Foreign Direct Investment in the US*, Washington, DC: Institute for International Economics, 1989.

Gravell, M. (ed.), *The Pentagon Papers: The Defense Department's history of the United States decision making on Vietnam*, Boston, Mass.: Beacon, 1971.

Grunberg, I., 'Exploring the "myth" of hegemonic stability', *International Organisation*, 44, 4, autumn 1990, pp. 431–77.

Guhin, M.A., *John Foster Dulles: A statesman and his times*, New York: Columbia University Press, 1972.

Haftendorn, H. and J. Schissler (eds.), *The Reagan Administration: A reconstruction of American strength?*, Berlin: Walter de Gruyter, 1988.

Halberstam, D., *The Best and the Brightest*, London: Barrie, 1972.

Halberstam, D., *The Reckoning*, New York: Morrow, 1986.

Halliday, F., 'The ends of cold war', *New Left Review*, 180, Mar.–Apr. 1990, pp. 5–24.

Halliday, F., *Iran: Dictatorship and development*, Harmondsworth: Penguin, 1979.

Halliday, F., *The Making of the Second Cold War*, London: New Left Books, 1983.

Harriss, N., *The End of the Third World: The newly industrialising countries and the decline of an ideology*, Harmondsworth: Penguin, 1987.

Havighurst, A.F. (ed.), *The Pirenne Thesis: Analysis, criticism and revision*, Lexington, Mass.: Heath, 1976, 3rd edn.

Hayek, F., *The Road to Serfdom*, London: Routledge, 1944.

Healy, D., *US Expansionism: The imperialist urge in the 1890s*, Madison, Wisc.: University of Wisconsin Press, 1970.

Hellman, R.G. and J.H. Rosenbaum (eds.), *Latin America: The search for a new international role*, New York: Wiley, 1975.

Hermann, C.F., C.W. Kegly, Jr and J.N. Rosenau (eds.), *New Directions in the*

Study of Foreign Policy, Boston, Mass.: Unwin Hyman, 1987.

Hersh, S., *Kissinger: The price of power – Henry Kissinger in the Nixon White House*, London: Faber, 1983.

Higgins, T., *The Perfect Failure: Kennedy, Eisenhower and the CIA at the Bay of Pigs*, New York: Norton, 1987.

Hobson, J.A., *Imperialism: A study*, London: Nisbet, 1902.

Hodgart, A., *The Economics of European Imperialism*, London: Edward Arnold, 1977.

Hofstadter, R., *The Paranoid Style in American Politics and Other Essays*, New York: Knopf, 1965.

Holland, H.M., *Managing Diplomacy: The United States and Japan*, Stanford, Calif.: Hoover Institute, Stanford University, 1984.

Honeywell, M. (ed.), *The Poverty Brokers: The IMF and Latin America*, London: Latin American Bureau, 1983.

Horowitz, D., *From Yalta to Vietnam: American foreign policy in the cold war*, Harmondsworth: Penguin, 1967.

Huntington, S.P., 'The US: decline or renewal?', *Foreign Affairs*, 67, 2, winter 1988, pp. 76–96.

Ikenberry, J., D.A. Lake and M. Mastanduno (eds.), *The State and American Foreign Policy*, Ithaca: Cornell University Press, 1988.

International Monetary Fund, *Balance of Payments Statistics Yearbook*, Washington, DC: IMF.

Iriye, A. and W. Cohen (eds.), *The United States and Japan in the Postwar World*, Lexington, KY: University of Kentucky Press, 1989.

Isaacson, W. and E. Thomas, *The Wise Men: Six friends and the world they made*, London: Faber, 1986.

James, W.E., S. Naya and G.M. Meier, *Asian Development: Economic success and policy lessons*, Madison, Wisc.: University of Wisconsin Press, 1989.

Jervis, R., *The Illogic of American Nuclear Strategy*, Ithaca, NY: Cornell University Press, 1984.

Joffe, J., 'Europe's American pacifier', *Foreign Policy*, 54, spring 1984, pp. 64–82.

Jones, C.A., *The North–South Dialogue: A brief history*, London: Pinter, 1983.

Kaldor, M., *The Disintegrating West*, London: Allen Lane, 1978.

Karabel, J., 'The failure of American socialism reconsidered', *Socialist Register*, 1979, pp. 204–27.

Kautsky, K., 'Ultra-imperialism', *New Left Review*, 59, Jan.–Feb. 1970, originally published in German, 1914.

Keegan, W., *Mrs Thatcher's Economic Experiment*, Harmondsworth: Penguin, 1985.

Kemp, T., *Theories of Imperialism*, London: Dobson, 1967.

Kennan, G., *American Diplomacy*, Chicago, Ill.: University of Chicago Press, 1984, expanded edn.

Kennan, G., 'The US and the Soviet Union, 1917–76', *Foreign Affairs*, 54, 4, summer 1976, pp. 670–90.

Kennan, G.F. *et al.*, *Encounters with Kennan*, London: Cass, 1979.

Kennan, G.F. *et al.*, *Decline of the West: George Kennan and his critics* (ed. M.F. Herz), Washington, DC: Ethics and Public Policy Center, Georgetown University, 1978.

Kennedy, J.F., 'Commencement address at the American University, Washington, June 10, 1963', *Public Papers of the Presidents of the United States: John F. Kennedy, 1963*, pp. 459–64.

Kennedy, P., *The Rise and Fall of the Great Powers: Economic change and military conflict from 1500–2000*, London: Unwin Hyman, 1988.

Keohane, R., *After Hegemony: Cooperation and discord in the world political economy*, Princeton, NJ: Princeton University Press, 1984.

Kiernan, V.G., *America, the New Imperialism: From white settlement to world hegemony*, London: Zed, 1978.

Kiernan, V.G., *Marxism and Imperialism: Studies*, London: Edward Arnold, 1974.

Kimball, J.P., *To Reason Why: The debate about the causes of US involvement in the Vietnam war*, New York: McGraw-Hill, 1990.

Kindleberger, C., 'Dominance and leadership in the international economy: exploitation, public goods and free rides', *International Studies Quarterly*, xxv, 1981, pp. 242–54.

King, A.D., *Global Cities: Post-imperialism and the internationalisation of London*, London: Routledge, 1989.

King, K., 'US monetary policy and the European responses in the 1980s', Chatam House Papers, no. 16, Royal Institute of International Affairs/Routledge, 1982.

Kirkpatrick, J., 'Dictatorships and double standards', *Commentary*, 68, 5, Nov. 1979, pp. 34–45.

Kirkpatrick, J., 'US security and Latin America', *Commentary*, 71, 1, Jan. 1981, pp. 29–40.

Kissinger, H., *American Foreign Policy*, New York: Norton, 1977, 3rd edn.

Kissinger, H., *The White House Years*, Boston, Mass.: Little Brown, 1979.

Knudsen, B.B., 'Europe versus America: Foreign policy in the 1980s', Atlantic Paper, no. 56, Paris: Atlantic Institute for International Affairs, 1984.

Kolko, G. and J. Kolko, *The Limits of Power: The world and US foreign policy 1945–54*, New York: Harper & Row, 1972.

Kolko, G., *Vietnam: Anatomy of a war 1940–75*, London: Allen & Unwin, 1986.

Kolkowicz, R. (ed.), *Dilemmas of Nuclear Strategy*, London: Cass, 1987.

Krasner, S.D., 'State power and the structure of international trade', *World Politics*, xxviii, 1976, pp. 317–47.

Krasner, S.D., *Structural Change: The Third World against global liberalism*, Berkeley, Calif.: University of California Press, 1985.

Lafeber, W., *America, Russia and the Cold War, 1945–84*, New York: Wiley, 1985, 5th edn.

Latham, E. (ed.), *The Meaning of McCarthyism*, Lexington, Mass.: Heath, 1973, 2nd edn.

Lekachman, F., *Greed Is Not Enough: Reaganomics*, New York: Pantheon, 1982.

Lenin, V.I., 'Imperialism, the highest stage of capitalism', in *Selected Works*, vol. 1, Moscow: Foreign Languages Publishing House, 1950.

Lever, H. and C. Huhne, *Debt and Danger: The world financial crisis*, Harmondsworth: Penguin, 1985.

Levinson, J. and J. de Onis (eds.), *The Alliance That Lost Its Way: A critical report on the Alliance for Progress*, Chicago, Ill.: Quadrangle, 1970.

Linderman, G.F., *The Mirror of War: American society and the Spanish–American war*, Ann Arbor, Mich.: University of Michigan Press, 1974.

Lipsey, R.G., *An Introduction to Positive Economics*, London: Weidenfeld & Nicolson, 1989, 7th edn.

Litwak, R., *Detente and the Nixon Doctrine: American foreign policy and the pursuit of stability 1969–76*, Cambridge: Cambridge University Press, 1984.

Louis, W.R. (ed.), *Imperialism: The Robinson and Gallagher controversy*, London: New Viewpoints, 1976.

Luxemburg, R., *The Accumulation of Capital*, London: Routledge, 1951.

Luxemburg, R., 'The accumulation of capital: an anti-critique', in N. Bukharin, *Imperialism and the Accumulation of Capital* (ed. K. Tarbuck), London: Allen Lane, 1972.

McClintock, M., *The American Connection: State terror and popular resistance in El Salvador*, London: Zed, 1985.

McNamara, R., *Blundering into Disaster: Surviving the first century of the nuclear age*, London: Bloomsbury, 1987.

Magdoff, H., *The Age of Imperialism: The economics of US foreign policy*, New York: Monthly Review Press, 1969.

Magdoff, H., 'How to make a molehill out of a mountain', *Insurgent Sociologist*, 7, 2, spring 1977, pp. 106–12.

Magdoff, H., 'The logic of imperialism', *Social Policy*, 1, 2, 1970, pp. 20–9.

Mandel, E., *Europe vs America?: Contradictions of imperialism*, London: New Left Books, 1970.

Mandelbaum, M., 'Ending the cold war', *Foreign Affairs*, 68, 2, spring 1989, pp. 16–36.

Mandelbaum, M., *The Nuclear Future*, Ithaca, NY: Cornell University Press, 1983.

Mandelbaum, M., *The Nuclear Question*, Cambridge: Cambridge University Press, 1979.

Marcuse, H., *One-Dimensional Man: Studies in the ideology of advanced industrial society*, London: Routledge, 1964.

Marshall, J., P.D. Scot and J. Hunter, *Iran-Contra: Secret wars and covert operations in the Reagan era*, Boston, Mass.: South End Press, 1987.

Martz, J.D. (ed.), *United States Policy in Latin America: A quarter century of crisis and challenge, 1961–86*, Lincoln, Nebr.: University of Nebraska Press, 1988.

Marx, K., 'The Eighteeneth Brumaire of Louis Napoleon', in *Selected Works*, London: Lawrence & Wishart, 1968.

Marx, K. and F. Engels, 'The manifesto of the Communist Party' in *Selected Works*, London: Lawrence & Wishart, 1968.

Mattelart, A., *Multinational Corporations and the Control of Culture: The ideological apparatuses of imperialism*, Hemel Hempstead: Harvester Wheatsheaf, 1979.

Melman, S., *The Permanent War Economy: American capitalism in decline*, New York: Simon & Schuster, 1974.

Miles, M.W., *The Odyssey of the American Right*, New York: Oxford University Press, 1980.

Miller, S.M., R. Bennett and C. Alapatt, 'Does the US economy require imperialism?', *Social Policy*, 1, 2, 1970, pp. 13–19.

Modelski, G. (ed.), *Transnational Corporations and World Order*, San Francisco, Calif.: Freeman, 1979.

Mommsen, W.J., *Theories of Imperialism,* London: Weidenfeld & Nicolson, 1981.

Moore, B., *The Social Origins of Dictatorship and Democracy: Lord and peasant in the making of the modern world*, Boston, Mass.: Beacon, 1966.

Morgan, H.W., *America's Road to Empire: The war with Spain and overseas expansion*, New York: Wiley, 1965.

Morgenthau, H.J., *Politics Among Nations: The struggle for power and peace*, New York: Knopf, 1948.

Mouffe, C. (ed.), *Gramsci and Marxist Theory*, London: Routledge, 1979.

Nau, H., *International Reaganomics: A domesticist approach to world economy*, Washington, DC: Georgetown Center for Strategic and International Studies, 1981.

Nearing, S. and J. Freeman, *Dollar Diplomacy: A study in American imperialism*, New York: Monthly Review Press, 1966.

Newell, N.P. and R.S. Newell, *The Struggle for Afghanistan*, Ithaca, NY: Cornell University Press, 1981.

Nixon, R.M., *The Memoirs of Richard Nixon*, London: Sidgwick, 1978.

Novak, M., *The Rise of the Unmeltable Ethnics*, New York: Macmillan, 1973.

Nowzad, B., *The International Monetary Fund and Its Critics*, Princeton, NJ: International Finance Section, Princeton University, 1982.

Nutter, G.W., *Kissinger's Grand Design*, Washington, DC: American Enterprise Institute, 1975.

Obey, D. and P. Sarbanes, *The Changing American Economy*, New York: Blackwell, 1986.

O'Brien, P. (ed.), *Allende's Chile*, New York: Praeger, 1976.

Olson, M., *The Rise and Decline of Nations: Economic growth, stagflation and social rigidities*, New Haven, Conn.: Yale University Press, 1982.

Olson, R.K., *US Foreign Economy and the New International Economic Order: Negotiating global problems 1974–81*, Greenwich, CT: Westview, 1981.

Owen, R. and R.B. Sutcliffe (eds.), *Studies in the Theory of Imperialism*, London: Longman, 1972.

Oye, K., D. Rothchild and R.J. Lieber (eds.), *Eagle Defiant: United States foreign policy in the 1980s*, Boston, Mass.: Little Brown, 1983.

Oye, K., D. Rothchild and R.J. Lieber (eds.), *Eagle Entangled: US foreign policy in a complex world*, New York: Longman, 1979.

Packenham, R., *Liberal America and the Third World: Political development ideas in foreign aid and social science*, Princeton, NJ: Princeton University Press, 1973.

Parboni, R., *The Dollar and Its Rivals: Recession, inflation and international finance*, London: New Left Books, 1981.

Parboni, R., 'The dollar weapon from Nixon to Reagan', *New Left Review*, 158, July–Aug. 1986, pp. 5–18.

Parsons, T. and N. Smelser, *Economy and Society: A study in the integration of economic and social theory*, London: Routledge, 1956.

Patterson, H.O., *Ethnic Chauvinism*, New York: Stein & Day, 1977.

Pearce, J., *Under the Eagle: US intervention in Central America and the Caribbean*, London: Latin American Bureau, 1982.

Peele, G., *Revival and Reaction: The right in contemporary America*, Oxford: Clarendon, 1984.

Petras, J., *The US and Chile: Imperialism and the overthrow of the Allende government*, New York: Monthly Review Press, 1975.

Petras, J. and R. Rhodes, 'The reconsolidation of US hegemony', *New Left Review*, 97, May–June 1976, pp. 35–53.

Pirenne, H., *A History of Europe from the Invasion to the 16th Century*, London: Allen & Unwin, 1939.

Pirenne, H., *Medieval Cities: Their Origins and the revival of trade*, Princeton, NJ: Princeton University Press, 1952.

Piven, F.F. and R.A. Cloward, *The New Class War: Reagan's attack on the welfare state and its consequences*, New York: Pantheon, 1982.

Podhoretz, N., 'The future danger', *Commentary*, 71, 4, Apr. 1981, pp. 29–47.

Podhoretz, N., 'The new American majority', *Commentary*, 71, 1, Jan. 1981, pp. 19–28.

Porter, M., *The Competitive Advantage of Nations*, London: Macmillan, 1990.

Poulantzas, N., *Classes in Contemporary Capitalism*, London: New Left Books, 1973.

Poulantzas, N., *Political Power and Social Classes*, London: New Left Books, 1973.

Ricardo, D., *On the Principles of Political Economy*, London: Dent, 1965.

Richardson, J.L., 'Cold war revisionism: a critique', *World Politics*, 24, 4, 1972, pp. 579–612.

Riddell, P., *The Thatcher Decade: How Britain has changed in the 1980s*, Oxford: Blackwell, 1989.

Robinson, R.E., J.A. Gallagher and A. Denny, *Africa and the Victorians: The official mind of imperialism*, London: Macmillan, 1961.

Rohatyn, F., 'America's economic dependence', *Foreign Affairs*, 68, 1, 1988/89, pp. 53–65.

Rosencrance, R. (ed.), *America as an Ordinary Country: US foreign policy and the future*, Ithaca, NY: Cornell University Press, 1976.

Rostow, W.W., *The Stages of Economic Growth: A non-communist manifesto*, Cambridge: Cambridge University Press, 1971, 2nd edn.

Rothstein, R.I., *The Third World and US Foreign Policy: Cooperation and conflict in the 80s*, Boulder, Colo.: Westview, 1981.

Rousseas, S., *The Political Economy of Reaganomics: A critique*, Armonk, NY: Sharpe, 1982.

Rowthorn, R., 'Imperialism in the 1970s', in H. Radice (ed.), *International Firms and Modern Imperialism*, Harmondsworth: Penguin, 1975.

Rubin, B., *Paved with Good Intentions: The American experience and Iran*, New York: Oxford University Press, 1980.

Russett, B., 'The mysterious case of vanishing hegemony: or, Is Mark Twain really dead?', *International Organisation*, 39, 2, spring 1985, pp. 207–31.

Sale, K., *Power Shift: The rise of the Southern Rim and its challenge to the Eastern establishment*, New York: Random House, 1975.

Samuelson, P.A. and W.D. Nordhaus, *Economics*, New York: McGraw-Hill, 1989, 13th edn.

Sau, R., *Unequal Exchange, Imperialism and Underdevelopment: An essay on the political economy of capitalism*, London: Oxford University Press, 1978.

Scammell, W., *The International Economy Since 1945*, London: Macmillan, 1989, 2nd edn.

Scheer, R., *With Enough Shovels: Reagan, Bush and nuclear war*, London: Secker, 1983.

Schlesinger, A.M. Jr, 'The cold war revisited', *New York Review of Books*, 10 Oct. 1979.

Schlesinger, A.M. Jr, *Robert F. Kennedy and his Times*, Boston, Mass.: Houghton Mifflin, 1979.

Schlesinger, A.M. Jr, *A Thousand Days: John F. Kennedy in the White House*, Boston, Mass.: Houghton Mifflin, 1965.

Schlesinger, S. and S. Kinzer, *Bitter Fruit: The untold story of the American coup in Guatemala*, London: Sinclair Browne, 1982.

Schmitt, H.O., 'Mercantilism: a modern argument', *The Manchester School*, 47, 2, June 1979, pp. 93–111.

Schumpeter, J.A., *Capitalism, Socialism and Democracy*, London: Allen & Unwin, 1987, 6th edn.

Schumpeter, J.A., *Imperialism and Social Classes* (ed. P. Sweezy), Oxford: Blackwell, 1951.

Schurrman, F., *The Logic of World Power*, New York: Random House, 1974.

Schwartz, D.N., *NATO's Nuclear Dilemmas*, Washington, DC: Brookings, 1983.

Secretaria de Relaciones Exteriores, *Cancun 1981: Framework, debate and conclusions of the meeting on international cooperation and development*, Mexico City 1982.

Shawcross, W., *Sideshow: Kissinger, Nixon and the destruction of Cambodia*, London: Hogarth, 1986, new edn.

Shoup, L. and W. Minter, *Imperial Brain Trust: The Council on Foreign Relations and United States foreign policy*, New York: Monthly Review Press, 1977.

Sigmund, P., 'Chile: what was the US role?', *Foreign Policy*, 18, fall 1974, pp. 142–66.

Singer, H. and J.A. Ansari, *Rich and Poor Countries: Consequences of International Disorder*, London: Unwin Hyman, 1989, fourth edn.

Sklar, H. (ed.), *Trilateralism: Elite Planning for World Management*, Boston: South End Press, 1980.

Skocpol, T., 'Political Responses to Capitalist Crisis: Neo-Marxist Theories of the State and the Case of the New Deal', *Politics and Society*, 10, 2, 1980, pp. 155–201.

Smith, A., *The Wealth of Nations*, Oxford, Clarendon, 1976.

Snidal, D., 'The Limits of Hegemonic Stability Theory', *International Organisation*, 39, 4, Autumn 1985, pp. 579–614.

Solomon, R., *The International Monetary System 1945–81*, New York: Harper, 1982, revised edn.

Sorensen, T., *Kennedy*, New York: Harper, 1965.

Southard, F.A., *The Evolution of the International Monetary Fund*, International Finance Section, Department of Economics, Princeton, NJ: Princeton University, 1979.

Spiegel, S.L., *The Other Arab–Israeli Conflict: Making America's Middle East policy from Truman to Reagan*, Chicago, Ill.: University of Chicago Press, 1985.

Steinfels, P., *The Neo-Conservatives*, New York: Simon & Schuster, 1980.

Stevenson, R.W., *The Rise and Fall of Detente: Relaxations of tension in US–Soviet relations 1953–84*, London: Macmillan, 1985.

Stewart, M., *The Age of Interdependence: Economic policy in a shrinking world*, Cambridge, Mass.: MIT Press, 1983.

Stockman, D., *The Triumph of Politics*, London: Bodley Head, 1986.

Strange, S., *Casino Capitalism*, Oxford: Blackwell, 1986.

Strange, S., 'The persistent myth of lost hegemony', *International Organisation*, 41, 4, autumn 1987, pp. 551–74.

Strange, S., 'Protectionism and world politics', *International Organisation*, 39, 2, spring 1985, pp. 233–59.

Sweezy, P.M. *et al.*, *The Transition from Feudalism to Capitalism*, London: New Left Books, 1976.

Szulc, T., *The Illusion of Peace: Foreign policy in the Nixon years*, New York: Viking, 1978.

Szymanski, A., 'Capital accumulation of a world scale and the necessity of imperialism', *Insurgent Sociologist*, 7, 2, spring 1977, pp. 35–53.

Szymanski, A., 'The decline and fall of the US eagle', *Social Policy*, 4, 5, 1974, pp. 5–13.

Szymanski, A., 'Is US imperialism resurgent?', *New Left Review*, 98, 101–2, Feb.–Mar. 1977, pp. 144–52.

Szymanski, A., *The Logic of Imperialism*, New York: Praeger, 1981.

Talbot, S., *Deadly Gambits: The Reagan administration and the stalemate in nuclear arms control*, New York: Knopf, 1984.

Terzian, P., *OPEC: The inside story*, London: Zed, 1985.

Tew, B., *The Evolution of the International Monetary System 1945–77*, London: Hutchinson, 1977.

Thompson, J.A., 'William Appleman Williams and the "American Empire"', *Journal of American Studies*, 7, 1, 1973, pp. 91–104.

Thornton, A., *Doctrines of Imperialism*, London: Wiley, 1965.

Treverton, G., *Making the Alliance Work: The US and Western Europe*, London: Macmillan, 1985.

Tsoukalis, L. (ed.), *The Political Economy of International Money*, London: Sage, 1985.

Ungar, S., *Estrangement: America and the World*, New York: Oxford University Press, 1985.

Valenta, J. and E. Duran (eds.), *Conflict in Nicaragua: A multidimensional perspective*, London: Allen & Unwin, 1987.

Vance, C., *Hard Choices: Critical years in America's foreign policy*, New York: Simon & Schuster, 1983.

Van der Pijl, K., *The Making of an Atlantic Ruling Class*, London: Verso, 1984.

Vernon, R., *Sovereignty at Bay*, New York: Basic Books, 1971.

Wallerstein, I., *The Capitalist World-Economy*, Cambridge: Cambridge University Press, 1979.

Wallerstein, I., *The Politics of the World-Economy*, Cambridge: Cambridge University Press, 1984.

Walton, R.J., *Cold War and Counter-Revolution: The foreign policy of John F. Kennedy*, Harmondsworth: Penguin, 1973.

Warren, B., *Imperialism: Pioneer of capitalism*, London: Verso, 1980.

Watson, A., 'Systems of states', *Review of International Studies*, 16, 2, Apr. 1990, pp. 99–110.

Watt, D.C., 'Rethinking the cold war', *Political Quarterly*, 49, Oct.–Dec. 1978, pp. 446–56.

Webb, M.C. and S.D. Krasner, 'Hegemonic stability theory: an empirical assessment', *Review of International Studies*, 15, 2, Apr. 1989, pp. 183–198.

Weisskopf, T., 'Theories of American imperialism: a critical evaluation', *Review of Radical Political Economics*, 6, 3, autumn 1974, pp. 41–60.

Welch, R.E. Jr (ed.), *Imperialists vs Anti-Imperialists: The debate over expansionism in the 1890s*, Itasca, Ill.: Peacock, 1972.

Williams, P., 'US–Soviet relations beyond the cold war?', *International Affairs*, 65, 2, spring 1989, pp. 273–88.

Williams, W.A. (ed.), *From Colony to Empire: Essays in the history of American foreign relations*, New York: Wiley, 1972.

Williams, W.A., *The Roots of the Modern American Empire: A study of the growth and shaping of social consciousness in a marketplace society*, New York: Random House, 1969.

Williams, W.A., *The Tragedy of Diplomacy*, New York: Dell, 1972, 2nd edn.

Wohlstetter, A. and R. Wohlstetter, 'Controlling the risks in Cuba', Adelphi Papers (April 1965), London: Institute for Strategic Studies, 1965.

Wolfe, A., 'The irony of anti-communism: ideology and interest in post-war American foreign policy', *Socialist Register*, 1984, pp. 214–29.

Wolfe, M. (ed.), *The Economic Causes of Imperialism*, London: Wiley, 1972.

Woodward, R. and C. Bernstein, *All the President's Men*, Quartet, London: 1974.

Woolf, L., *Economic Imperialism*, London: Swarthmore, 1921.

Wyden, P., *Bay of Pigs: The untold story*, New York: Simon & Schuster, 1979.

Yergin, D., *Shattered Peace: The origins of the cold war and the national security state*, New York: Houghton Mifflin, 1979.

Young, M.B. (ed.), *American Expansionism: The critical issues*, Boston, Mass.: Little Brown, 1973.

Zevin, R., 'An interpretation of American imperialism', *Journal of Economic History*, 32, 1, March 1972, pp. 316–60.

INDEX

Afghanistan,
  and the Carter administration, 148
  Soviet invasion of, 59, 82, 148, 157,
    185
Africa, 5, 146
Allende, Salvador, 104
anti-communism, 143
  and American ideology 41–2
  and Vietnam, 118
  and the cold war, 53–4
  and Jimmy Carter, 149
  and Richard Nixon, 59, 139
Argentina,
  relations with the US, 105
Aron, Raymond,
  and imperialism, 26
Asia,
  and American involvement, 111
  and economic development, 105–7
  and the world economy, 91
atomic bomb, 49
Ayatollah Khomeini, 147

Baker, James, 164
balance of power, 6, 7, 27, 35, 52, 117
balance of payments/trade, US, 32–4,
  69–70, 163, 185
Berlin blockade, 111
black Americans, 190
Brandt report, 135
Brazil,
  relations with the US, 105
brinkmanship, 111
Britain/United Kingdom,
  and empire, 2, 72, 90–1, 100
  Heath government, 150 n9
  macro-economic policy and overseas
    capital, 76, 87 n9
  and the origins of the cold war, 49
  Thatcher government, 150 n9, 172 n17
Brzezinski, Zbigniev, 152 n43

Bukharin, Nikolai, 11
Bush, George,
  administration of,
  and American decline, 186–7
  and Congress, 187
  and Eastern Europe, 187
  and relations with Japan, 187

Cambodia, 122, 126
Cancun conference, 162
Carter, Jimmy
  administration of, 144–50
  and Afghanistan, 148
  and Africa, 146–7
  and anti-communism, 149
  and the Camp David accords, 148
  and Chile, 148–9
  and détente, 59
  and human rights, 144
  and Iran, 147–8
  liberal approach to foreign affairs,
    196
  and the Trilateral Commission, 145
  and Vietnam, 126–8
Castro, Fidel, 113
CBS (Columbia Broadcasting System),
  and Japanese capital, 73
Central America,
  Contradora group, 166
  and European/American differences, 83
  and the Reagan administration, 165–6,
    185
Chile,
  American involvement in, 104–5
  and the Carter administration, 148–9
China,
  Chinese revolution, 48, 94, 111
  and détente, 138–9, 142, 143
  and the Nixon-Kissinger opening, 41
  Soviet relations, 48, 56, 117
CIA (Central Intelligence Agency), 26

Coca-Cola, 72
cold war,
 debate on the origins of, 46
comparative advantage, principle of, 2, 3,
  19, 20, 81, 90, 176
comprador classes,
 in the Third World, 102
Congress, the US,
 and 'burden sharing', 73
 and the Bush administration, 187
 and military expenditure, 38, 159
 and Watergate, 142,
containment,
 and American hegemony, 48–9, 56,
  111
 and *détente*, 57–60, 179
 and the Kennedy administration, 112
 and Soviet ideology, 51–2
corporatism, 80, 106
cruise missiles, 84, 167
Cuba,
 and American brinkmanship, 56
 Bay of Pigs, 112–13
 liberation movement, 94
 missile crisis, 183
  American handling of, 113–14
  Soviet reactions, 56, 114
Czechoslovakia,
 and the cold war, 47

dependency theory, 90–5, 181–2
dependent development, 101–4
détente,
 and American decline, 75, 137–42
 and China, 138–9
 and containment, 57–9, 179
 and the Nixon administration, 123–4,
  184
 weaknesses of, 59–60, 141–3, 184
Disney characters, 72
Dulles, John Foster, 111

Eastern Europe, 18
 and the Bush administration, 187
 and the cold war, 47
 and the collapse of communism, 60,
  179
 European and American attitudes to,
  82
 and the Reagan administration, 169
Egypt,
 and the Camp David accords, 148
Eisenhower, Dwight D.,
 administration of, 111–12
  Bay of Pigs, 113
El Salvador,
 and the Reagan administration, 166

environment, the
 global, 100
 Third World, 102
European Community,
 and defence, 74
 and the globalization of capitalism,
  79–80

favelas, 102
flexible response, concept of, 84–5
Ford, Gerald, R., 124
 administration of, 131
France, 76
free rider problem, 81
free trade, 2, 4, 34, 81, 134, 161, 188
Fulbright, Senator, William J., 127
functionalism,
 and American history, 25
 and Marxism, 23 n35
 and the theory of imperialism, 16, 19

GATT (General Agreement of Tarrifs
  and Trade), 78, 187
Germany,
 and American decline, 67, 180, 195
 and the domination of Europe, 62
 and military expenditure, 39
 and nuclear defence, 74
 and the world economy, 62
globalism/globalization of capitalism, 15,
  18, 20, 29, 34, 67, 68, 77–9, 85–6,
  89, 99, 145, 181–2, 184, 188,
  192–5
Goldwater, Barry, 154
Gorbachev, Mikhail, 171
Great War, 17, 18
Grenada,
 American invasion of, 40 127, 192
Guatemala,
 American intervention in, 112
Gulf, the,
 war, 175
  and American strategy, 189, 192–3
  and Iraqi domination, 192
  and post-war reconstruction, 191

Hanoi, 120
hegemony,
 American, 3, 4, 27, 29, 33, 34, 43, 68,
  178, 193–6
 benign, 15, 70
 and the Carter administration, 184–5
 and the decline of communism, 181
 and development, 108
 and economic decline, 180
 and the globalization of capitalism,
  77–8, 194

and the Gulf war, 175
and the origins of the cold war,
48–50
and the Third World, 163, 181–2
as tribute, 31
and imperialism, 32, 178
meaning of, 27–8
and multipolarity, 7, 67, 170, 178, 192
and stability, 26, 28
Hitler, Adolph, 47
Hobbes, Thomas, 5
Hobson, J.A.,
and the theory of imperialism, 9–10, 15
Hong Kong, 95, 105

ideology,
American, 40–2
and anti-communism, 140
and the cold war, 50
and the communist bloc, 117–8
and consensus, 47
and the Reagan administration, 158–9
and the Soviet Union, 51–4
and Vietnam, 126–7
IMF (International Monetary Fund), 78,
91, 92, 132
imperialism,
and American history, 24–26
and American ideology, 40–2
and capitalism, 2
definition of, 1
and the United States, 24
Hobson's theory of, 9–10
Marxist theories of, 2, 10–20, 29, 176
as applied to the US, 30–43, 176,
193
non-Marxist theories of, 2–8, 177
psychological basis of, 7–8
and Raymond Aron, 26
and the Soviet Union, 5, 18, 26, 55
and the Third World, 99
Indonesia, 106
International Energy Agency, 151 n20
internationalization of capitalism, 3,
14–15, 30, 67, 68, 77, 81, 159,
171, 175, 193
Iran,
American involvement in, 112
and the Carter administration, 147–8,
153, 185
-Contra affair, 166
and hostage taking, 59, 147
and the Nixon administration, 141,
143, 148
Shah of, 147, 148
Tehran, 148
Iraq, 189, 192

Islam, 158
isolationism,
and American ideology, 42
Israel,
and the Camp David accords, 148
and the Nixon administration, 141

Japan,
and American decline, 67, 69, 180,
188, 195
as part of the American sphere of
influence, 26
and the Bush administration, 187
and free trade, 82
and homogeneity, 190
as the inverse of the United States, 33
investment in the US, 30
and military expenditure, 39
as a model of economic development,
182
and the 1930s, 18
and the Nixon administration, 134–5
and nuclear defence, 74
and the Reagan administration, 159
and the origins of the cold war, 48, 49
and trade with the United States, 34
and the world economy, 62, 91, 105–6
Johnson, Lyndon B.,
administration of,
and Vietnam, 117–21, 183

Kautsky, Karl,
and the theory of imperialism, 18–19
Kennan, George, F.,
and containment, 53–4
and perspectives on the Soviet Union,
51, 54–5
Kennedy, John F.,
administration of,
Alliance for Progress, 115
approach to foreign affairs, 112–16, 183
American University speech, 115
Bay of Pigs, 112–13
Cuban missile crisis, 113–14
Nuclear Test Ban Treaty, 115
and Vietnam, 116
Kent State University, shootings at, 122
Keynesianism, 9, 10
and macro-economic policy, 156, 158,
159
and military expenditure, 36–7
Kissinger, Henry,
and *détente*, 57–9, 140, 179
and strategy for American decline,
131–3
and Vietnam, 121–4, 128
Korea, 54

Korean War,
    American involvement in, 111
    South, economy of, 95, 105
Kuwait, 189

Latin America,
    Alliance for Progress, 115
    relations with the US, 56, 92, 104, 107
    and the world economy, 91
Lebanon, 127
Lenin, V. I.,
    and Hobson, 10
    and the theory of imperialism, 16–19
Levis, 72
Libya, bombing of, 165
linkage, concept of, 59, 117–18, 121
Luxemburg, Rosa,
    and the theory of imperialism, 11–15,
        30

McCarthyism,
    and American imperialism, 41
    and the cold war, 53
McDonald's, 72
Marshall Plan, 47, 49, 187
Marx, Karl, 12
    and the globalization of capitalism, 99
    and the peasantry, 94
Marxism,
    and dependency theory, 90
    and the Soviet Union, 51–2
    and the theory of imperialism, 2,
        10–20, 29,
        as applied to the US, 30–43, 193
    and ultra-imperialism, 76
mercantilism, 81, 108, 188, 190
    and the Carter administration, 145
    and Japan, 134
    and the nation-state, 81
    and the Nixon administration 133–4,
        184
    and the Reagan administration, 161
merchants, 90, 95
Mexico,
    relations with the US, 105
Middle East,
    and American involvement, 56, 141,
        189
    and European/American differences, 83
    and the Reagan administration, 166–7
military expenditure,
    and American decline, 73–4
    and American foreign policy, 36–40
    and the origins of the cold war, 49
    and the Reagan administration, 157,
        159, 164, 186
    and the Soviet Union, 61

modernization theories, 93
Moscow, 146
multinational corporations, and American
        foreign policy, 30–1
    and free trade, 145
    and an international capitalist class, 180
    and Lenin's theory of imperialism, 17,
        18
    and nation states, 77, 86
    and oil, 136
    and overseas profits, 30
    and perfect competition, 4
    and the Reagan administration, 162
    and the Third World, 101
mutual assured destruction (MAD),
    concept of, 64, 83, 85, 167

National Rifle Association, 154
National Security Council, 141
nation-state, 5, 7, 15, 20, 26, 68, 77–9,
        86, 194
Nato, 56
    European–American divisions, 84–5
    fundamental doctrines of, 83–4
Nazism, 18
neo-conservative, 154
New England, 43
New Right, 154, 170, 185
Nicaragua,
    Contras, 166
    and the Reagan administration, 165–6
    Sandinistas, 166
Nixon, Richard,
    and anti-communism, 59, 139
    administration of,
        and American decline, 71, 131–3,
            136–42
        and China, 138–9, 184
        and *détente*, 57–9, 123–4, 137–42,
            179, 184
        and Iran, 141
        and Israel, 141
        and Japan, 134–5, 184
        and mercantilism, 133–4
        and the Middle East, 141
        Nixon Doctrine, 123, 140–1, 166
        Nixon shocks of 1971, 131–2
        and the Third World, 135
        and Vietnam, 121–4, 128, 183–4
        and Watergate, 59, 124–5, 142
NSC-68, 51
    and McCarthyism, 53
nuclear weapons
    and American decline, 74

OECD (Organisation for Economic
        Cooperation and Development),
        78, 79

OPEC (Organisation of Petroleum
   Exporting Countries), 135–6
Oval Office, 155

Panama,
   canal, 165
US invasion of, 192
Pareto optimality, 3, 29
pax americana, 188
peasantry, 94
Peking, 120
perfect competition, 4
Phillipines,
   Acquino regime, 167
Marcos regime, 106, 167
Pinochet, Augusto, 104, 105, 148
pluralism,
   and American decline, 108
   and the international system, 194
Poland,
   and the cold war, 47
popular culture,
   and American influence, 71–3
post-industrialism,
   and the American economy, 72–3
and the Third World, 90
post-modern world, 196

raw materials,
   and US foreign policy, 34–6
Reagan, Ronald
   as Governor of California, 154
   administration of, 32
   and American decline, 153–8, 185,
      186, 187–8
   and American exceptionalism, 171
   and Central America, 165–6, 185
   compared to the Carter
      administration, 162
   and defence spending, 37
   and *détente*, 60, 168
   and the 'evil empire', 165
   and Grenada, 127, 165, 166
   and the internationalization of
      capitalism, 161–2
   and the Iran–Contra affair, 166
   and Japan, 159
   and Lebanon, 127, 166
   and Libya, 165
   and the Middle East, 166–7
   and military expenditure, 157, 159,
      186
   and multinational corporations, 162
   and the New Right, 154
   1980 election campaign, 149
   1984 election, 162
   compared to the Nixon
      administration, 161

and the Phillipines, 167
Reagan Doctrine, 165
and social inequality, 188
and the Soviet Union, 167–70, 186
and the state, 155
and the Strategic Defence Initiative/
   'Star Wars', 168
and terrorism, 158
and the Third World, 158
and the US dollar, 160, 162–4
and Vietnam, 127–8, 156–7, 165, 166
realism, theory of,
   and the globalization of capitalism, 78
   and the theory of imperialism, 5–7, 20
   and nation-states, 177, 193
realization problem, 11, 13–14, 16, 20, 31
realpolitik, 124, 135, 144, 149
Regan, Donald, 164
Republican Party,
   1964 convention, 154
Ricardo, David, 2

San Francisco, 119
Say's law, 9
Schumpeter, Joseph,
   and the theory of imperialism, 3, 4,
      17, 34
Singapore, 95, 105
Smith, Adam, 2
social democracy, 28
socialism,
   and American life, 40, 156
   and American working class
      conservatism, 93–4
   transformation of, 75
Southern California, 13
Soviet Union/USSR, 18
   and Afghanistan, 59, 82, 148, 185
   American view of, 51–7
   and colonialism, 3
   communist revolution, 46
   and *détente*, 57–9, 138, 143, 179
   and hegemony, 27
   and imperialism, 5, 18, 26, 55
   and nuclear weapons, 50, 63–4
   and the origins of the cold war, 46–8,
      52–3
   relations with the Reagan
      administration, 167–70, 179
perestroika,
   American reactions to 60–4
   and nuclear defence, 75
   and strategic relations, 50–1
   and superpower relations, 43, 186
   and totalitarianism, 51–2
Spain, 24
Spanish Civil War, 48

Spenglerian perspective, 137
Sputnik, 112
state, the, 9,
 American, 31–2, 34
 and corporatism, 106
 and the theory of imperialism, 17, 21
 and the Reagan administration, 155
 welfare, 10, 156
Strategic Defence Initiative/'Star Wars',
 168
Sunbelt, 154
surplus value, 11, 90, 95–6

Taiwan, 95, 105
Texas-Mexico border, 190
Third World,
 and authoritarianism, 103–7
 and corporatism, 106–7
 and dependency theory, 90–5, 181–2
 and dependent development, 101–4
 and the development of capitalism,
  95–100
 and globalization, 89–90
 and the Nixon administration, 135
 and oil, 136
Titanic, 103
totalitarianism, 51
Trilateral Commission,
 and the Carter administration, 145, 184
 creation and purpose of, 80–81
 and the 'Fourth World', 151 n21
 and an international capitalist class, 180
Truman, Harry
 and the origins of the cold war, 48

ultra-imperialism, 18, 64, 68, 76, 81
uncertainty, the problem of
 and the theory of imperialism, in
  superpower relations, 55
unequal exchange, 3
United Nations, 146, 192
US Constitution, 142
US dollar,
 changing role of, 69–71
 and the Nixon administration, 131–2
 and the Reagan administration, 160
US working class,
 and dependency theory, 93–4
 and socialism, 93–4

Vance, Cyrus, 152 n43
Vietnam,

and American reactions to defeat,
 125–6, 192
and American ideology, 41–2, 126–7
and American intervention, 36, 56
and bombing of Haiphong, 58
and the Carter administration, 126–8
and the cold war, 49–50
and containment, 183
and *détente*, 57, 137, 143
Diem coup, 116
and the Johnson administration 117–21,
 183
and the Kennedy administration, 116
liberation movement, 94
and the Nixon administration, 121–4,
 123–4
and the Nixon doctrine, 141
and the Reagan administration, 127–8,
 156–7, 165
and relations with the USSR and
 China, 118, 123
Tet offensive, 121
and US dollar, 70–1
and US withdrawal, 119
Viet Cong, 116

Wallace, George, 154
Warren, Bill, 100
Warsaw Pact, 83–4, 112
Watergate, 153
 and *détente*, 59–60
 and Vietnam, 124–5
Western economic summits, 79, 145
Western Europe,
 as part of the American sphere of
  influence, 26
 and the origins of the cold war, 48
 and Marshall aid, 49
 and the Third World, 91, 93
Williams, William Appleman,
 and American imperialism, 25
World Bank, 78, 79, 91
World War Two/Second World War, 37,
 46, 47

Young, Andrew, 146

zero-sum relations, 4, 50, 59, 97, 108,
 117, 140, 143, 146, 183
Zimbabwe, 146
ZANU, 146